LIFE SCIENCE LIBRARY

FLIGHT

LIFE SCIENCE LIBRARY

CONSULTING EDITORS
René Dubos
Henry Margenau
C. P. Snow

FLIGHT

by H. Guyford Stever, James J. Haggerty

and the Editors of **TIME-LIFE BOOKS**

TIME-LIFE BOOKS   NEW YORK

ABOUT THIS BOOK

THE WORLD OF MANNED FLIGHT—from its primitive beginnings through the sophisticated present to the science-fiction future—makes up the scope of this book. It covers the history of flight, the theory of aerodynamics, propulsion, navigation and air-traffic control, testing, design and other aspects of this world.

The volume consists of alternating text chapters and picture essays. Some essays contain complementary material (for example, Chapter 3 and the accompanying essay deal with aerodynamics); others supplement the text chapters (Chapter 6 is a general discussion of navigation; Essay 6 describes one aspect of navigation, air-traffic control).

The Appendix comprises a glossary of airmen's slang and a chronological list of the highlights of manned flight.

THE AUTHORS

H. GUYFORD STEVER is president of the Carnegie Mellon University. A specialist in aeronautics and astronautics, he was Chief Scientist for the Air Force in 1955 and 1956. Later he served as consultant for the National Aeronautics and Space Administration and the Congressional Committee on Science and Astronautics. As a professor at Massachusetts Institute of Technology, he headed two departments from 1961 to 1965.

JAMES J. HAGGERTY has won several awards for aviation and space writing, flew 52 missions as a navigator in World War II, and is himself a licensed pilot. He was aviation editor of *Collier's* magazine from 1953 to 1956.

THE CONSULTING EDITORS

RENÉ DUBOS, a member and professor of The Rockefeller University, is a distinguished microbiologist and experimental pathologist who was awarded the Arches of Science Award in 1966 and the Pulitzer Prize in 1969 for his book *So Human an Animal: How We Are Shaped by Surroundings and Events*. He is also the author of *Mirage of Health* and *Man Adapting* and coauthor of *Health and Disease* in this series.

HENRY MARGENAU is Eugene Higgins Professor of Physics and Natural Philosophy Emeritus at Yale, and an authority in spectroscopy and nuclear physics. He wrote *Open Vistas, The Nature of Physical Reality*, and is coauthor of *The Scientist* in this series.

C. P. SNOW has won an international audience for his novels, including *The New Men, The Affair* and *Corridors of Power*, which explore the effects of science on today's society.

ON THE COVER

The 34-foot-high tail section of a Boeing 727 jetliner rises dramatically against the afternoon sky at John F. Kennedy Airport in New York. On the back cover is a stylized depiction of the basic airflow over a wing that results in the lift that makes flight possible.

CONTENTS

TIME-LIFE BOOKS

EDITOR
Maitland A. Edey
EXECUTIVE EDITOR
Jerry Korn
TEXT DIRECTOR   ART DIRECTOR
Martin Mann   Sheldon Cotler
CHIEF OF RESEARCH
Beatrice T. Dobie
PICTURE EDITOR
Robert G. Mason
Assistant Text Directors:
Harold C. Field, Ogden Tanner
Assistant Art Director: Arnold C. Holeywell
Assistant Chief of Research: Martha T. Goolrick

PUBLISHER
Rhett Austell
Associate Publisher: Walter C. Rohrer
Assistant Publisher: Carter Smith
General Manager: Joseph C. Hazen Jr.
Business Manager: John D. McSweeney
Production Manager: Louis Bronzo

Sales Director: Joan D. Manley
Promotion Director: Beatrice K. Tolleris
Managing Director, International: John A. Millington

LIFE SCIENCE LIBRARY

SERIES EDITOR: Martin Mann
Editorial staff for *Flight:*
Editor: Robert Claiborne
Associate Editor: Robert G. Mason
Text Editors: Leon Greene, Percy Knauth,
Alfred Lansing
Picture Editor: Robert W. Bone
Designer: Arnold C. Holeywell
Associate Designer: Edwin Taylor
Staff Writers: Peter M. Chaitin, Jonathan Kastner,
Harvey B. Loomis
Chief Researcher: Thelma C. Stevens
Researchers: Beatrice M. Combs, Edward Brash,
Adrian G. Condon, Owen Fang, Ann Ferebee,
Helen Greenway, Rosemary Haverland, Alice Kantor,
Frank Kendig, Irene J. Kleinsinger,
Victor H. Waldrop, Anthony Wolff

EDITORIAL PRODUCTION
Color Director: Robert L. Young
Assistant: James J. Cox
Copy Staff: Rosalind Stubenberg,
Suzanne Seixas, Florence Keith
Picture Department: Dolores A. Littles,
Barbara Simon
Traffic: Arthur A. Goldberger
Art Assistants: Patricia Byrne, Charles Mikolaycak

This book, from its conception to final editing, was under the professional direction of H. Guyford Stever. The text chapters were written by James J. Haggerty, the picture essays by the editorial staff. The following individuals and departments of Time Inc. were helpful in producing the book: LIFE staff photographers Ralph Crane and Yale Joel; Editorial Reference, Peter Draz; Picture Collection, Doris O'Neil; Photographic Laboratory, George Karas; TIME-LIFE News Service, Murray J. Gart; Reprints Editor, Paula Arno; Assistant Reprints Editor, Alice Kantor.

INTRODUCTION

THE DYNAMIC NATURE of the growth of science and technology in our century, and their impact on society and on the individual, are nowhere better evident than in the fulfillment of man's ancient dream to fly through the air. Born within the lifetime of many of us, aviation has grown, slowly at first and more rapidly later, until it has removed the barriers of space and time between the peoples of the earth.

Aviation was one of the earliest of the technologies of this century to require the intimate partnership of scientists, engineers and industrialists of many skills to accomplish rapid progress at the frontiers of knowledge. No single human mind could comprehend all the knowledge embodied in the design, construction and operation of a jet transport. Today we have many such difficult and complex technological developments, including nuclear energy, high-speed electronic computers and space vehicles. But aviation was one of the earliest to move from the individual creation of the pioneer inventor to the product of a new social invention, the design team of specialists working in harmony like the members of a symphony orchestra to produce a result far beyond the capability of any individual.

H. Guyford Stever and James J. Haggerty here review for us how all this came to pass. They acquaint us in layman's language with essentials of the scientific and technological problems of flight.

We are introduced to the mysteries of the flow of the invisible air about the airplane, the lift that holds the airplane in the air and the changing look of airplanes as their speed has been increased from 100 to 4,000 miles per hour.

We learn of piston engines and propellers, of modern jet engines deriving thrust from reaction to the discharge of hot gases, and of rockets that operate in space carrying their own oxygen.

We follow the changes in materials from wood, wire and cloth to steel, aluminum and titanium, and the changes in structure from bridgelike trusses to thin, metal shells reinforced by metal beams.

We become acquainted with navigation and traffic control along the airways, with electronic devices to guide through darkness and fog and to improve stability and control.

Finally we catch a glimpse of the future, the supersonic transport and the embryonic hypersonic airplanes which may reduce the travel time between any two points on the earth to two and a half hours.

All of these threads are woven together to illustrate the complexities of the pattern of human effort underlying modern air transportation.

—HUGH L. DRYDEN
Late Deputy Administrator
National Aeronautics and Space Administration

1
Realization of an Age-old Dream

PIONEERING FINISH
As two bystanders vigorously cheer, Henri Farman guides his biplane across the finish line at Issy in France to win the 50,000-franc Grand Prix d'Aviation by flying more than a kilometer in a circle. Although the flight covered less than a mile and lasted only about a minute and a half, it was, in January 1908, by far the longest and most impressive yet made in Europe.

"How i yearn to throw myself into endless space and float above the aweful abyss." With these words the German poet Goethe expressed the dream of men since the beginning of time. Man, incontestably the most advanced of creatures, has only to watch the flight of birds to feel the weight of his earthly imprisonment. And so the desire to fly has been ever present in the mind of man; but the reality was long in coming.

True flight with power and control is a product of the 20th Century. Its meaningful beginning, however, can probably be found somewhere in the Middle Ages when the vanguard of a long succession of "tower jumpers" trusted their lives to homemade wings built on the assumptions that the bird's wing was the source of its lift and the flapping motion the source of its propulsive power. While basically correct, these deductions did not go far enough. Early tower jumpers did not come close to understanding the amount of lift required to support a human body, and they failed to grasp the significant difference between birds and humans.

The fact is that a human being is simply not designed to fly. He is heavy and unstreamlined, and his bone structure and muscle arrangement are completely unsuited to handling wings. An average-sized person of 150 pounds would have to have a breastbone protruding six feet in order to accommodate the muscles needed to power a set of wings capable of lifting him off the ground. It was not until 1680, after many centuries of tower-jumping, that anyone pointed out this fact. An Italian named Giovanni Borelli published a serious and detailed study of human muscle as it applied to flight, concluding: "It is impossible that men should be able to fly craftily by their own strength." Borelli's findings may have deterred a few prospective jumpers, but the bone-shattering research went on.

Until the end of the 18th Century, little or no progress was made in the art of flight. The only work worthy of serious consideration was done by one man: Leonardo da Vinci, the genius of the Renaissance. Leonardo (1452-1519) approached flight in a scientific spirit; he made detailed studies of bird motion, of airflow and of air's resistance to a body moving through it. He designed a parachute, a pyramidal "tent made of linen" with which he claimed that man could descend "from any great height without sustaining injury." In a series of sketches, Leonardo designed several flying machines, one of which included an elevator control section to be operated by a harness attached to the pilot's head.

For all Leonardo's advanced thinking, however, his aircraft designs had one major flaw: they depended on human muscle for their propulsive force. Today Leonardo's work is interesting only as an illustration of his versatile intelligence in a scientifically unenlightened era.

For more than 200 years after Leonardo, flight progress was stalled.

Then, late in the 1700s, man's yearning for flight took a new turn. The age-old idea of imitating the birds was temporarily abandoned in favor of lighter-than-air craft. By then, experimenters had discovered the lifting properties of both heated air and hydrogen, and inventors began to apply this knowledge in the construction of man-carrying balloons. It was a means to an end—at least of getting human beings airborne—but it was not the answer to the persistent dream of true, birdlike flight.

The brains behind flight

Historically, the accomplishment of true, powered flight owes a basic debt to the genius of four men—Sir George Cayley (1773-1857), Otto Lilienthal (1848-1896) and the brothers Wright, Wilbur (1867-1912) and Orville (1871-1948). Important, though lesser, contributions came from William S. Henson (1812-1888), Octave Chanute (1832-1910), Samuel Pierpont Langley (1834-1906), Sir Hiram Maxim (1840-1916) and Alphonse Pénaud (1850-1880).

The first, Cayley, was a Yorkshire baronet with an incredible range of interests. In the course of his 84 years, Cayley investigated such diverse subjects as drainage and land reclamation, hot-air engines, endless-tread tractors and artificial human limbs. He was also a natural philosopher, a promoter of education, a Member of Parliament and a founding father of the British Association for the Advancement of Science.

Cayley has been called by historians "the true inventor of the airplane." The title may be an exaggeration, but incontestably Cayley laid the groundwork for later aeronautical research. He was the first to assemble in theoretical form the many elements necessary for practical flight. He thought of the wing not only in terms of lift but also of drag—the resistance produced by a body moving through air. He investigated the amount of lifting surface which supported a given weight in birds, and he recognized that the lifting properties of wings varied with the angle at which the wing moved through the air mass. He proposed a mechanical power system—an engine, which he called a "first mover." He realized that it should necessarily be light and he suggested that it might operate "by the sudden combustion of inflammable powders or fluids"—the internal-combustion engine. Furthermore, he recognized the need for providing stability and control.

In a remarkably succinct statement, Cayley summed up the task confronting aerodynamicists. "The whole problem is confined within these limits: to make a surface support a given weight by the application of power to the resistance of the air."

Born in 1773, Cayley was 10 years old when the world was astonished by early balloon flights. Those gas-bag adventures fired his imagination for the possibilities of flight, but he made an early decision "to make use

A LEGENDARY FLYING MACHINE, representing one of man's earliest attempts to travel by air, dates from a Chinese myth of about 1500 B.C. One medieval rendering *(above)* suggests that the carriage may have had a prototype of the propeller. A later drawing of the craft *(below)* shows what appear to be screw-bladed rotors, an indication that the ancient Chinese speculated on the principle of powered cross-country flight.

of the inclined plane propelled by a light first mover," rather than to work on lighter-than-air craft.

Cayley started, as had so many before him, with painstaking studies of bird flight. But he coupled this research with parallel investigations of air's reaction to objects passing through it by building model wings to study air resistance and pressures.

In 1804, after years of careful research, Cayley built his first aircraft, a model glider which many historians accept as the original airplane. In test flights it was sufficiently practical so that five years later Cayley constructed and successfully flew an unmanned, full-sized version with some 200 square feet of wing area.

Cayley sought to apply power to his glider, but in that respect he was too far ahead of his time. The only available power source was the steam engine, which was in fairly wide use at the time, but it was far too heavy for use in aircraft. Cayley made studies of other forms of propulsion, but in the end he failed to come up with a power system light enough for flight. So his attention returned to aerodynamics. Cayley discovered the importance of streamlining an aircraft, and he sketched shapes which would encounter the least resistance from air. He devoted additional effort to studies of movable tail surfaces and theorized about the stabilizing effect of "dihedral"—positioning the wings at an upward angle from the fuselage.

Drawing upon this theory, Cayley built and tested a second full-sized glider. On one flight a young boy served as test pilot and was reported to have flown "several yards" down a hill. Cayley experimented with this glider, or a modified version of it, for several years. Then, around 1853, he persuaded his coachman to make a flight from a hill across a small valley. Few details of the flight are available but it appears to have been moderately successful. The coachman, however, had little of the bold determination of later airmen. He quit on the spot, according to Cayley's granddaughter, shouting, "I was hired to drive, not to fly."

As the 19th Century advanced, interest in aeronautics quickened, and numerous designs were proposed while theories were expounded and experiments conducted. Only a few Victorian inventors, however, made any contribution to the ultimate success of the airplane.

An ambitious idea

Among these was William S. Henson, Cayley's leading admirer. Using Cayley's work as a basis, he designed an enormous "Aerial Steam Carriage" with which he hoped to carry "letters, goods and passengers from place to place." The vehicle had a wing span of 150 feet, and was to have been driven by a pair of six-bladed pusher propellers turned by a steam engine. The design was advanced for its time but it faced the same drawback Cayley had encountered: the weight of the steam engine. The "Aerial Steam Carriage" was never built.

Henson's contribution came when he lowered his sights, and teamed up with an engineer named John Stringfellow. The two men built a 20-foot scale model of the steam carriage, powered by a relatively light and compact steam engine. In an 1848 test, the model "flew" after a fashion, but the engine could not sustain flight. The model was only capable of gliding, with a rate of descent slower than would have been possible without power. The test, however, was the first attempt to apply mechanical propulsion to aircraft.

Rubber-band power

The next aviation pioneer was Alphonse Pénaud, who stepped onto the aeronautical stage in the 1870s. He produced the first design which had inherent stability; its dihedral wing tips and tail plane set a pattern for most of the airplanes to come. His 20-inch-long "planophore," as he called his rubber-band-powered, pusher-propeller model, was flown successfully in public in 1871.

Pénaud then turned his attention to man-carrying aircraft and designed a remarkably advanced full-sized amphibian with many of the features of modern planes—the tractor, or pulling, propeller, wing dihedral, retractable landing gear, a rear-mounted tail plane with fixed vertical fin, rudder and elevators, and a single control for all flight operations. Pénaud estimated that his design could fly at 60 miles per hour—if he could only find financial backing. But he never did and the plane was never built. In 1880, bitterly discouraged and in poor health, Pénaud committed suicide.

He died without knowing of an indirect contribution he had made to the future of flight. In 1878, one Milton Wright, a bishop of the United Brethren Church in Cedar Rapids, Iowa, brought his two younger sons, Wilbur and Orville, one of Pénaud's rubber-powered airplane models. The little toy made a lasting impression on the boys, and started them thinking of larger models.

The greatest contribution to pre-Wright aeronautics, aside from Cayley, came from Germany's Otto Lilienthal. He made detailed studies of birds and published his findings in *Bird Flight as the Basis of Aviation*, a work which influenced later researchers, including the Wrights.

Lilienthal's real contribution, however, was his decision to concentrate on obtaining experience in actual flight. Starting in 1891, Lilienthal built and flew a series of gliders. In his later designs, takeoff was accomplished by Lilienthal himself, running down a hill until sufficient speed was attained for lift. When the glider took to the air, Lilienthal supported himself by gripping a frame and letting his legs dangle be-

THE BEGINNINGS OF AERONAUTICS were made at the turn of the 19th Century by the English inventor Sir George Cayley. An amateur engraver, he commemorated on a silver disk in 1799 *(above)* his concept of designing a plane with fixed wings. In 1804 he built and flew the first true airplane—a five-foot glider with a kite for wings *(below)*.

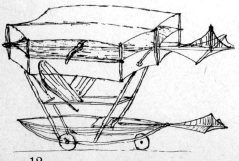

THE FIRST MAN-CARRYING GLIDE was made in this improbable contrivance designed and built by Cayley in 1849. He recorded, "a boy about ten years of age was floated off the ground for several yards." The three-wheeled flying machine—the first full-sized airplane to incorporate inherent stability—was launched by rolling it downhill.

neath the craft. By shifting his body weight, he achieved a crude form of stability and control. With his gliders, Lilienthal made more than 2,000 flights over a six-year period, traveling on some occasions more than 270 yards. Although his total flight experience was short by modern standards, he amassed more time in the air than all his predecessors combined. Most importantly, he demonstrated once and for all that a properly designed wing would support the weight of a man in the air.

In 1896, Lilienthal started work on a powered glider. He used a novel approach: a carbonic-acid gas motor was to supply power to the wing tips and cause a birdlike flapping action. But Lilienthal's luck ran out before he could succeed with the new plane. On August 9, 1896, he was making a routine hop in one of his unpowered gliders when a gust of wind stalled the craft and it crashed from an altitude of about 50 feet. Lilienthal died of his injuries the following day.

Contemporary with Lilienthal was a man who built and experimented with large powered aircraft prior to 1900. An American expatriate living in England, Sir Hiram Maxim concentrated on power application while all but ignoring the associated problems of lift and control. He built an aerodynamically crude biplane powered by two 180-horsepower steam engines, each of which drove a propeller 18 feet in diameter. On a test run in 1894, the engines generated sufficient power actually to lift the heavy plane off the ground, even though there was a guard rail intended to keep it from taking off. Incredibly, Maxim considered his work complete; he had demonstrated that adequate power could lift even a three-and-a-half-ton vehicle, and he concluded his tests.

Another pre-Wright experimenter was Octave Chanute, an American civil engineer who became interested in flying in 1875 and spent the rest of his life collecting and disseminating the work of other researchers. Not until 1896 did he decide to design gliders of his own. Already in his sixties, Chanute refined a biplane glider designed by Lilienthal, making one important contribution to future structures by introducing the bridge builder's Pratt truss, a method of bracing the wings by struts and diagonal wires still employed on planes manufactured in the 1930s. Chanute's gliders made hundreds of successful flights, many of them covering more than 100 yards. Chanute had hoped to go on into powered craft, but in 1900 he became confidant and consultant to the Wrights.

A catapult and a houseboat

Another of the greats of prepowered-flight was Samuel Pierpont Langley, architect, astronomer, physicist, mathematician and, in later life, Secretary of the Smithsonian Institution. He conducted extensive theoretical and laboratory research into aerodynamics from 1886 until his death in 1906. Of particular interest was his attempt to fly a full-scale

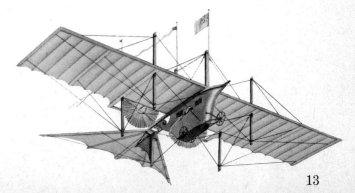

MODERN AIRPLANE STRUCTURE was anticipated in 1842 by Cayley's leading admirer, William S. Henson, when he patented this prophetic design. Though never built, it was to have fixed wings braced by strong spars, twin propellers and flying controls—features that became standard in many airplanes some 65 years later.

powered airplane called an "Aerodrome," a term Langley applied to his airplanes. After the search for a light and powerful engine, Langley's associate engineer, Charles M. Manly, designed a remarkable engine of his own which provided 52 horsepower at a weight cost of only 125 pounds, a ratio not bettered until the end of World War I. The Aerodrome with its 48-foot wing was to be launched by catapult from a houseboat especially built for the tests.

The beginnings of a breakthrough

With Manly as pilot, Langley's plane was first tried on October 7, 1903. The houseboat was anchored in the Potomac River near Widewater, Virginia, and Manly gave the signal for launch. The Aerodrome started forward, but the launching device fouled and the Aerodrome tumbled into the Potomac. Pilot Manly was drenched but unhurt.

The plane was repaired and a second attempt was made two months later. Again the launch gear snarled; this time, although Manly survived, the Aerodrome was severely damaged. After Langley's death, his admirers insisted that the Aerodrome was the first airplane capable of sustained powered flight. Only the catapult, they said, was faulty in design.

The stage was now set for the introduction of true manned flight. That achievement waited for Wilbur and Orville Wright, the bicycle makers from Dayton, Ohio. In 1900, after considerable study, they decided to build a full-sized glider. It was a tailless biplane with a horizontal control surface forward of the wings. The design was similar to Chanute's, but with an important improvement: wing-warping, or twisting, to obtain lateral control of the craft. Where others made use of shifting body weight, the Wrights worked out an imaginative method by which the pilot could twist the wing tips by means of wires. These cables moved one wing tip up, the other down and, theoretically, would provide effective control.

In October 1900, at Kitty Hawk, North Carolina—a beach site specially selected for its consistently steady winds and the absence of obstacles like trees—the Wrights made a dozen brief manned flights, totaling about two minutes in the air. Although the glider had less lifting capability than they had estimated, the Wrights were encouraged and returned to Dayton to build a larger craft.

Their second glider, flown in July and August of 1901, again at Kitty Hawk, was disappointing. The larger craft had poorer control and stability. More research was needed. Prior to 1901, the Wrights had done considerable research of their own, but they had also accepted without question the findings of others. Now they took a second look at the work of their predecessors. "We saw," they later wrote, "that the calculations upon which all flying machines had been based were unreliable, and that

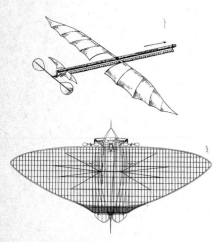

ALPHONSE PÉNAUD'S 20-inch "planophore" *(top)* had inherent lateral and longitudinal stability, his major contribution to flight. He was only 21 when he introduced the model. It was powered by a twisted rubber band, a Pénaud invention. In 1876 he patented a plan for a full-sized amphibious monoplane *(bottom)*, but killed himself at 30 because he failed to find backing for the project.

all were simply groping in the dark. Having set out with absolute faith in the existing scientific data, we were driven to doubt one thing after another, till finally, after two years of experiment, we cast all aside. . . . Truth and error were everywhere so intimately mixed as to be indistinguishable."

Back in Dayton, the Wrights built their own wind tunnel and conducted tests on a variety of wing shapes in monoplane, biplane and triplane configurations. This work led to the very important conclusion that they could build a more efficient and stable wing by using less camber, or curve, coupled with a greater ratio of wing length to width. This knowledge, together with the technique of wing-warping and other findings, was incorporated in the design of their third glider, a biplane with a wing span of 32 feet.

At Kill Devil Hills, near Kitty Hawk, the brothers made almost 1,000 flights with Glider No. 3 in a period of only 39 days in September and October 1902. The tests were completely successful; they had found a way to cope with stability and control, and they were now ready for the big move: the application of power.

Calculating their needs, the Wrights designed and built their own engine. It weighed only 180 pounds although it produced 13 horsepower. Of equal importance were the propellers. After much investigation, the Wrights produced a propeller in which the blade itself was an airfoil, aerodynamically similar to a wing. In the Wrights' eventual success, the propeller's high degree of efficiency was as important a factor as their aerodynamic and power-plant designs.

The Wrights' first powered machine was constructed in the summer of 1903. It was a biplane with a wing span of 40 feet four inches, and weighed 605 pounds. Its two propellers were driven by bicycle-type gears and chains connected to the engine shaft. For launching, the Flyer, as they once later referred to it, rested on a small wheeled truck, mounted on a wooden launching rail. The plane was transported in pieces to the Wrights' camp at Kill Devil Hills in September 1903.

Finally, on December 14, Wilbur, who had won the right by a toss of a coin, made the first attempt. The Flyer moved down the launching rail, climbed briefly, then lost flying speed and fell onto the sandy beach. Unhurt, Wilbur admitted that he, not the plane, was to blame.

December 17, 1903

The Flyer was only slightly damaged and it was ready for another flight attempt three days later. This time it was Orville's turn. After a brief run on the rail, the Flyer left its truck and wobbled 120 feet over the sands of Kill Devil Hills. "This flight lasted only 12 seconds," Orville reported, "but it was, nevertheless, the first in the history of the

OTTO LILIENTHAL, the world's earliest true aviator, is shown in photographs of two of his more than 2,000 glider flights. He was the first man consistently and successfully to build and fly heavier-than-air craft. The Wright brothers were strongly influenced by his experiences with such gliders as the monoplane *(below)* which he flew in 1893-1894, and his biplane of 1895-1896 *(above)*. They also drew on theories from his book *Bird Flight as the Basis of Aviation*. Lilienthal died in 1896, of injuries received when a gust of wind caused his glider to crash.

world in which a machine carrying a man had raised itself by its own power into the air in full flight, had sailed forward without reduction of speed, and had finally landed at a point as high as that from which it had started."

With the brothers alternating at the controls, there were three more flights that day, each setting a new record for duration of powered flight. On the last, Wilbur remained aloft for 59 seconds and traveled 852 feet.

The age-old dream had been realized. Many had tried. The Wrights succeeded.

In the years since Kitty Hawk, the airplane has undergone a dramatic evolution. The Wright Flyer managed to reach 30 miles an hour. Modern military aircraft exceed 2,000 miles per hour and a passenger on the ordinary airliner can cross the United States in four and a half hours. Aircraft construction and operation is a major factor in the nation's commerce and economy. The revenues of airlines in the U.S. alone amount to about $8 billion annually, their earnings exceed $300,000,000. Manufacturers sell more than $6 billion worth of airplanes in the civil market and export commercial aircraft worth well over $2 billion annually; they employ close to three quarters of a million workers. But aeronautical progress is still accelerating. Its future impact on man and his world is quite beyond measure.

The Wright Brothers: Fathers of the Airplane

Wilbur and Orville Wright did more than invent and fly the first powered airplane: they compiled a body of accurate knowledge in the little-explored science of aeronautics. Although their invention was in some part the logical extension of the work of others, they brought clarity for all time to a subject obscured by centuries of myths, guesses and erroneous calculations. Approaching their task with little more than good minds, deft hands and determination, the brothers developed into engineers and aeronautical theoreticians of towering stature. They did pioneering work to solve such problems as the control of wings in unstable air and the design of efficient propellers. They achieved a scientific breakthrough in charting the lifting effect of wind on curved wings. Popular legend has Wilbur and Orville Wright as inspired tinkerers who made good. History, however, knows them as original thinkers whose ideas changed the world.

FIRST FLIGHT
On the opposite page bits of history, on a bed of Kitty Hawk sand, recall the event of December 17, 1903. The airplane photograph records the first powered flight: Orville piloting, Wilbur running alongside. The Wright brothers' stopwatch rests on their diary, and their anemometer—to gauge wind speed—lies on Orville's telegram to their father, announcing the extraordinary success.

MACHINE

...t Can Really Fly

Successfully Navigated
By Dayton Brothers.

Huge Kite Soars Above
the Carolina Coast

Under Perfect Control and
at a Rapid Speed

In the Teeth of a Stiff
and Steady Storm

Gasoline Engine Puts the
Propellers in Motion.

The Ohio Inventors Sought To
Hide the Secret of Their
Apparatus By Choosing
an Isolated Spot

Orville Wright

Wilbur Wright.

Form No. 168.

THE WESTERN UNION TEL

INCORPORATED

23,000 OFFICES IN AMERICA.   CABLE S

This Company TRANSMITS and DELIVERS messages only on conditions limiting its liability. Errors can be guarded against only by repeating a message back to the sending station for comparison, and the Company will not hold itself liable for errors or delays in transmission or delivery of Unrepeated Messages, beyond the amount of tolls paid thereon, nor in any case where the claim is not presented in writing within sixty days after the message is filed with the Company for transmission. This is an UNREPEATED MESSAGE, and is delivered by request of the sender, under the conditions named above.

ROBERT C. CLOWRY, President and

RECEIVED at

176 C KA CS 33 Paid.   Via Norfolk Va

Kitty Hawk N C Dec 17

Bishop M Wright

7 Hawthorne St

Success four flights thursday morning all against twenty one mile

wind started from Level with engine power alone average speed

through air thirty one miles longest 57 seconds inform Press

home ~~there~~ Christmas .

Orevelle Wright   525P

Two Minds Working as One

"Orville and myself lived together . . . worked together and, in fact, thought together," said Wilbur Wright. Despite a four-year difference in age—Wilbur was born in 1867, Orville in 1871—their affinity of mind was complete. The Wrights' father, a Dayton, Ohio, clergyman, encouraged his sons to investigate whatever struck their fancy. "Dear Father," wrote Orville at age nine, "The other day I took a machine can and filled it with water then I put it on the stove I waited a little while and the water came squirting out of the top about a foot." As youths, the Wrights built a press and published a newspaper. Then they opened a bicycle shop. When Otto Lilienthal, the German gliding pioneer, crashed fatally in 1896, their interest focused on aviation. Within three years, they were conducting their own experiments with gliders.

THE ORDERLY CLUTTER OF GENIUS
Builders as well as thinkers, the Wrights were master craftsmen. In their bicycle shop, where Wilbur is shown *(above)*, they made whatever they needed. Their desk, now at Greenfield Village, Dearborn, Michigan, reflects their varied interests: a copy of their *West Side News;* carving tools; books on flight; a clutter of papers and parts. The picture is of their father.

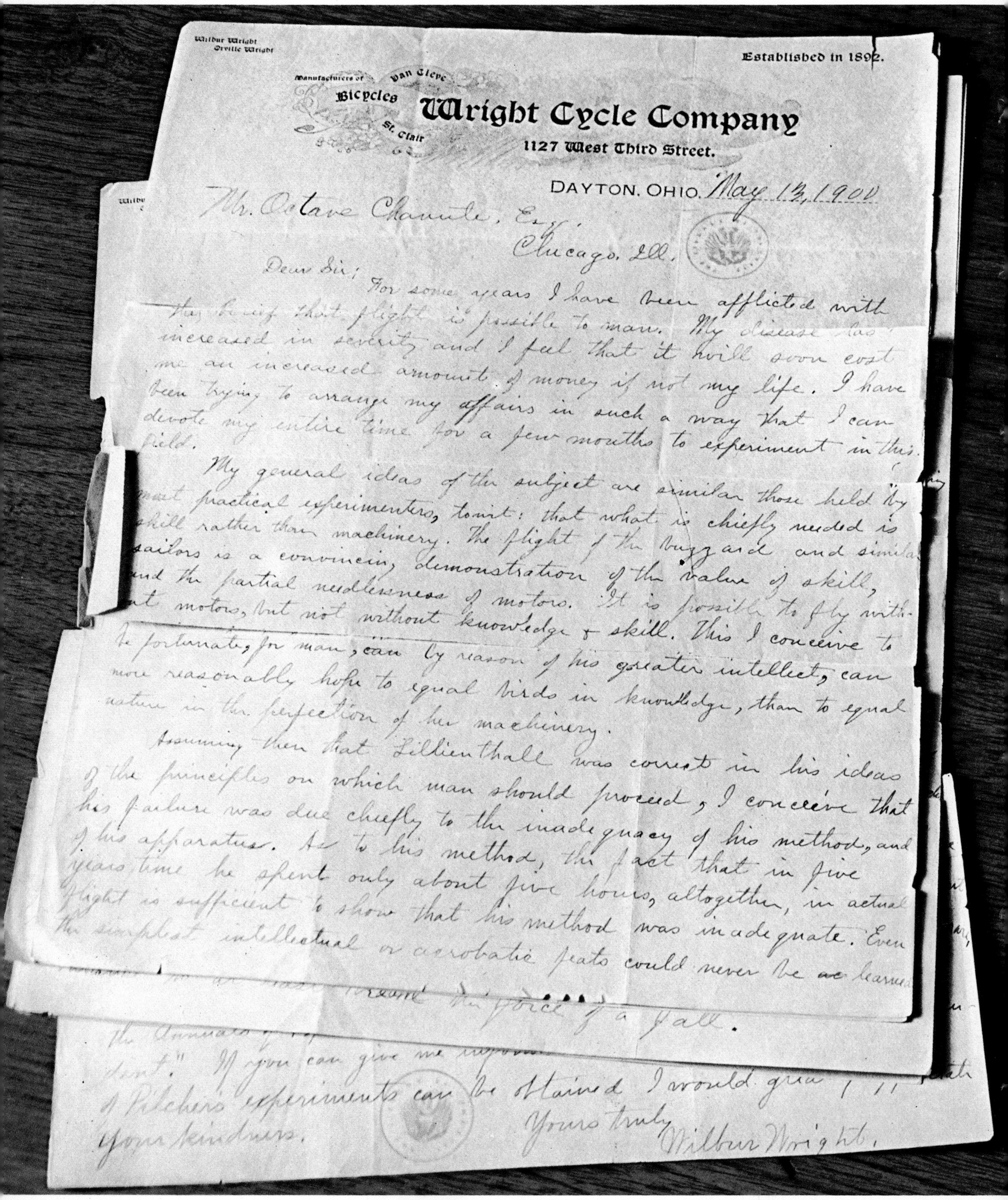

Manufacturers of

Van Cleve

Bicycles

St. Clair

Wright Cycle Company

1127 West Third Street.

DAYTON. OHIO. May 13, 1900

Mr. Octave Chanute, Esq.

Chicago, Ill.

Dear Sir;

For some years I have been afflicted with the belief that flight is possible to man. My disease has increased in severity and I feel that it will soon cost me an increased amount of money if not my life. I have been trying to arrange my affairs in such a way that I can devote my entire time for a few months to experiment in this field.

My general ideas of the subject are similar to those held by most practical experimenters, to wit: that what is chiefly needed is skill rather than machinery. The flight of the buzzard and similar sailors is a convincing demonstration of the value of skill, and the partial needlessness of motors. It is possible to fly without motors, but not without knowledge & skill. This I conceive to be fortunate, for man, can by reason of his greater intellect, can more reasonably hope to equal birds in knowledge, than to equal nature in the perfection of her machinery.

Assuming then that Lillienthall was correct in his ideas of the principles on which man should proceed, I conceive that his failure was due chiefly to the inadequacy of his method, and of his apparatus. As to his method, the fact that in five years time he spent only about five hours, altogether, in actual flight is sufficient to show that his method was inadequate. Even the simplest intellectual or acrobatic feats could never be ac learned

the force of a fall.

the Annuals of ... dent." If you can give me inform... of Pilcher's experiments can be obtained I would grea... your kindness.

Yours truly,

Wilbur Wright,

Finding a Key to Control

By the time they were ready to begin practical experiments in 1899, the Wrights had read omnivorously in aeronautics and had studied birds in flight. The more they learned, the more convinced they became that the basic element of flying was control—maintaining balance in unstable air. They noted that soaring birds, when a gust forced one wing down, could restore their balance by angling that wing up to the wind and the other one down. How could this be duplicated in a machine? Wilbur found the answer while toying with a cardboard box *(upper right):* wings could be angled by warping, or twisting, them to offer varying surfaces to the wind. That year the Wrights built a biplane kite with wings that could be warped by manipulating strings. The system worked, and in 1900 and 1901 the brothers embodied the idea in full-sized gliders. The basic control factor was established; sustained flight was now possible.

A SECRET IN A CARDBOARD BOX
Hands twist a box, simulating Wilbur's discovery that led to the warping of wings. As Wilbur explained, writing to Octave Chanute: "If you will make a square cardboard tube . . . and choose two sides for your planes you will at once see the [twisting] effect of moving one end of the upper plane forward and the other backward . . . without sacrificing lateral stiffness."

KITE-FLYING AT KITTY HAWK
On a North Carolina beach at Kitty Hawk the Wrights found an ideal spot for their gliding tests, with a steady wind over the sand dunes. Flying their glider as a kite in 1901 *(right),* they held cables which warped the wings, allowing the brothers to control the craft effectively.

SCIENTIFIC CORRESPONDENCE
Wilbur described wing-warping in his first letter *(opposite)* to aeronautics pioneer Octave Chanute, opening a correspondence that lasted 10 years. Chanute, who had many contacts in scientific circles, became the Wrights' trusted adviser and later helped publicize their work.

BICYCLE BUILT FOR TESTING
In their first effort to observe and evaluate the performance of model wings the Wright brothers used this bicycle-mounted device. A curved surface *(right)* and a flat surface *(left)* were mounted opposite each other on a free-turning wheel; the unknown lifting powers of the curved surface could then be compared with the known lift capabilities of the flat piece.

Applying the Scientific Method

The Wright brothers left Kitty Hawk in 1901 with a fundamental problem still unsolved: their glider had failed to develop the lift they anticipated. They had designed its wings in accordance with the data compiled by Otto Lilienthal, which the German had tested with actual experience in the air. But in terms of the Wrights' experience, these calculations had proved erroneous: it was evident to the brothers that reliable data could only be worked out in the controlled conditions of the laboratory. They decided to make their own calculations "to accurately determine the amount and direction of the pressure produced on curved surfaces by winds at . . . various angles. . . ." To do this they designed and built a wind tunnel, through which air was driven by a fan at 25 to 35 miles per hour. In the tunnel they suspended on delicate balances miniature wings of varying design and measured the forces working on them. Charting these figures, the Wrights were able to discover the optimum profile of curve which would enhance lift. Now they were able to construct full-sized wings of predictable performance. This utilization of scientific method liberated them from complete dependence on trial and error, and enabled Orville to say that by 1902 he and Wilbur knew more about curved surfaces, "a hundred times over, than all our predecessors put together."

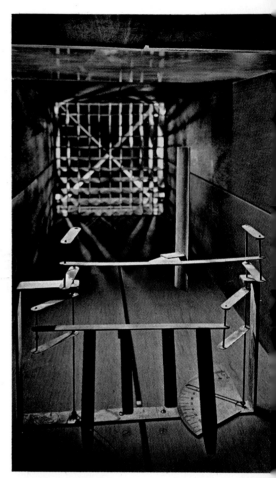

INSIDE THE TUNNEL
Ready for a test, the balance, seen inside the tunnel, stands under the viewing window. The lift of a model wing, mounted vertically on the top crossbar, was compared to the known resistance of the four flat surfaces beneath it. Readings were taken off the balance's scale.

INSTRUMENTS TO CONQUER AIR
The Wrights' wind tunnel (shown in replica at left) was equipped with a balance *(foreground)* to measure the lifting abilities of model wings. The balance was placed inside the tunnel, and by peering through a window the Wrights could note the performance of the wing. Readings from earlier tests in a prototype tunnel were traced directly on wallpaper scraps *(right)*.

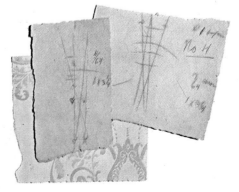

On the Verge of Triumph

When the Wrights returned to Kitty Hawk in 1902, they brought a glider which they knew would develop sufficient lift. But now they met an unforeseen problem. When a wing was dropped by a gust and was then warped to bring it up again, it often failed to rise—the warping increased the wing's resistance to the air, slowing its speed and robbing it of lift. As part of the same process, the glider turned toward the lowered wing. Further warping intensified the turn, which became uncontrolled. What could be done? Orville puzzled out the answer: a rudder to counteract the turn. To this innovation Wilbur added another by connecting wing and rudder controls. Now the pilot could not only correct unintended turns but also make smooth turns at will, warping wings and turning rudder with a single motion. With these great improvements the Wrights had reached the verge of practical flight: all that remained was to add power.

A PATENT FOR FLIGHT
The patent granted the Wright brothers for "certain new and useful improvements in Flying-Machines" was based on the 1902 glider's system of controls. It was this machine that really conquered the air and made the addition of power a practical and inevitable final step.

A SCENE OF TRIUMPH
The flights in the 1902 glider led Orville to exult: "We now hold all the records! The largest machine, the longest time in the air, the smallest angle of descent. . . ." Replicas of this craft and the brothers' hangar and cabin stand today at the Wright memorial in Kitty Hawk.

IN HIS FLYING MACHINE
Soaring through the air in the 1902 glider, Wilbur controls by hand the front elevator which varies the glider's pitch; his hips rest in a movable cradle to which are attached wing and rudder wires. By shifting his position, he could warp the glider's wings and turn the rudder.

The First True Airplane

Designing an airplane for powered flight was no longer a problem for the Wrights. Nor did the motor present unusual difficulties; when no suitable model could be found, they built one. Propellers proved perplexing. The brothers recognized a salient point: that a propeller is really a wing moving in a spiral course. Just how it worked, however, baffled them. "With the machine moving forward," they later wrote, "the air flying backward, the propellers turning side-wise, and nothing standing still, it seemed impossible . . . to trace the . . . reactions." It took months, but in the end they had formulated and built an efficient propeller, and on December 17 at Kitty Hawk all was ready for the final test. At 10:35 a.m. Orville climbed into the pilot's cradle. The securing rope was slipped, the craft moved slowly along a track and then, like an uncertain bird, it lifted itself into the air. In Wilbur's words, "the age of flight had come at last."

THE ORIGINAL WRIGHT PLANE

During its single day of glory this airplane made four flights. The first lasted 12 seconds, the last and longest, 59 seconds. Now restored, it hangs in the Smithsonian. The plane's twin propellers were chain-driven by a 12-horse-power motor. Minutes after its last flight the plane was overturned by a gust of wind. But it had done its job, though it never flew again.

A PROPELLER THAT WORKED

The efficiency of this original Wright propeller was a marvel for its day: it could translate 66 per cent of its engine's rotational energy into forward thrust. After more than six decades of research in aeronautics the best of today's air-screws achieve about 85 per cent efficiency.

Toward Practical Flight

OVER AN OHIO FIELD

Better controls, a more powerful engine and stronger propellers made this 1905 airplane more useful than its 1903 prototype. To the Wrights it was the first practical airplane. It is shown here on a 21-mile, 33-minute flight. This aircraft's fine performance was made possible not only by its mechanical refinements but also by the brothers' greater piloting skill.

The historic day at Kitty Hawk had its inevitable sequel: more work to be done. The airplane had leaped ahead of its inventors; the Wright brothers now had to learn the art of flying before they could demonstrate the value of their invention. By 1905, both plane and pilots were considerably improved: flights of more than half an hour had been achieved near Dayton (left). For two years, the brothers engaged in abortive correspondence with the War Department. Meanwhile several foreign governments became interested. In 1908, while Wilbur flew in Europe, Orville at last began his flight trials before American officers. A year later the Signal Corps bought a plane. Flying was out of the experimental stage and practical aviation had begun.

FRONT ELEVATOR

WARPABLE WING

MOTOR

PROPELLER

PROPELLER

RUDDER

SIGNAL CORPS I
Passenger and pilot sat, instead of lay, on the lower wing of the U.S. Army's first airplane, built in 1909. Its exact replica *(left)* is in the Air Force Museum, Dayton. Like all the Wright brothers' planes, it included the essential features to be incorporated in all later prejet aircraft: motor, propellers, warpable wings—the precursor to modern ailerons—elevator (here in front) and rudder. The last two were shortly to be combined in a single tail section.

2
The Essentials of Flight

IN THE OFFICE of an aircraft manufacturer there is a framed drawing that illustrates the eternal battle of compromise which is the essence of aircraft design. In cartoon fashion, the drawing pictures the ideal plane as seen by each of several design specialists.

The aerodynamicist, for instance, sees a highly streamlined ship with razor-thin wings and knifelike fuselage—not the slightest bulge to increase air resistance. The power-plant man grudgingly concedes a tiny cockpit, but the rest of his design is an enormous engine. To the structural engineer, the airplane is simply a pair of crossed I beams strong enough to withstand the blows of a pile driver. The navigation specialist would clutter the external surfaces with a variety of antennae; the focal point of his design is a huge cockpit crammed with every conceivable type of instrument.

The spoof simply exaggerates the attitudes of the design specialists, who must live with compromise. But it also makes an important point: if an airplane is to perform a useful function, it must be designed as an integrated system, not as a collection of components, efficient only when operating by themselves. The final blueprint must take into consideration the interaction among the four basic essentials of aircraft design: aerodynamics, propulsion, structure and control.

These design essentials, properly incorporated in an airplane, will enable it to overcome the pull of gravity and fly. But flight in a winged plane—with or without an engine—is not the only method that man uses to rise above the surface of the earth. Before the first flyable planes were built, escape from gravity was accomplished by means of lighter-than-air balloons. And today, even as swifter and more powerful jet planes crowd the airlanes, space scientists are launching rockets that conquer gravity by brute force—that simply generate more upward thrust than the weight of the entire vehicle.

It was the buoyancy of balloons, though, that first turned the dream of flight into reality. The big, man-carrying bags became a possibility after the late-18th Century discovery that hydrogen actually is lighter than air. Around 1766 the famed British scientist, Henry Cavendish, filled a bladder with hydrogen, which he called a kind of "factitious" (or "artificial") air, and discovered that the bladder weighed less.

To Cavendish, however, this was purely a physical phenomenon, and he did not consider its aeronautical applications. It remained for another scientist, Jacques Charles, to harness the lifting power of hydrogen 17 years later and achieve flight. But the first practical application of balloon buoyancy was made by the Montgolfier brothers of France.

How the Montgolfiers got into the field of ballooning has been told and retold so often that it has become difficult to separate fact from fantasy. The most popular version of the story has it that Joseph Montgolfier, elder of the brothers, was idly staring into his fireplace one evening in 1782, watching the smoke curl lazily up the chimney. The tale goes on to say that Joseph borrowed a piece of silk from his housekeeper and fashioned it into an open-bottomed bag. Then, holding the bag above the fire, he let it fill with heated air and smoke. When he released it, the bag rose to the ceiling.

Command performance for a balloon

After this initial success, the Montgolfier brothers tried other, more ambitious experiments using larger balloons. Within six months, utilizing an outdoor bonfire as a source of heat, they had sent a balloon aloft to a height of a little more than a mile, a feat that was witnessed by a large crowd of spectators.

News of the Montgolfier flights reached King Louis XVI, who ordered a command performance at Versailles. For the occasion, the brothers built an elaborately decorated balloon and, as an added attraction, decided to find out whether animal life could survive in the upper air. A sheep, a duck and a rooster were sent aloft from Versailles on September 19, 1783, in a tub-shaped basket suspended from the balloon. The flight lasted eight minutes and the balloon traveled a mile and a half. On landing, the animal passengers showed no ill effects. The Montgolfiers immediately set about building a man-carrying balloon.

The new model was provided with its own airborne furnace for sustained flight. It took two months to get the balloon ready, and several trials were held with the balloon tethered to the ground. Finally the Montgolfiers decided that everything was ready.

News of the impending flight had spread throughout France and excitement ran high. King Louis himself took an active interest, and even offered to provide two condemned criminals to serve as passengers. At this, Jean-François Pilâtre de Rozier, a young historian and a ballooning enthusiast, became indignant.

"Shall vile criminals have the honor of first rising into the sky?" he stormed. "I myself shall go!"

On November 21, 1783, before a cheering throng gathered on the grounds of a Paris chateau, Rozier and another volunteer, the Marquis d'Arlandes, climbed aboard the circular, bunting-draped "gallery" at the base of the balloon. The mooring lines were cast off, and the big balloon began to rise.

At first it lifted very slowly, and Rozier began stoking the fire with straw. The balloon began to ascend more rapidly, but at the same time several small fires broke out in its fabric; the two aeronauts raced around the gallery with wet sponges, extinguishing the flames.

ZEPPELIN DEVELOPMENT is depicted by the trio of German airships below. Fitted with an aluminum framework that streamlined and sustained its mammoth gas bags, the zeppelin was the first aircraft to fly passengers commercially. The maiden flight of the first zeppelin *(left)* proved the feasibility of a rigid design, and larger ones were built, like the giant *(center)* used for reconnaissance and bombing in World War I. When the sumptuous *Hindenburg (right)* was launched in 1936, the zeppelin reached its zenith, only to have its era end abruptly a year later when the hydrogen-filled airship crashed in flames.

1900: FIRST ZEPPELIN, 420 FEET   1917: WARTIME MODEL, 740 FEET

Once the fires were out, the remainder of the ride was sheer exaltation as the balloon sailed over the rooftops of Paris for 25 minutes before it landed safely five and a half miles away. For the first time in the history of the world, man had achieved free flight.

Ten days after the Montgolfier flight came the second manned flight. This time, under the same Parisian sky, some 200,000 Frenchmen witnessed the pioneering physicist Jacques Charles and a companion make a two-hour, 27-mile flight in a hydrogen-filled balloon. They landed safely. But when Charles's companion climbed out of the gondola, he automatically lightened it; the balloon, with Charles in it, soared back up into the air, inadvertently making Charles the first human being to take a solo flight. It was now dark, and the balloon climbed to a record height of 9,000 feet. By the time Charles got back to earth, he was so shaken that he swore never to set foot in another balloon.

Despite Charles's defection, the ballooning craze swept all of Europe. Soon there were professional balloonists making exhibition flights, even including a stunt man who once ascended on horseback, with the horse standing on a platform underneath the gas bag.

Since balloons were prey to the whimsy of the wind, even the earliest balloonists realized the need for some kind of propulsion. Paddles, oars and sails were tried; one theorist proposed using masses of tethered birds. True powered flight, however, had to await the 1852 marriage of the steam engine and the balloon.

Tragic end to an era

The powered balloon was brought to its highest development beginning in 1910, when Germany inaugurated commercial airship service. Subsequently the 775-foot *Graf Zeppelin* joined the fleet. Named for Count Ferdinand von Zeppelin, father of the rigid airship, it was a balloon built around a stiff frame as its predecessors had been. The *Graf Zeppelin* made a number of successful voyages from its homeland to the Mediterranean and to North and South America. In 1936 the German Government built a larger zeppelin with a greater range, the 804-foot *Hindenburg*. Like its predecessor, the *Hindenburg* was hydrogen-inflated. Launched in March 1936, the *Hindenburg* was the last word in luxury transportation. There were double-occupancy cabins for its 72 passengers, hot and cold water, a dining room, a bar and lounge complete with a grand piano, and promenades for the transoceanic traveler's traditional walk around the deck.

In the 14 months of its existence, the *Hindenburg* made 63 flights; 37 of them were across the Atlantic, and 21 of those were between Germany and the United States. On May 6, 1937, the *Hindenburg* was preparing to moor at Lakehurst, New Jersey, after its first North American

1936: *HINDENBURG*, 804 FEET

trip of the year. As a crowd of horrified spectators watched, a burst of fire appeared just forward of the upper vertical fin. Within seconds the fire spread from stern toward the bow and the great zeppelin fell slowly to earth, a mass of flaming wreckage. The exact cause of the fire was never determined, but it was generally believed that leaking hydrogen had been ignited by atmospheric electricity. The loss of 36 lives in the disaster brought an end to the hydrogen airship.

A drag on velocities

Safety aside, lighter-than-air craft have other inherent drawbacks as a means of airborne transportation. For their size, balloons and dirigibles have very feeble lifting power. To carry any substantial payload, such vehicles must have enormous proportions. These enormous proportions in turn result in a large amount of "bag drag"—wind resistance that limits speed to very modest velocities by aircraft standards.

At the other end of the flight-speed spectrum, there are rocket engines that can generate enormous high speeds—but there are also serious drawbacks. To achieve the power necessary for flight, enormous quantities of fuel must be burned. Consequently the period of powered flight is limited to only a few minutes at the very most, because there are limits to the amount of fuel a plane can carry. The stubby Messerschmitt 163 Komet, used during World War II to attack Allied bombers, carried only enough fuel for eight to 10 minutes in the air, and thus was limited to powered flights of up to 100 miles. After the war, the U.S. produced an experimental rocket-powered airplane, the X-15. Launched from a large jet plane at high altitudes, it reached speeds of 4,520 mph, more than six times the speed of sound, before it was retired in 1968. But its function was purely experimental.

Practical, economical flight within the atmosphere is confined chiefly to flight achieved by aerodynamics, literally, "air motion." Basically, to build a flyable, aerodynamic airplane, four fundamental factors must be taken into account: weight, lift, drag and thrust.

Weight includes the airplane, its fuel and a payload.

Lift is the force by which an airplane overcomes the pull of gravity.

Drag is the retarding pull of several assorted air currents.

Thrust is the force which, overcoming drag, drives the airplane through the air.

Let us examine how the airplane designer deals with these four factors:

Lift, be it in a bird or an airplane, is generated primarily by the flow of air over the wings—with a small assist from the body and tail surfaces. The flow of air necessary for lift can be produced in two ways. One impractical method would be to blow wind past a parked aircraft. But with

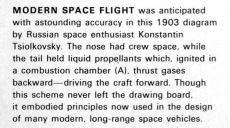

MODERN SPACE FLIGHT was anticipated with astounding accuracy in this 1903 diagram by Russian space enthusiast Konstantin Tsiolkovsky. The nose had crew space, while the tail held liquid propellants which, ignited in a combustion chamber (A), thrust gases backward—driving the craft forward. Though this scheme never left the drawing board, it embodied principles now used in the design of many modern, long-range space vehicles.

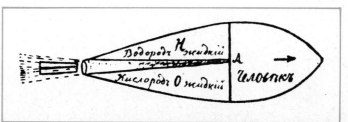

even a modest-sized plane like the familiar old DC-3, such a wind would have to be of hurricane force to produce sufficient lift to get the machine off the ground. It is far more practical to drive the airplane through the air at speeds sufficient to produce lift.

The term "lift" should be taken quite literally. An airplane is, for the most part, actually lifted into the air by the behavior of wind streaking past its wings. The wing configuration is such that the rush of wind creates a condition of imbalance; the pressure on the upper surface of the wing is lower than the pressure on the bottom side. Thus the wing is forced upward, carrying the airplane with it.

Whereas lift is a relatively clear-cut matter, drag is a combination of forces working to retard the forward motion of the plane, particularly along the wings. There are three varieties of drag, each different from the other, but all adding up to a rearward force.

The final basic element needed for flight is thrust. Whatever provides it—motor-driven propeller, a jet engine or a rocket power plant such as the X-15 used—the thrust must be sufficient to drive the airplane fast enough to produce enough airflow for lift. At the same time the thrust must overcome the drag that is also created by the moving air. In level flight, the thrust exactly equals the force of drag.

This is an application of Newton's famed first law of motion, which states that a body in motion tends to remain in motion unless acted upon by an outside force. Once an airplane has reached cruising altitude and cruising speed, it is a body in motion and tends to remain in motion at precisely that speed. But there is a force acting upon it: drag. To continue flying at this same speed, it therefore becomes necessary for the plane's engine to provide only sufficient thrust to overcome the rearward pull of drag. The same balance must exist between lift and weight.

The sophistication of stabilization

These are the basic elements. But in order to achieve true flight, the airplane must also be stable. In the pre-Wright era, the lack of a light-weight propulsion source was one of the main deterrents to flight. But many of the 19th Century designs would not have been successful even if such an engine had been available. The Frenchman Clément Ader, for instance, claimed until his death that he had achieved flight in 1897 with his steam-driven *Avion III*. Historians discount his claim and the eminent British student of flight, Charles H. Gibbs-Smith, adds that the Ader machines "were woefully lacking in effective wing design, stability and control, and, even with suitable propulsion, could never have satisfied the proper criterion of the practical airplane."

Sir Hiram Maxim's steam-powered biplane had sufficient propulsive energy, but if it had taken to the air, it would have come down in short order for lack of stability and control. The consensus of flight historians is that Professor Samuel P. Langley's Aerodome might have been capable of taking off, but would never have become a successful airplane, also because of its fundamental lack of stability and control.

Stability is the characteristic of an airplane to right itself and return to level flight when, for some reason—a gust of wind, for instance—its equilibrium is disturbed. There are three components of disturbing motion: "pitch," in which the plane noses up or down; "yaw," in which it slues to the side; and "roll," in which the aircraft moves about its longitudinal axis, dipping its wings to one side or the other.

Dihedral to inhibit roll

The stabilizing force needed to counteract pitch and yaw comes mainly from the tail of the airplane, which works exactly like the feathered vanes of an arrow. Air rushing past the fixed upright portion of the airplane's tail section counteracts the wagging action of yaw, while the fixed, horizontal stabilizers on the tail tend to damp the up-or-down motion of pitch.

The stability needed to counteract roll is a bit more complex and involves the slant of the wings—the "dihedral" (for "two planes"), which is most easily visible in a front view and resembles a flattened V. When an airplane rolls, say, to the left, the left wing lowers and the right wing comes up. In this position, the lowered left wing presents a higher angle of attack to the wind than does the uptilted right wing. The increased lift tends to twist or roll the plane back to level flight.

Curiously, all the best of aerodynamics are embodied in what is essentially the earliest sort of airplane—the kind that took the life of Lilienthal and so many other pioneers of aviation. This is the glider, or more properly, the sailplane.

Even sitting on the ground at rest it *looks* like the aerodynamic marvel that it is. The surfaces of its wings and fuselage are at least as smooth as glass. There is not the smallest rivet head protruding above the surface to roil the air in its passage.

There are many wrong notions about how sailplanes achieve flight. It is widely believed that they "ride updrafts," rising thermal currents of air. While true, this is only part of the story. A sailplane rides thermals to gain *altitude*. But it flies by *gliding downward*. Since it lacks an engine, the only way a glider can obtain a flow of wind over its wings is to be in a diving situation relative to the wind. But this is the shallowest possible dive imaginable. It is usually an angle so slight that if the sailplane were an automobile on a downgrade, the slope would not be enough even to get the car rolling. Consequently, a sailplane, being so perfectly balanced and so aerodynamically efficient, will rise while rid-

PITCH

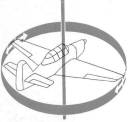

YAW

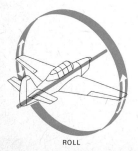

ROLL

THREE BASIC MOVEMENTS of which an airplane is capable—called "pitch," "yaw" and "roll"—are based upon rotation around its three axes, shown here. In pitching, the nose moves up or down about the lateral axis of the plane. A yawing plane slues to one side or the other around the vertical axis extending through its body. When rolling, the wings dip to one side or the other around the long axis of the fuselage.

ing a thermal updraft—even though the plane itself is in a diving situation, if it can be called that. A high-efficiency sailplane, on a day of dead calm winds, is thus able to glide 15 miles from a height of only 2,500 feet.

There are other misconceptions about sailplanes, too. One is that they are slow. Another half-truth. While the speeds at which they normally operate are indeed slow, say, 40 to 50 mph, some sailplanes are entirely capable of diving at speeds of up to 150 mph every bit as safely as airplanes. Another misconception has it that the maneuvers of which a sailplane is capable are limited. Not so at all. Sailplanes can do most of the aerobatic tricks of which airplanes are capable, including an outside loop, one of the most strenuous maneuvers an airplane does. An outside loop begins with the sailplane in normal level flight. Then it successively dives, flies upside down, and climbs back to level flight.

Furthermore, sailplanes can reach altitudes that few propeller-driven planes can achieve. Paul F. Bikle, Director of the National Aeronautics and Space Administration's Flight Research Center, currently holds the record. On February 25, 1961, Bikle reached a height of almost nine miles in an unpowered soaring craft specially equipped with an oxygen system. Taking off from Lancaster at the edge of California's Mojave Desert, Bikle was towed to 10,000 feet by an airplane and cut loose. For more than an hour he deftly manipulated the high-performance plane into rising air drafts, climbing higher and higher until his altimeter needle touched 46,267 feet. He might have gone even higher, but his flight plan allowed him only five minutes above 40,000 feet, since he was not wearing a pressure suit.

While this flight was unusual, weekend soarers frequently climb to 18,000 to 20,000 feet. Sailplanes have made cross-country trips of as much as 647 miles and endurance flights up to 76 hours.

Design for specialization

The sailplane, of course, is a specialized design. But in a sense so are all airplane designs. All the refinements of modern science and engineering still adhere to the same basic principle which guided the Wright brothers: the need to design a plane for a particular job. The purpose of the Wrights' 1903 Flyer was simply to lift one man into the air and carry him a reasonable distance by powered flight. Once this was achieved, aircraft design progressed to increasingly sophisticated purposes. But the concept of compromise in order to achieve a specific purpose remains unchanged.

Speed is generally achieved at the expense of range, maneuverability at the expense of speed. Payload—passengers, freight, armament, navigation and guidance instruments, cabin-pressurizing systems and other on-board equipment—dictates the lift and thrust requirements, in turn

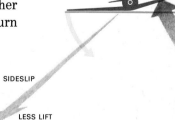

STABILITY FOR ROLL is achieved by "dihedral," or the upward angle of an airplane's wings. In level flight, both wings have equal lift *(top)*. But if a wind gust should tilt up one wing, the plane rolls, then slips sideways toward the lowered side *(middle)*. The sideslip creates an additional flow of air under the lowered wing. This "relative wind," and the greater lift on the lowered wing, swings the plane back to level flight.

affecting aerodynamics, power plants and structure. All of these considerations must be balanced in the functional flying machine.

The importance of compromise in aircraft design was dramatically demonstrated during the Korean War, which pitted the U.S. Air Force's F-86 Sabrejet against the Soviet-built MIG-15. The two airplanes were of approximately the same dimensions, but the F-86 was also considerably heavier; the manufacturers, North American Aviation, had given the Sabre a generous coating of armor plating and added an automatic computing fire-direction system weighing several hundred pounds. The MIG designers scorned such frills; the Soviet fighter had a little armor and a simpler, lighter cannon-sighting device. As a result, the MIG had an edge in altitude capability and maneuverability. But by the end of the year, F-86 pilots had compiled a record of 14 MIG kills for every Sabre lost, a ratio which astounded even the Air Force brass and their Sabre contractor. The high professional skill of the American pilots was certainly a factor in the extraordinary kill ratio; but there is no doubt that the F-86's armor saved many a plane that might otherwise have been lost, and the deadly accuracy of the heavy fire-control system gave the American pilots a significant advantage over the enemy.

The battle of compromise in the design of an airplane has been aptly summed up by one aerospace engineer: "You can't take it *all* with you."

Nature's Flying Machines

In 1901, two years before his historic flight, Wilbur Wright remarked that a bird's skill as a flier "is not apparent. . . . We only learn to appreciate it when we try to imitate it." Birds are not the only living flying machines, but they are the most versatile. As man has mastered flight in machines, his appreciation of natural flight has grown. In the sky, man and bird face similar problems and have arrived at remarkably similar solutions. Propeller, wings, flaps, stabilizers —each has its equivalent in the bird. The problem of how to combine maximum power with minimum weight, which long taxed man's technological prowess, was solved by nature in the course of eons—in the fast-flapping flight of insects, then in the aerodynamically more sophisticated flight of birds. Thus animals, like men, attained flight only after a long process of trial and error. At the end of that process were speed and the ease of being completely at home in the air.

PUTTING THE WIND TO WORK
On nearly motionless wings, a flock of ring-billed gulls *(opposite)* sails into a 25-mile wind above Lake Erie. Watching birds like these as they altered the pitch of their wings or the angle of their tails, early students of aviation learned of nature's designs for sustained, controlled flight. But it was not until men built their own flying machines that they understood how these designs worked.

FLYING SQUIRREL

TRIO OF SHORT-TERM GLIDERS

Putting gravity to work, specialized species of squirrel *(above)* and lizard *(right)* spread membrane "wings" to turn free falls into controlled glides. Taking off from treetops, the lizard can glide 50 feet, the squirrel 150 feet or more. Steering with their legs, the squirrels balance themselves with their tails. A flying fish *(below)* can glide as far as a flying squirrel but has to develop its own takeoff power first. Slanting up through the water and strongly propelled by its thrashing tail, the fish unfurls its wide fins as it enters the air. The gliding flight of each of these three animals is a brief one, seldom lasting longer than two or three seconds.

FLYING LIZARD

FLYING FISH

CLUMSY RUNNER, MASTER FLIER

Ungainly on land, the short-legged Laysan albatross *(above)* spreads its six-foot wings and runs for the takeoff. Albatrosses need a good breeze, a sharp drop or a long run, but once airborne they may not touch land again for four or five years, although they do land on the sea.

The Gliders or the Soarers

Man's first attempts to fly had more in common with the quick glide of the flying squirrel than with the serene soaring of the albatross *(above)*. Early experimenters, jumping from towers with crude wings strapped to their outstretched arms, at best could hope to achieve planing flight, with no chance to maneuver. A fatal plunge frequently was the result. The more astute of aviation's pioneers realized that such winged men could never truly fly, that only a larger machine capable of lifting a man with it could realize the dream of flight. The result was the construction of glid-

ers. One of the fanciest to get off the ground was built in France in 1856. It was modeled after the albatross. But appropriately shaped wings were not enough for the long-range gliding known today. Yet another secret of flight remained to be discovered. What was missing was an understanding of the bird's instinctive use of air currents. Land birds, such as eagles and hawks, are experts at riding rising columns of heated air, and sailing around in easy ascending circles. Seabirds, such as the albatross, can exploit layers of wind moving at various speeds to sail on for hours without exertion.

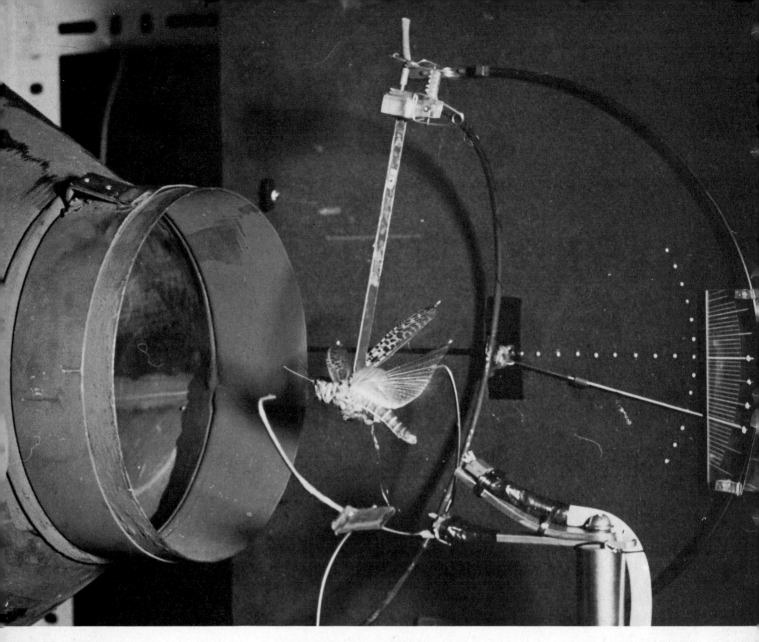

FLIGHT TEST FOR A LOCUST
Facing a wind tunnel, a harnessed locust beats its wings with remarkable efficiency at the rate of 17 stroke cycles per second, to attain a computed speed of 12 feet per second. The rod attached to the locust is suspended from a balance which, by measuring reduction of weight during each wing flap, measures lift. A scale *(right)* indicates the insect's angle of flight.

The Insects: Tiny Helicopters

Small, light and charged with energy, insects were the natural pioneers of animal flight, venturing into the air 300 million years ago, some 100 million years before the first vertebrates began to glide. Aerodynamically speaking, insects fly more like helicopters than airplanes. Their oscillating wings, like the helicopter's rotor, provide both lift and thrust. Like helicopters too, many insects are able to hover, fly backward and rise or descend nearly vertically.

Most insect flight is characterized by very-high-frequency wingbeats. Bees average 200 to 300 beats per second, midges as high as 1,000. The swiftest of insects—hawkmoths and dragonflies—can cruise at about 25 miles per hour, speeding up to 40 when pressed. But nimble and high-powered though they are, insects are not adapted to exploit wind currents as birds do. Their habit of taking off and flying straight into the wind often leads them into trouble. Flying into a wind blowing inland from a lake or ocean, swarms of insects may end up exhausted and too far out over the water to get back to land.

FIGURE-8 WING STROKE
In insect flight, each wing moves not simply up
and down but in a looping, figure-8 pattern.
As shown in the side view, the downstroke is
also a forward stroke and accomplishes the
work of lifting and propelling at the same time.
As the wings are brought back and up again,
they are feathered to minimize wind resistance.

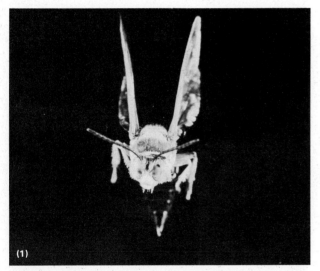

(1)

CICADA-KILLER WASP'S WINGS POSITIONED FOR DOWNSTROKE.

(2)

WINGS FLATTENED FOR LIFT HALFWAY THROUGH THE STROKE.

(3)

WINGS FAR FORWARD AND TWISTING BACK FOR THE UPSTROKE.

(4)

NEARING END OF UPSTROKE, WINGS KNIFE UP FOR A NEW CYCLE.

WINGS LIFTED AS UPSTROKE ENDS.   BEGINNING OF THE DOWNSTROKE.   PRIMARIES TWISTING UP AND OUT.

The Birds: Living Airplanes

Although men studied the flight of birds for centuries, seeking to learn their secrets, it was finally man's own invention—the propeller airplane—that gave him the key to understanding. For while an airplane is far from being a bird, a bird is actually a living airplane. In the bird each wing functions efficiently as a combined wing and propeller. The inner half of a bird's wing, its "arm," supplies most of the required lift. The outer half, or "hand," serves as the propelling agent (above). The primary feathers on the outer half of the wing twist out at an angle to the rest of the surface to attack the air. The pitch of the primaries can be altered to accelerate or brake (right). During gliding flight, the primaries lie flat so that the outer wing becomes an extended part of the lifting "arm."

Wings are adapted to the living habits of particular species of birds. A glider like the gull, for instance, has light, long, narrow wings with loose primaries that can respond to delicate wind shifts. A strong flier like the racing pigeon, which can fly as fast as 90 miles an hour, has short and heavy wings with tightly fitted primaries to form a strong propeller.

CONCLUSION OF THE DOWNSTROKE.

BEGINNING OF THE UPSTROKE.

WINGS SWEEPING BACK FOR NEW CYCLE.

A CYCLE OF THRUST AND LIFT

Six stages in the stroke cycle of a Canada goose *(above)* show the downstroke *(2 and 3)* bringing the outer half of the wing far forward as well as down. Air pressure during the downstroke twists the flexible, long primary feathers into propelling position. While the outer wing provides thrust, the inner part arches to provide the bird with a constant maximum of lift.

FULL STRETCH TO A STOP

A sparrow hawk's descent to a landing is caught in one fell swoop in this high-speed stroboscopic picture by photographer Gjon Mili. To end gliding flight, the wings are stretched fully outward and tilted vertically *(left)*. In this position they act as an effective air brake. From the very start of the landing, the hawk's tail spreads out in a wide fan to slow the bird down.

PREHISTORIC PROTOTYPE

The earliest known bird, flourishing 150 million years ago, *Archaeopteryx*, or "ancient wing," was short-winged, long-tailed and crow-sized, as this reproduction shows. Too unwieldy and weak for active flight, this "glorified reptile" probably fluttered out of trees for a glide.

EARLY BIRD IN FOSSIL FORM

Head bent back below outspread wings, *Archaeopteryx* lies perfectly preserved in a fossil *(right)* found in a Bavarian quarry in 1877. A lizard-like head, toothed jaws, bony tail and wing bones ending in sharp claws are all evidence of a reptile past, but the feathers prove it a bird.

A FRAME MADE FIT FOR FLIGHT

Archaeopteryx's skeleton, compared in this anatomical drawing to a pigeon's *(right)*, was poorly adapted to flight. In the pigeon, the bony tail has become a knob for tail feathers, the breast-bone a deep, strong anchor for flight muscles powering the wings. Hand bones are welded into one structure, and the brain has grown to accommodate keen senses of vision and balance.

Evolution of an Airframe

Birds evolved from four-legged lizards, which changed their structure as they changed their habitat. From the land they first moved to trees, from trees they took to the air. Forelimbs that had been used first for walking, then for climbing, were modified again for flight, becoming wings. The scales that armored the ground-running lizard were also gradually transformed, eventually becoming light, overlapping feathers.

Once started on an aerial life, the reptile body was altered in more subtle ways. The long lizard frame became a compact structure with a strong rib cage and shoulder girdle to support a body suspended from wings. At the same time, the lightness required of any flying machine was achieved by shedding most of the cumbersome tail and by a unique change within the bones—they were hollowed out *(page 48)*. A hard, adaptable bill took over the functions of the clawed forefeet, capturing and manipulating food, grooming the feathers, even acting as a weapon. Finally, responding to a new medium where coordination and sharp vision were crucial to its survival, the bird's brain expanded in a lighter skull.

ALULA

PRIMARIES

SECONDARIES

A Model for Flying Machines

Efficient power and a light, strong structure are two basic requirements for any flying machine. Both are consummately achieved in birds. In their bodies, bulk is pared down to a minimum. Even some bones are hollow (right). Their feathers, stronger for their weight than any wing structure achieved by man, are supremely adaptive to the varying pressures of the air. Powerful breast muscles, a big, rapidly beating heart and a high rate of metabolism furnish the motive power which makes birds not only enduring fliers, but also the swiftest of all animals. Heat generated by the driving muscles as they burn up high-calorie fuel is regulated by the most efficient respiratory system to be found among the vertebrates. About three quarters of each air intake spreads through lungs and a network of supplementary air sacs in the bird's body for cooling during flight. In some birds these air sacs extend right down to their toes. The use of fuel is equally efficient. After a 2,400-mile nonstop migratory flight, the golden plover weighs only two ounces less than it did at the start.

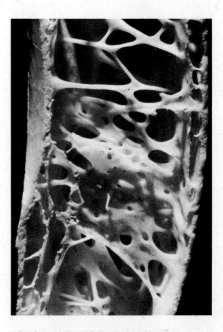

TOUGH AND VERSATILE BONES
A hollow girder stiffened with struts, an eagle's upper arm bone (above) is perfectly adapted for flight. The honeycomb of air spaces in such bones not only contributes to the bird's light weight, but may also form a working part of its extensive combined respiratory and cooling system.

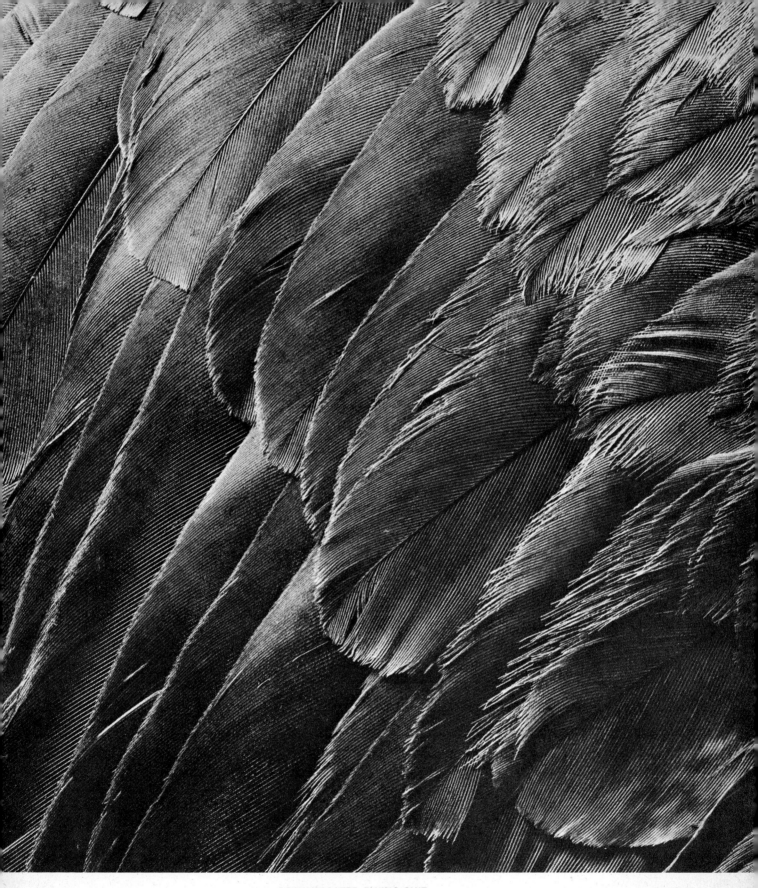

SOPHISTICATED FLYING SUIT

Streamlined, strong and flexible, feathers fulfill many purposes. This trim row *(above)*, covering part of a buzzard's wing, provides a properly contoured lift surface. Extended primaries at the end of the wing propel. Compact body feathers offer a surface with low friction. When properly groomed, they are waterproof and help water birds to float. Underneath, short, fluffy feathers, or down, effectively insulate the bird. Protected by feathers, penguins, skuas and other birds are able to thrive in parts of the Antarctic far too cold for other animals to withstand.

The Pioneers
of Distance Flying

When men at last found it possible to make not only short hops but also lengthy journeys in airplanes, they faced the new problem of aerial navigation. It was a problem millions of birds seemed to solve every spring and fall as they traveled between winter feeding grounds and distant breeding grounds. What equipment did the birds employ? At least a part of the bird's ability to navigate appears to depend on its visual perception of landmarks—but only a part. Albatrosses flown by airplane thousands of miles from their Midway Island nests have found their way back over unfamiliar stretches of ocean: one returned after covering more than 4,000 miles in 32 days. Recent experiments have shown that certain species of birds make use of the sun and stars to navigate, and may even possess an "internal clock" capable of making time corrections for the changing position of the sun. To equal the mysterious mechanism by which birds chart their course, man had to invent complex instruments and build a widespread communications network—a bulky substitute for the instinct at work within the light skull of a migrant bird.

V-FORMED FOR EASIER FLIGHT
Following a leader makes flying easier for this flock of graylag geese *(right)* on its annual fall flight from Scandinavia to Southern Europe and North Africa. While the leader "breaks trail" through the air, each following bird gains lift from an updraft off the wing of the bird ahead.

3

The Science of Aerodynamics

SMOKE TRAIL OF A STALL
Lines of smoke in a wind tunnel mark the flow of air around a wing model. The nature of the airflow over a plane's wing is the basic factor that determines whether the aircraft will stay aloft. Smooth flow generates lift; but if, as in this case, the flow breaks away from the wing's top surface, turbulence results and lift is destroyed. The wing is then said to be stalled.

THERE IS AN OLD SAYING in the aviation world: "Give me an engine powerful enough and I'll fly a barn door." It is true enough. Sufficient power applied to a propeller can pull a remarkably inefficient wing into the air. However, a much more efficient method of achieving flight is to shape the vehicle so that its surfaces produce the greatest amount of lift while creating the least amount of drag.

As explained in Chapter 2, lift and drag are the predominant aerodynamic forces that act upon an airplane. As a consequence, they are the primary factors which influence the shape of the plane. In particular, they influence the shape of the wing, the basic lifting surface for either bird or airplane. Nature's wings, designed to suit the needs of the individual bird, dictate the type of flying the bird may perform. A sea gull, for example, would be hopelessly out of place attempting to hover while sipping nectar from a flower hummingbird-fashion. In manned flight, the characteristics of an airplane's wing have the greatest influence on its performance.

The concept of lift is not often understood by the layman. The prevalent idea seems to be that lift is the result of an upward pushing of the air against the bottom of an airplane wing. This is only partially correct; it overlooks the force acting on the upper side of the wing, where the bulk of lift is created. In reality, lift is actually produced by the differences in the pressure of the air above and below the wing.

There is an area of low pressure above the wing which is explained by a principle advanced by the Swiss mathematician Daniel Bernoulli. In 1738 Bernoulli published a paper entitled *Hydrodynamica*, which discussed the forces exerted by fluids in motion. One part of this work contained the formula known as Bernoulli's principle, which explained how the pressure of a moving fluid (which also covers gases) changes with its speed of motion.

Water moving through a hose exerts a uniform pressure on the hose. Bernoulli's principle states that if the flow of water in the hose is speeded up, the pressure on the hose actually decreases. One way to increase the speed of water flowing through a hose is to pinch the hose, thereby constricting the space through which the water must pass; this will also have the effect of decreasing the pressure of the water on the hose. The same effect could be achieved by inserting an object into the hose, and it is by this principle that an airplane's wing achieves lift. In effect, an airplane in flight is an object inserted into a moving stream of air. If an airplane's wings in profile were the shape of a teardrop, the speed of the air passing over the top and bottom would be identical, and the lowered air pressure that resulted from this speedup would be the same on both sides.

However, if this teardrop-shaped wing were cut in half, a shape resembling a basic airplane wing would result. With this configuration, air molecules moving over the curved upper surface would have farther to go, and would have to move faster to keep pace with molecules moving along the flat bottom of the wing. The speedup of air on the top would result in a comparative drop in pressure. This difference in pressure produces lift.

High pressure from below

While most lift comes from the low pressure on *top* of the wing, a certain amount is generated from beneath by the air striking the lower part of the wing. Here the effect is the reverse of what happens on the wing's upper surface. The airflow on the underside of the wing is stopped at a point close to the leading edge. It then gradually picks up speed until, near the trailing edge of the wing it has reached the same velocity as the air on the upper surface of the wing. In accordance with Bernoulli's principle, during the course of its passage beneath the wing, this slowed air was at a higher pressure and thus created a positive, upward pressure against the wing.

There are several things that influence the amount of lift. Wing area is one, because the larger the surface exposed to the air, the greater the lift. Speed is another factor, because the more swiftly the air passes over the upper surface, the greater the pressure differential. A third factor is the "angle of attack," the up or down tilt of the wing as it strikes the airflow. Within certain limits, the more a wing is uptilted—that is, the greater the angle of attack—the greater the resultant pressure differential between the top and bottom of the wing. It is a matter of simple mechanics. With an uptilted wing, the air passing over the top has a greater distance to travel and thus is speeded up more. The larger the pressure differential, the greater the lift will be.

A pilot, of course, alters his angle of attack continually in the course of a flight. But additional lift produced by an increased angle of attack is most essential in landing. It may seem odd that a pilot descending to a runway is concerned with getting *more* lift—a condition usually associated with gaining altitude. Since he wants to land at the slowest possible safe speed, he is continually reducing speed as he approaches the touchdown point. In slowing forward motion, he is losing lift. He is forced to compensate for this by increasing his plane's angle of attack. In addition he uses his flaps.

Every regular airline traveler is familiar with these devices, the large extensions of the wing located at the trailing edge. Normally retracted into the wing during cruise flight, most flaps are rolled downward and rearward when the pilot wants extra lift. The extra lift is partly the result of a larger wing area provided by the flaps. The downward extension

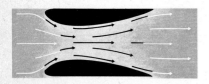

BERNOULLI'S PRINCIPLE, which explains how lift is created by an airplane's wing, is depicted in these three diagrams. A fluid traveling through a constriction in a pipe *(above)* speeds up, and at the same time the pressure it exerts on the pipe decreases.

THE CONSTRICTED AIRFLOW shown here, formed by two opposed airplane wings, is analogous to the pinched-pipe situation above: air moving between the wings accelerates, and this increase in speed results in lower pressure between the curved surfaces.

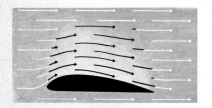

THE SAME PRINCIPLE applies when the air is disturbed by a single wing. The accelerating airflow over the top surface exerts less pressure than the airflow across the bottom. It is this continuing difference in pressure that creates and sustains lift.

of the flaps also increases the angle of attack since there is a new, lower trailing edge. Apocryphal or otherwise, there is a story among pilots which dramatically illustrates the lifting power flaps provide. During World War II, the pilot of a large C-87 cargo plane had taken off from the airport at Agra, India, with a heavy load on board. He had specifically asked for a small load of fuel, but the ground crew had put on a full load, and failed to tell the pilot. Not until the plane began to lurch down the runway did the pilot realize the added weight he was carrying—about a three-ton overload. By then he was committed to take off and seconds later the plane was headed for one of the towers on the Taj Mahal, which was being repaired and was swarming with workmen. The pilot gave the plane full throttle but it still refused to rise. Desperate, he ordered full flaps lowered. Instantly, as it lost some of its forward speed due to increased drag, the plane ballooned upward a hundred feet, clearing the famed tomb, to the immense relief of the workmen.

In a landing situation, this combination of flaps and a greater angle of attack provides a substantial increase in lift. Without this compensation, there would be insufficient lift to sustain flight at the slow speeds involved; the plane would "stall" and could possibly crash. Fundamentally, stall is the failure of lift. When a pilot increases his angle of attack, the effect is to create added lift. However, this is true only up to a certain point. On the average airplane when the angle of attack reaches about 14°, the airflow of the upper surface of the wing begins to break away from the wing and create turbulence far greater than is normally present near the trailing edge of the wing. As the angle of attack is increased, this turbulence begins to occur over a greater and greater percentage of the wing.

If the pilot continues to increase his angle of attack, separation of the airflow and the resulting turbulence occur over the entire upper surface of the wing, the amount of lift becomes inconsequential, and the plane stalls.

Three types of drag

While lift is the force which enables an airplane to rise into the air, the forward motion of the airplane—along with the lift itself—generate the retarding force termed "drag," of which there are three basic types: friction drag, form drag and induced drag. The first two are the results simply of the effect of moving a body through a substance—in this case an airplane through the air. Induced drag, on the other hand, is a byproduct of the lift generated by the wings.

Friction drag is caused by what aerodynamicists call the "boundary layer." The boundary layer is actually made up of a number of extremely thin layers of air, collectively constituting a thickness measured in inches. As the airplane flies along, the thin layer in immediate contact with the wing sticks to the surface. The next layer rubs against the surface layer, the third layer against the second and so forth. The effect is similar to that which occurs when a deck of playing cards is tossed on a table: the bottom card sticks to the table, those immediately adjacent move a little, those next in line move a bit more and so on.

Near the leading edge of the wing, the frictional layer is smooth, or, to use the aerodynamicists' term, "laminar." But at some point on the wing, depending on its design, the boundary layer becomes turbulent in the way smoke from a cigarette, after rising cleanly, breaks up into a whirling pattern a few inches above the tip. Similarly, boundary-layer turbulence increases as the air moves rearward, and the boundary layer reaches its greatest thickness near the trailing edge.

A payoff in power

Where the air is smooth, the drag force is considerably less than in the turbulent portion of the boundary layer. It is obvious, then, that if the boundary-layer flow could be kept laminar, there would accrue a tremendous benefit to airplane performance. The airplane's engine would not have to expend so much of its power overcoming boundary-layer drag, and the available power could be utilized more efficiently to provide greater speed, range or payload.

Control of the boundary layer has attracted considerable attention from flight researchers. One experiment devised to investigate possible reduction of drag through laminar-flow control involved the conversion of two weather reconnaissance planes; their twin jet engines were moved to mountings at the aft end of the fuselage and a pair of pumps was installed where the engines had hung beneath the wings. Slot lines, running outward from the fuselage to the tips, were cut in both the upper and lower surfaces of the wing. In flight, the turbine-driven pumps drew the turbulent air into the wing, smoothing the flow; the "inhaled" air was then discharged from the rear of the pods. Test instrumentation showed that the suction system was able to maintain laminar flow over most of the wing, thus substantially lowering friction drag.

The advent of more powerful engines, which in itself offered substantial improvement of range or payload, has lessened interest in boundary layer research, but recently some authorities have recommended renewed efforts to apply its efficiencies. Many questions about the pumped-laminar flow system remain to be answered; how does the system perform under operational conditions? How much of a problem is maintenance? How costly is it in routine use?

Even if aeronautical science eventually does conquer friction drag, there still remain the two other basic drag components with which to

LAMINAR-FLOW CONTROL, an experimental technique to reduce drag caused by air friction across the surface of a plane's wings, was first successfully tested in 1963. A special wing was built with numerous slots running its length *(above)* and rigged with two turbine-driven pumps underneath *(below)*. As the layer of churning air swirled past the wing's surfaces, it was sucked through the slots by the pumps, then blown rearward from under the wing, resulting in a smooth flow.

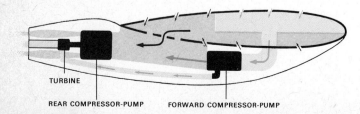

TURBINE

REAR COMPRESSOR-PUMP   FORWARD COMPRESSOR-PUMP

deal: form drag and induced drag. They can each be reduced, but neither can be eliminated completely. Form drag is simply the resistance of the air to the passage of a body through it. A blunt shape—such as a box—creates a great deal of form drag, whereas a streamlined airfoil creates very little.

The advantages of streamlining are considerably more dramatic than they would appear. For example, a streamlined wing traveling 210 mph with a maximum thickness of 10 inches actually produces slightly less drag than a round—and therefore unstreamlined—wire *one* inch in diameter. Mindful of this, it becomes apparent how incredibly inefficient early biplanes were with their maze of struts and cross-bracing wires. Though early fliers were aware of drag, the problem was relatively minor at low speeds. It was not until planes became faster that the niceties of streamlining and other drag-reducing techniques became major design factors.

Induced drag, the third type, is traceable to the fact that the wing is a lifting surface. In short, induced drag is the penalty exacted for creating lift. The pressure difference in air passing over an airplane's wing, by which lift is created, results in lower pressure on the upper surface and high pressure underneath. This imbalance in pressure causes a downwash, or wake; in addition, high-pressure air tends to flow toward an area of low pressure. This occurs primarily at the tips of the wings, where there is nothing to impede the process. So high pressure from below curls upward into the low pressure above, forming two spiral-shaped vortices as the plane flies along.

The creation of the downwash and these vortices results in a rearward force which must be overcome by a forward force or thrust, provided by the engines.

A lingering menace

In still air, these vortices, particularly those created by large planes, do not dissipate immediately and can be a genuine menace to small craft. Some years ago, a single-engine Piper Tri-Pacer was flying near Dover, Delaware, in clear weather. Unknown to the pilot, a four-engine C-124 cargo plane had flown by a short time before, leaving a huge but invisible wake in its path. The Tri-Pacer hit the wake, and the turbulence was so violent that the little plane's wings were folded upward and it crashed.

There is one other source of drag which does not qualify as basic because it is not common to all aircraft; it exists only in those planes which fly near or faster than the speed of sound. That speed varies with temperature; at sea level in moderate weather it is about 760 miles per hour, but at high altitude, where the temperature is lower, it falls off to

660. Whatever its actual measurement in miles per hour, the speed of sound is known to modern airmen as Mach 1, in honor of Ernst Mach (1838-1916), an Austrian physicist and psychologist who did lengthy studies on the behavior of sound. Mach numbers are used over the entire range of high-speed flight. They stand for a percentage of the speed of sound. Mach 0.8 is 80 per cent of the speed of sound, or slightly more than 525 miles per hour at 30,000 feet. (Planes flying near or above the speed of sound operate at high altitudes, and thus compute their Mach numbers using 660 mph as the speed of sound.)

The thunderclap of jets

The near-sonic/supersonic drag phenomenon is known as wave drag, and it is caused by abrupt pressure changes in the air brought about by the onrushing airplane. A plane moving at any speed sends a "signal" of its approach to the air ahead. That signal, a pressure wave moving at the speed of sound, "warns" the air to begin moving out of the way. However, when a plane is moving faster than its warning wave, the air ahead has no time to part. Billions of tiny air molecules, instead of moving out of the airplane's path, are abruptly shoved to the side and compressed by the intruding body. This creates a region of compressed air, a cone-shaped shock wave. A plane in this situation develops a series of such shock waves at the nose, the leading edges of the wing and tail surfaces and along the fuselage. There is a similar series of shock waves behind these wing and tail surfaces, where the moving air comes together again. The lower section of these conical waves extends to the ground in the thunderlike clap known as the sonic boom.

Like induced drag, which is the detrimental but unavoidable by-product that accompanies the creation of lift, wave drag is the detrimental but inescapable price paid for traveling near or above the speed of sound. The power necessary to build up the region of high pressure which accompanies a plane's passage into the area of sonic speeds must be supplied by the engines of the airplane and constitutes wave drag. The shock-wave buildup starts at about Mach 0.8 for most planes. Even though the plane is not then moving as fast as sound, the accelerated air moving over the top of the wing reaches supersonic speed and a small shock wave is formed. The region from about Mach 0.8 to Mach 1.2 is called the transonic region because some of the airflow is subsonic and some supersonic.

The swept-back wing design so common in fast airplanes is a result of minimizing the problem of flying in and beyond this transonic region. The fact is that even a subsonic plane like the 707 could never operate at the speeds it does unless its wings were swept back. This is because the 707 does in fact cruise at speeds of around 600 mph at altitudes of

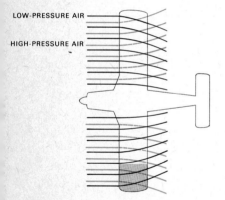

LOW-PRESSURE AIR

HIGH-PRESSURE AIR

WING-TIP VORTEX *(below)* produces part of the induced drag that cuts aerodynamic efficiency. As a plane's wings move through the air *(above)*, a low-pressure flow forms on top which bends inward *(black lines)*, and an outward-bending high-pressure flow forms beneath *(blue lines)*. The outward flow at the wing tip curls up and over the edge and, turned by the wing's forward motion into a twisting trail of air, it sucks in part of the upper stream *(below)*. The energy expended to create this vortex is part of the unavoidable price a plane must pay for lift.

UPPER WING SURFACE NEAR TIP

LOW-PRESSURE AIR

HIGH-PRESSURE AIR

25,000 feet or over. This is more than 90 per cent of the speed of sound.

At such speeds, a straight-winged 707 would have an airspeed over the wings, due to the acceleration needed for lift, of supersonic levels. Assuming such a 707 had sufficient power to overcome the drag created at these speeds, the shock waves set up could cause severe buffeting and a lack of control.

However, by sweeping back the wings, the formation of shock waves is delayed. In flight, the swept-back wing meets the air at an angle. The effect of this is that now the velocity of the wind relative to the wing acts in two directions—one at a right angle to the leading edge of the wing, and the other along the span of the wing. Neither of these components is equal to the original velocity of the wind striking the forward edge of the wing—which, in fact, is the speed of the airplane.

It is only that part of the wind passing at a right angle to the leading edge of the wing which is accelerated in its passage in order to obtain lift. Since the speed of this wind is less than the forward speed of the airplane, it becomes possible for the airplane to fly much closer to the speed of sound before shock waves begin to form on the wings.

Designers express the relationship between the amount of lift and the amount of drag in a plane with a figure known as the "lift-to-drag ratio." An extremely efficient wing, designed for low-speed flight, with a lift-to-drag ratio of as much as 30, would have 30 times more lift than its drag force. Transport aircraft generally have lift-to-drag ratios of about 15. With the onset of wave drag at high subsonic speed and the resulting increase in overall drag, L/D ratio drops off sharply. A wing that produces eight times as much lift as drag at Mach 3 is well designed.

The L/D ratio determines how far a plane will "glide" should it suddenly lose power. That is, a plane with an L/D ratio of 30 will, for every 30 feet of forward motion, descend one foot in altitude. All gliders have a very high L/D ratio so that they will descend very slowly when not riding an updraft.

Long and lean for soaring

The L/D ratio is directly dependent upon another factor, which the aerodynamicist calls "aspect ratio." Aspect ratio is the relationship between the length or span of a wing and its chord, the average distance between the leading and trailing edges. A high-aspect-ratio wing is one wherein the span is many times greater than the chord length. Wing area, of course, is a consideration in the creation of both lift and drag, but two wings with identical area yet different aspect ratios will have very different lift and drag characteristics, due mostly to differences in the vortices which create induced drag. Wing aspect ratio helps determine how far a plane can fly with a given fuel load, and the high-aspect-ratio wing is employed where range is the dominant factor in the design. For example, all soaring planes have high-aspect-ratio wings, as do certain specialized aircraft like the Grumman Albatross, a Coast Guard/Navy/Air Force search-and-rescue plane, or the Lockheed U-2, a very-high-altitude reconnaissance craft which was the subject of some less-than-diplomatic exchanges of opinion between the U.S. and the Soviet Union a few years ago. There is also a parallel in nature. The soaring birds—the eagle, hawk, albatross, condor, gull—have long glide and long range capability because of their high-aspect-ratio wings.

A form for every function

All of the foregoing must be taken into consideration by the aerodynamicist as he shapes the design of an airplane. To combat the slowing effects of friction drag, he shapes the cross section of the wing in a manner designed to keep the airflow laminar as long as possible. He attempts to minimize the simple air resistance caused by form drag by making the airplane as streamlined as possible. For high-speed aircraft he employs the extremely thin, swept-back wing and slender fuselage as a countermeasure to wave drag because such a design offers a lesser degree of air compression leading to the formation of shock waves. If the plane is to fly at supersonic speed, the leading edge of the wing becomes knifelike and the fuselage nose is tapered to a sharp point, further decreasing the drag due to shock-wave formation.

The thin, swept wing is most efficient at high speeds, but the desired drag reduction is obtained at the expense of lift. The fastest airplane must still land and take off at low speed, and in this portion of the flight profile a Mach 3 wing is inefficient. Thus the ideal wing for a high-performance aircraft is one which presents an almost straight leading edge to the air at low-speed operation and a swept-back edge at supersonic speed. After years of study and experiment, researchers have produced such a hybrid airfoil: the variable-sweep wing.

This innovation offers the best of two aerodynamic worlds: high lift at low speed, low drag at high speed. Variable sweep wings are employed by the Air Force's General Dynamics F-111 fighter and FB-111 bomber which take off with their wing leading edges swept back only 16 degrees. During flight the pilot can change the angle through a full range of positions up to the 72.5° of sweep considered best for these airplanes' maximum speed. Prior to landing, the wing is swung forward once again to the nearly straight configuration required for low speeds. The design of the Navy F-14 and the Air Force F-15, fighter planes intended for use during the 1970s also incorporate the swing-wing. It is applicable to commercial supersonic transports as well but was not used on early models because of its weight and complexity.

60

An airplane's function, of course, may dictate emphasis on other performance values, for instance, a large weight-lifting capability coupled with high subsonic speed, as is the case in modern airliners. The plane must carry upward of a hundred passengers, so its fuselage must have sufficient volume, but it is made relatively thin with respect to its length. For 600-mile-an-hour speeds, the transport needs a moderately swept wing to delay the formation of shock waves. The lift requirements of a heavy aircraft demand a rather large wing area, and the plane's operational employment on transcontinental or transoceanic routes calls for the high-aspect-ratio wing.

The designer of the light private plane takes a completely different approach. If his craft is to operate in the 100- to 200-mile-per-hour-zone, the matter of drag presents less of a problem. He does not want the thin, swept-back wing which would cost him lift and bring on stability and control problems. He does not want a great wing span with its attendant structural difficulties. He employs the short-span wing with reasonable thickness for structural strength, and the straight leading edge for low-speed lift and stability.

In the design process, an aerodynamicist may employ a number of special devices which increase wing efficiency in one way or another or offer a solution to a specific problem of flight. For example, it is possible to vary the angle of attack of a wing mechanically rather than by elevating the nose of an aircraft for landing lift, a remedy for a problem peculiar to naval aircraft operations. Nose-lifting presents difficulties to the pilot attempting to land on an aircraft carrier. High-speed aircraft frequently have poor visibility because the cockpit canopy is sharply streamlined as a drag-reduction measure. When the nose comes up, it blocks the pilot's forward view of the landing strip. In the Navy's F-8 Crusader, the wing is movable so that the pilot can increase the angle of attack without pulling up the nose.

A rein on speed

The pilot of a military fighter might want to dive at a steep angle without building up excess speed which could make it difficult to pull out of the dive. For this purpose, some aircraft are fitted with dive brakes, aerodynamic panels which look like flaps and which pop out of the wing or fuselage at a near-perpendicular angle to the line of flight, increasing drag.

In providing the high-speed airplane with a swept wing for retarding the shock wave, the designer encounters a new problem: the airflow tends to follow the sweep angle; that is, it curves outward toward the wing tips. As a result, the boundary layer becomes turbulent on the outer parts of the wing, then separates and causes drag. The designer's

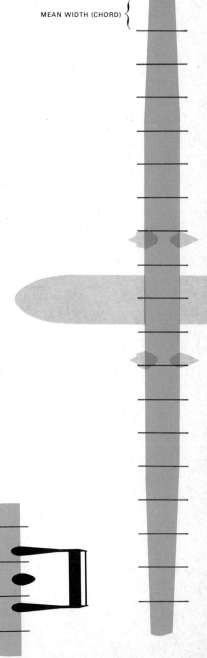

MEAN WIDTH (CHORD)

THE ASPECT RATIO OF A WING, obtained by dividing the wing's mean width into its span, is an important factor in determining flight performance. The aspect ratio will vary widely according to a plane's purpose. Thus, the Hurel-Dubois 31 *(far right)*, built for great range at high altitudes, has long, slender wings and a high aspect ratio of 20.2. The OV-10A Bronco, a stubby-winged, highly maneuverable light reconnaissance plane, has an aspect ratio of only 5.5.

remedy is the aerodynamic fence, a thin, metal strip jutting above the wing and running fore to aft. The fence serves as a barrier to the airflow, blocking its movement toward the tips. A large wing may have several fences to channel the air in a direction roughly parallel to the longitudinal axis of the airplane, thereby delaying the boundary-layer buildup and cutting down on drag.

Another tool used by the aerodynamicist is the vortex generator. This is a small, wing-shaped object mounted on the upper surface of the wing; on an airliner there are often long rows of these airfoils in front of the ailerons and flaps. The airflow acts on the vortex generator just as it does on the main wing of the airplane, and a series of small vortices is created. These air whirlpools serve to energize the boundary layer by mixing high-speed air with the sluggish air of the boundary layer. Such an accelerated airflow tends to follow the surface of the wings so that when the ailerons or flaps are positioned down, the end result is much better control of the airplane.

These are the essentials of the fascinating science of aerodynamics, the constant struggle to effect a balance between lift and drag, a compromise consistent with the purpose of the airplane. Design ingenuity is the real basis for manned flight, and aerodynamics has been rightfully termed "The Queen of the Flight Sciences."

The Key to Practical Flight

Basic to powered flight are the aerodynamic forces created by an airplane's interaction with the air. As a plane moves it creates a wind, which reaches hurricane speeds or higher. Airmen call this "relative wind." The pressures exerted by this rushing air as it passes over wings and tail surfaces are what make stable flight possible. On the curved wings, the relative wind generates lift, a force that counters gravity. The horizontal tail surfaces act in the wind like a weather vane lying flat, holding the plane level. In similar fashion, the vertical fin holds the airplane straight. And by presenting various movable surfaces (*opposite*) at varying angles to the relative wind, the pilot "bends" the air to do his bidding and thus controls his airplane's flight. Maneuvers shown in this essay are exaggerated to emphasize the interplay of relative wind and airplane surfaces.

AGENTS OF CONTROL
Movable surfaces on wings and tail *(opposite)* govern the attitude and actions of an aircraft. Ailerons *(blue)* tipping in opposite directions on the trailing edges of the wings deflect the airflow to force wing ends up or down. On the horizontal tail plane, a movable trailing edge, the elevator *(yellow)*, governs fore-and-aft pitch—and thus controls the angle at which the wing meets the air, the so-called angle of attack. The rudder *(red)*, on the vertical tail fin, controls lateral rotation.

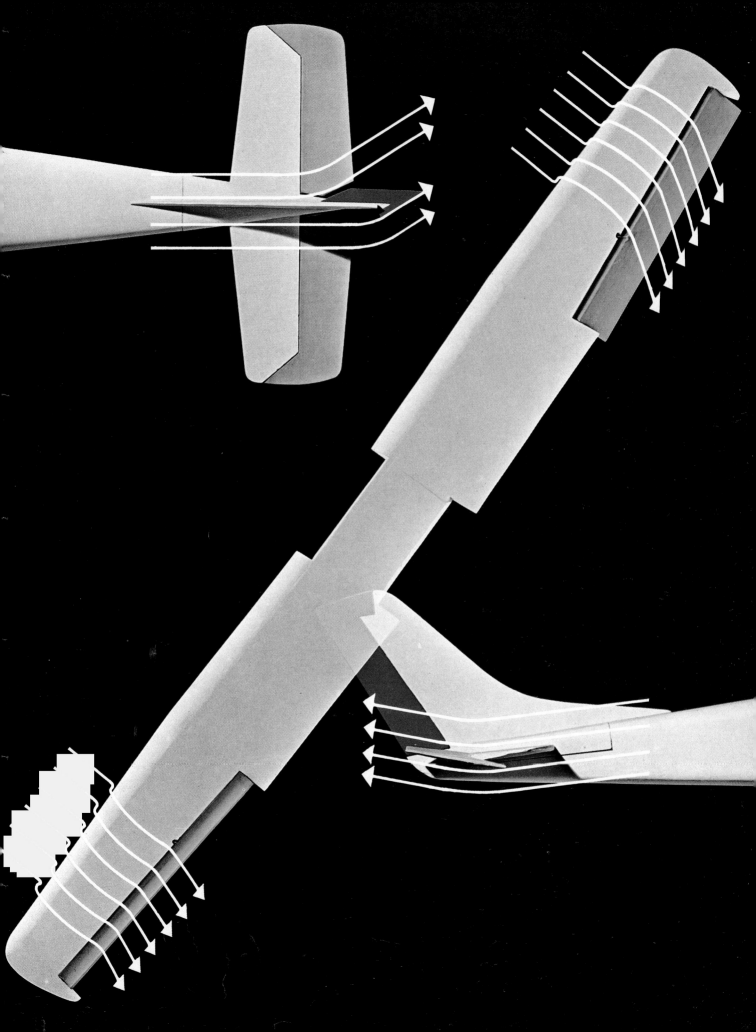

Multiple exposures reveal four stages of a takeoff. As the plane nears flying speed, its elevator is deflected; the tail is forced down,

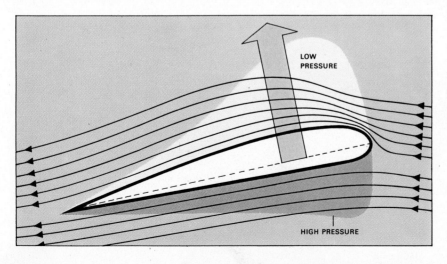

AIR OVER WING YIELDS LIFT
Streaming across a wing *(left)*, moving air creates a low-pressure area *(light blue)* over the wing, a high-pressure area *(dark blue)* beneath it. In this case the resultant force *(arrow)* is directed upward; but if the wing's attitude changes, so will the direction of the lifting force, since it always acts perpendicularly to the wing.

THE ROLE OF THE ELEVATOR
During takeoff the elevator is raised *(opposite)*, increasing the lifting force of the tail surface. Here, however, the lift force is exerted downward, forcing the tail down. This raises the nose and tilts the wing into a high angle of attack.

tilting the wings into a more pronounced angle of attack. Off the ground, the plane levels off to pick up speed before resuming its climb.

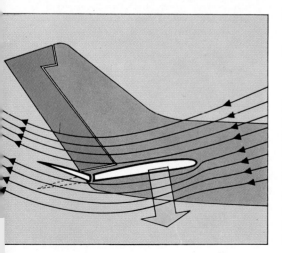

The Takeoff: Wing vs. Gravity

Moving down a runway, an airplane approaches flying speed. Wind rushing across the wing is generating lift: because the curve on the wing's upper surface makes the distance from leading to trailing edge greater than on the underside, air over the wing speeds up and pressure becomes less than below. But the lift force is yet insufficient. The pilot deflects the elevator, rotating the nose up and steepening the angle at which the wing attacks the air. To overcome the increased curve, air speeds up still more, generating greater lift. But a high attack angle also creates more drag: it is harder to pull the craft through the air. So after the plane is aloft it is leveled off, momentarily reducing drag to speed up for a climb.

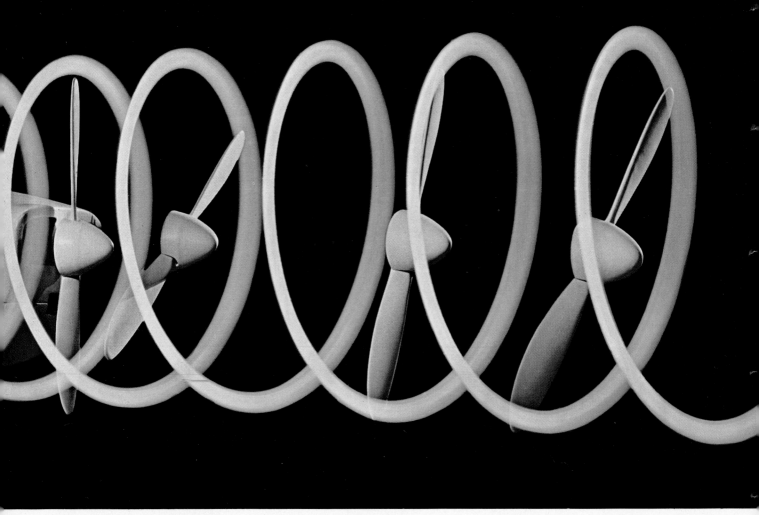

A propeller blade moving through the air and pulling an airplane describes a corkscrew path. Shown here, in a spiral of blue, is the pattern

The Propeller:
A Twisted Wing

The primary factor in flight is forward motion: an airplane must be moving fast enough for the relative wind to create the lift it needs to stay in the air. But what makes it move? Surprisingly, the answer once again is lift—only in this case it is lift directed forward, by the whirling propeller blades. For the propeller is actually a wing that revolves in a vertical plane: the lift force it generates is called "thrust."

This may be more easily understood if a propeller blade is viewed in cross section, as opposite. Now it reveals its classic wing shape: a convex curve on the upper—now forward—surface, with the bottom—or rear surface—relatively flat. As the blades turn, air flowing over them reacts exactly as with a wing: a low-pressure

area is created on the forward face because the airflow speeds up there, and the pressure differential between the front and rear surfaces results in forward thrust.

But why is a propeller twisted? The answer is startlingly simple: like all things that turn around a central hub, the outer parts of the propeller travel faster through the air than the inner ones. In other words, more air is attacked at a greater speed toward the tip than toward the hub. This, combined with the forward velocity of the airplane itself, dictates a relatively flat pitch toward the tip; near the hub, however, the blades must be set at higher pitch to generate maximum thrust. The twist is simply the result of the changing pitch from the tips of the blades inward.

HOW A PROPELLER WORKS
From the tip to the hub, a propeller blade in cross section shows its airfoil shapes pitched at constantly increasing angles. The paths followed by blade elements as they attack the air are shown in curved black lines; the angles of attack to the relative wind are described between these lines and the chord lines, drawn from the leading edge to the trailing edge of each blade cross section. As on a wing, the net force is perpendicular to the chord line (arrow).

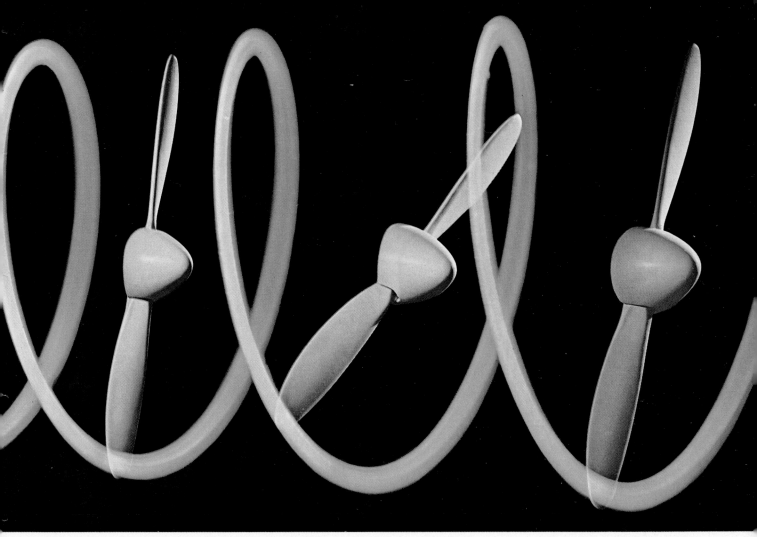

made by one point on the blade as it rotates. As thrust increases, the plane is pulled forward: the widening spiral shows it picking up speed.

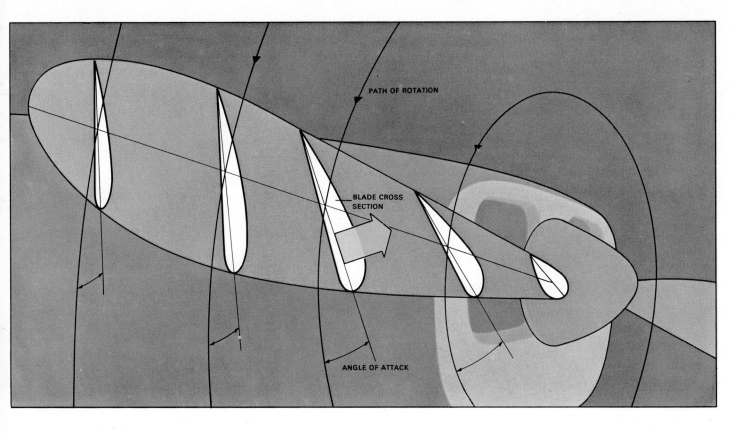

PATH OF ROTATION

BLADE CROSS SECTION

ANGLE OF ATTACK

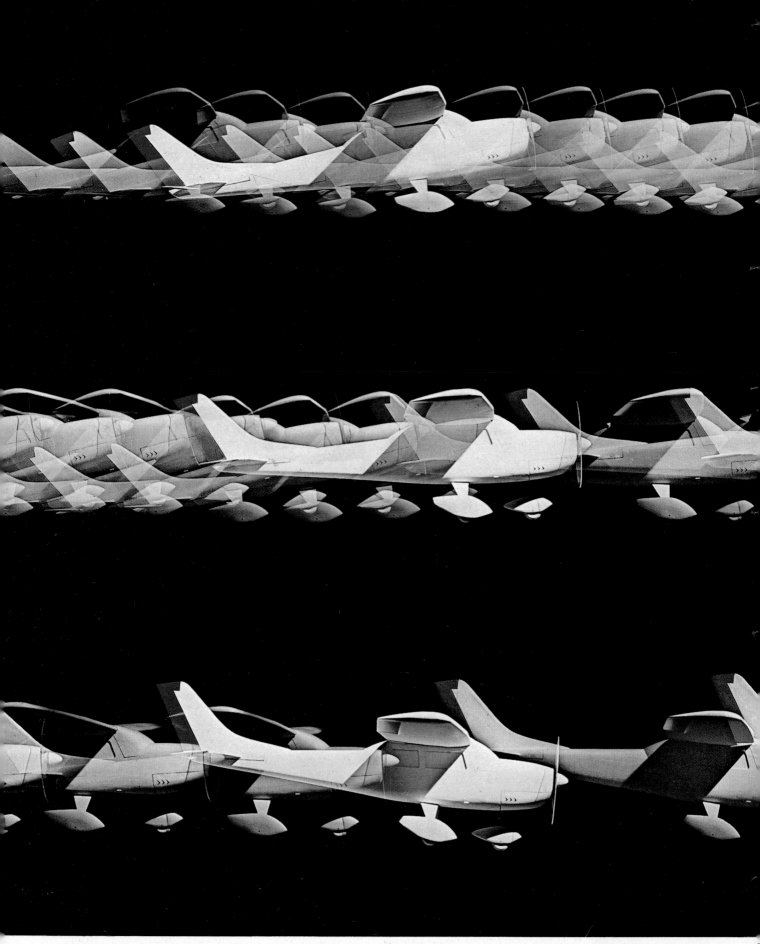

Speed and lift are directly related. At low speed *(top line)*, the angle of attack is high. At cruising speed *(middle line)*, the angle of attack

Three Kinds of
Straight and Level

After it has climbed to cruising altitude, the airplane levels off and starts its journey. Now, in straight and level flight, all forces working on it are in balance. Thrust equals drag, lift compensates exactly for the airplane's weight. Should any of these forces be unbalanced, the craft will automatically alter its flight path up or down in search of equilibrium. To hold to level flight the pilot must precisely coordinate both the angle of attack and thrust. If thrust decreases —i.e., his engine slows down slightly —speed decreases, and lift becomes less than weight: the plane will start descending. To bring it to level flight again, the pilot can open his throttle to reestablish his previous force of thrust—or he can pitch the airplane up slightly, increasing the wing's angle of attack to generate additional lift. In this case, he will have changed the conditions of his flight—though on a level flight path, he will now be flying more slowly *(top row, left)*.

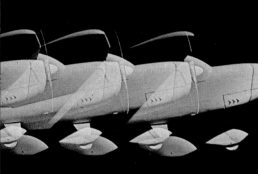

LOW SPEED

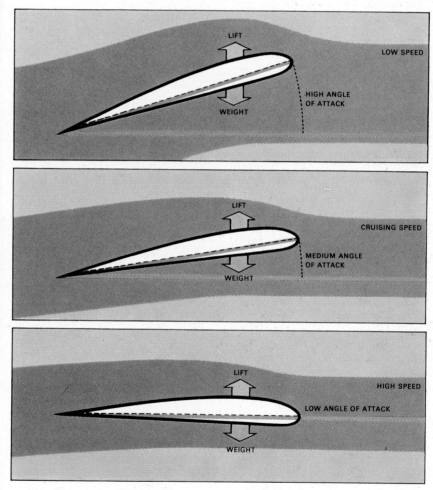

SPEED AND ANGLE OF ATTACK
Level flight may be sustained at speeds from very slow to very fast. In the sequence pictures at top left, the airplane is going into "mushing" flight: nose-high, with little thrust and a high angle of attack, its speed has dropped close to the minimum *(diagram, above)*. In the middle row, the nose has been lowered for cruising speed: thrust and angle of attack are coordinated for optimum performance. At high speed *(bottom row)*, greatly increased thrust—i.e., throttle opened wide—must make up for the extremely small angle of attack: in theory, level flight even at a slight negative angle of attack is possible at extreme high speed. In the diagram, arrows show the lift remaining equal to weight in spite of the changing attitude of the wing.

CRUISING SPEED

HIGH SPEED

is less. At high speed the angle is about zero.

This greatly compressed sequence photograph shows the stages of a right turn: first, ailerons deflected to bank wings; then ailerons

The Turn: Inward Lift

How does an airplane turn? A pilot flying a straight course decides to turn right *(above)*. He momentarily deflects his ailerons to force the right wing tip down and the left wing tip up, putting his plane into a banked attitude. The wing's lift now operates inwardly as well as upwardly, with the force of inward lift pulling the plane into a curving flight path. But now centrifugal force reacts to the turn, pulling the plane in the opposite direction, to the left. This counterforce balances inward lift, and thus held in equilibrium the plane turns smoothly. The rudder is used only to counteract yaw *(opposite)*. During the turn the elevator is tilted up slightly to force the wings to a higher angle of attack; this compensates for the sacrifice of upward lift.

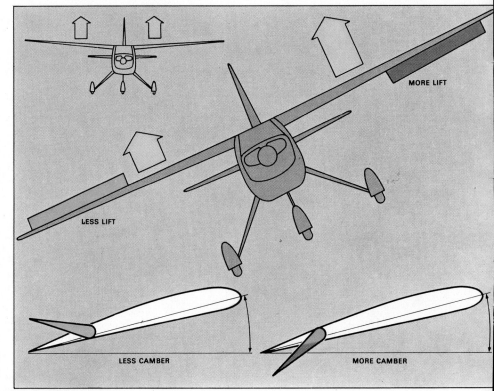

MORE LIFT

LESS LIFT

LESS CAMBER

MORE CAMBER

70

neutralized as turn begins; elevator held up to increase lift; finally, as turn ends, ailerons deflected in the opposite direction to level wings.

HOW AILERONS WORK

In level flight the wings generate equal lift as the sketch *(opposite)* shows. To bank an airplane a differential in lift has to be created. The pilot deflects the ailerons, which work together; when one goes down *(dark blue)*, the other goes up *(light blue)*. The result is more lift on one wing tip than on the other; the airplane responds by rolling into a banked attitude.

AN AERODYNAMIC ODDITY

As a plane tilts into a bank a seeming paradox occurs: its nose tends to head against the turn *(right, top)* as increased drag on the rising wing slows that wing and pulls it back. To correct this yaw the rudder is deflected toward the lower wing, creating a compensating force.

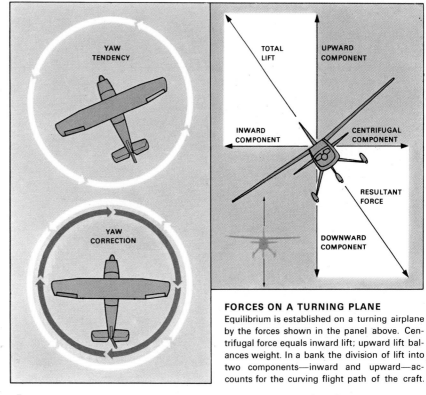

FORCES ON A TURNING PLANE

Equilibrium is established on a turning airplane by the forces shown in the panel above. Centrifugal force equals inward lift; upward lift balances weight. In a bank the division of lift into two components—inward and upward—accounts for the curving flight path of the craft.

The Stall: When Lift Fails

Up to a point, airmen can trust the axiom that lift increases as the wing's angle of attack steepens. At constant airspeed, raising the angle from 4° to 8°, for instance, will about double the lift force. On most wings, however, the axiom begins to lose its validity when the wing reaches an attack angle of approximately 14°: the threshold of a condition called a stall. At this point air flowing over the wing starts to break away from the surface; it becomes turbulent. The low-pressure area above the wing begins to dissipate, and with it lift. If the pilot continues to force the wing into an ever steepening angle of attack, he will increase the separation until at about 18° the stall becomes complete: air moving over the entire surface of the wing is now turbulent. There is less pressure differential between the upper and lower surfaces: lift, for all practical purposes, has vanished. Deprived of lift, the plane falls, nose down. Diving, the wings automatically assume a favorable angle as they meet the relative wind. As airspeed picks up quickly, lift is restored and the pilot, regaining control, can again bring the airplane into a level flight path.

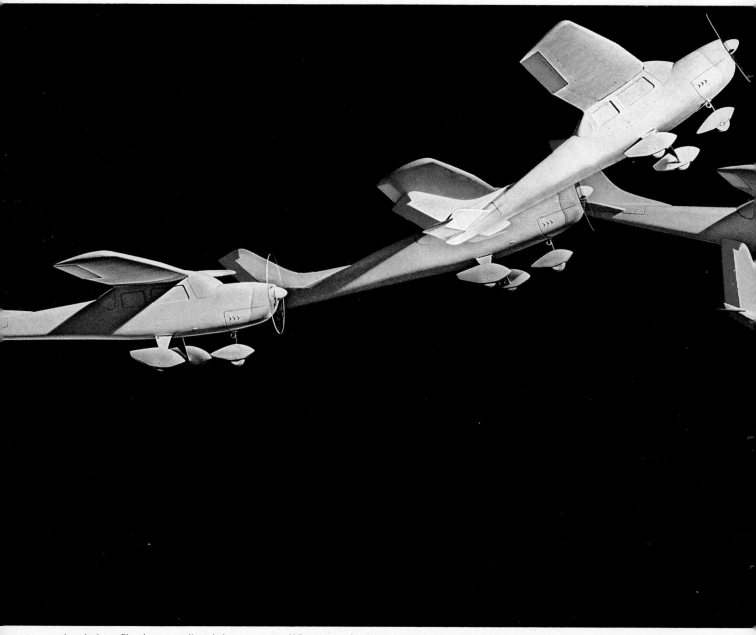

An airplane flies into a stall and then recovers. Wings are raised to an extremely high angle of attack, and at the point when airflow over

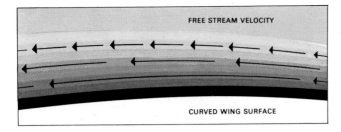

FREE STREAM VELOCITY

CURVED WING SURFACE

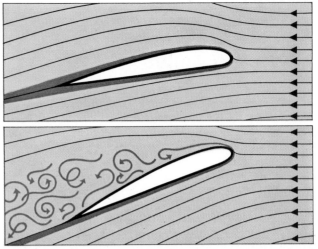

TROUBLE WITH THE BOUNDARY LAYER

The nature of airflow over a wing *(upper right)* is the result of a certain "stickiness," or viscosity, of air *(above)*. The first layer actually sticks to the wing, not moving at all; the second layer, in friction against the first, moves slowly over it; the third layer moves somewhat faster, still following the curvature of the wing. Thus, layer by layer, the flow builds up to "free stream velocity," or airspeed. But when a wing is stalled, all these successive tiers of air, which form the so-called boundary layer, lose their grip on the surface *(lower right)* and break away into turbulence.

the wings becomes separated and turbulent, the craft begins to dive, forcing wings into a lower angle to reestablish a lift-producing airflow.

The Landing:
Steep and Slow

Many factors determine the pattern followed by an airplane when it lands —its type and size, its load, prevailing wind and weather. But the aim is always the same: to set down at the slowest possible speed. A textbook approach, like the one shown here, has three stages. First the pilot reduces power: the nose drops and the plane enters a shallow dive. When the airport is near, he cuts power still more and deflects his elevator to force the wing into a high attack angle. The result is a steep mushing descent. As he reaches the runway the pilot increases the attack angle to the maximum: the plane "flares out" and floats at minimum flying speed. With wings near a stall, the craft touches down, smoothly, slowly, without a bump.

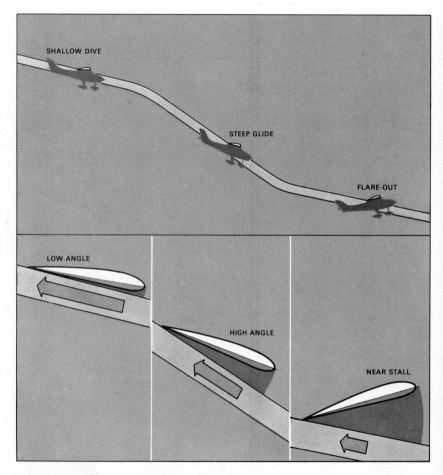

SHALLOW DIVE

STEEP GLIDE

FLARE-OUT

LOW ANGLE

HIGH ANGLE

NEAR STALL

A FLIGHT PATH FOR LANDING
Landing tactics are shown in diagramatic form in the panels above. The plane *(top panel)* follows textbook maneuvers, moving from shallow dive to slow, steep glide to "flare-out." The three panels below chart the wing's changing angle of attack during these phases: first a low angle for a shallow glide, then a high angle for steep descent, finally an extreme angle for touchdown.

BACK TO EARTH
Seen head on in this greatly foreshortened sequence of pictures, an airplane approaches the runway and lands in the classic fashion. As the rear wheels of the craft touch the ground, the nose drops and in an instant the plane is earthbound, now rolling firmly on its tricycle gear.

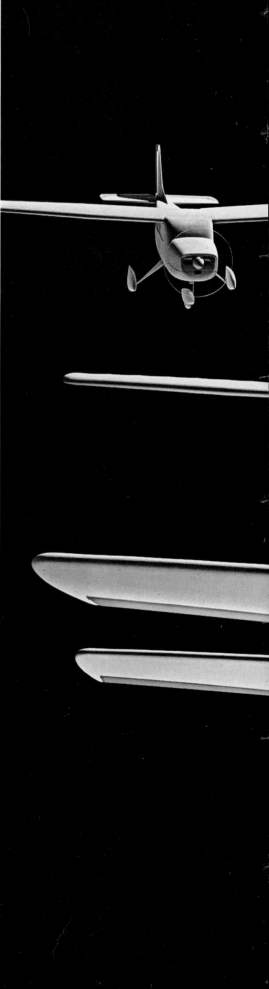

4
Power
for Lift

JOHN WIMPENNY is the biggest frog in what is perhaps the world's smallest pond. Among the handful of persons who have flown under their own power, Wimpenny holds the international record. In 1962 he flew a specially designed aircraft more than half a mile. It had a fuselage, wings, tail and a propeller. But Wimpenny himself was the engine.

He had been experimenting with man-powered flight for years, but his efforts were given added impetus in 1959 when a British plastics manufacturer named Henry Kremer offered a £5,000 prize for the first successful flight of an aircraft based on a human propulsion system. In November 1961 a group of aircraft engineers and technicians headed by Wimpenny completed construction of a plane, the *Puffin*, built primarily of wood and covered with a plastic skin. Fundamentally, it was a cross between an airplane and a bicycle, because the "cockpit" enclosed a single-wheel cycle; the pilot pumped the pedals, turning the wheel for takeoff momentum and at the same time spinning the propeller for in-flight thrust.

On May 2, 1962, Wimpenny, who had warmed up for the flight cycling five miles to work every day, pedal-powered *Puffin* to an altitude of eight feet and traveled for 993 yards. The flight set a record, but won no prize because the contest specified a longer flight and a figure-8 course. Although Kremer has since upped the prize to £10,000, it still awaits a winner.

Quite obviously, whatever the future of human propulsion may be, it has no place in *purposeful* flight because of its extremely low power-to-weight ratio. The fact remains that during the long centuries in which man strove and finally learned to fly, he generally patterned his flying apparatus on birds and put movable wings on his airplanes. But after the death of scores of wing-flapping tower jumpers, it became lethally apparent that to propel these birdlike machines some substitute had to be found, both for the bird's flight muscles and for the "sculling" action of the bird's wing tips, which converts muscle power into forward thrust.

A flyable airplane, of course, begins with a practical aerodynamic design. But there must also be a power source capable of lifting, not only its own weight and that of the aircraft, but also a payload, be it simply the pilot himself or tons of cargo. In developing power for airplanes, the biggest difficulty was the weight of the engine. In the 19th Century, experimenters tried engines powered by steam, by carbonic acid and by electric power. All these engines weighed too much to lift the airplanes for which they were designed.

Oddly enough, the gasoline engine that made the power-to-weight breakthrough was fastened to an airplane that was an aerodynamic failure. For the first efficient engine was not the Wrights', but that modified by Charles Manly from an earlier engine built by Stephen M. Balzer for

POWER APLENTY

The mouth of a Rolls Royce turbojet engine, power plant of many modern aircraft, appears hardly more imposing than a kitchen exhaust fan. But it is one of the most powerful and efficient engines devised. In the time it takes to reach cruising altitude, one of these engines gulps enough air to fill the *Graf Zeppelin*, more air than a normal man breathes in 20 years.

use in Professor Langley's ill-fated Aerodrome. Manly was an engineer and a skilled machinist, and the engine he built in 1901 was better than the Wrights' in the power it gave for its weight and probably could have provided power for flight in a flyable airplane. Manly's five-cylinder engine proved itself when it produced 52 horsepower during a 10-hour run. The engine weighed only 207 pounds, and delivered one horsepower for every 3.9 pounds of its weight, a power-to-weight ratio that was not bettered in a water-cooled engine until 1918.

The Wright brothers' engine, however, must be considered the first successful aircraft power plant, because it made possible the first powered, man-carrying flight. The Wrights calculated that they needed an engine which would produce at least eight horsepower, at a ratio of not more than 20 pounds of engine weight per horsepower.

The search for an engine

In December 1902 the Wrights wrote to about a dozen automobile and gasoline-engine manufacturers, citing their requirements. No such engine was then being manufactured and most of the companies replied politely that they were much too busy to undertake a special assignment. So the Wrights decided to build their own engine. In less than six weeks they had it ready for testing. It was a four-cylinder engine which developed 12 horsepower—four more than the Flyer needed—and with its accessories weighed over 200 pounds, or 16.6 pounds per horsepower. It was adequate for flight only because of the Flyer's large wing area, its lightweight structure and the efficiency of the propellers designed by the Wrights. Within five years the brothers were able to modify the basic engine so that it delivered 30 horsepower, or one horsepower for every six pounds of engine weight.

The Wright engine was basically a modified automobile engine of an "in-line" design, with the cylinders one behind the other. Manly's engine was a liquid-cooled "radial," with the cylinders arranged in a circle and the pistons driving a crankshaft in the center. Each design had its advantages and each its drawbacks. Because its cylinders are arranged in the form of a wheel, a radial engine sets up more air resistance than the in-line type. On the other hand, Manly's engine provided more horsepower for its weight and the space it occupied.

Manly was ahead of his time, and the radial configuration did not appear again until 1909 with the so-called "rotary engine," in which the crankshaft remained stationary while the engine itself, with the propeller attached to it, spun around in a circle. In order to feed fuel and oil to the engine, the crankshaft was hollowed out and over this tortuous route was pumped a mixture of gasoline to run the engine and castor oil to lubricate it. Castor oil was generally used in aircraft engines

THE FIRST "TAKEOFF" in a powered airplane with a man aboard was made in this rickety-looking contraption at Brest, France, about 1874. Based on a design patented in 1857, it had curious, forward-swept wings, retractable landing gear, and a propeller turned by a piston-powered, hot-air engine. According to scanty contemporary accounts, this contrivance rolled down an inclined ramp and actually rose momentarily into the air.

because of its heat tolerance and excellent lubricating properties.

Unorthodox as it seems, the engine was a great success in fighter planes during World War I. Developed by the French, it was widely used in planes on both sides.

But the most distinctive feature of the rotary engine was not the peculiarity of its spinning cylinders, but the fact that it was the first successful air-cooled engine, and thus eliminated the excess weight of the radiator and cooling liquid. Earlier attempts had been made to produce an air-cooled in-line engine, but this design invariably developed hot spots in various parts within the engine. With the rotary engine, all of its cylinders were equally exposed to the wind, and this, plus the spinning motion, produced effective cooling. It was not until the early 1920s that the development of aluminum cylinder heads brought about effective air cooling without having the engine itself whirling around, and the radial engine became practical.

The rotary engine, however, had at least two drawbacks. One came from the castor-oil fumes and spray which poured back constantly into the pilot's face. Old photographs show pilots wearing scarves knotted around their necks, which gave them a dashing appearance. Actually the scarves were useful, not only to keep the wind from blasting down the pilots' necks, but also to provide a cloth to wipe the oil off their goggles.

The second drawback in rotary-engine-powered airplanes was the gyroscopic action set up by the whirling engine, which, in effect, gave the airplane a mind of its own. Because of the spinning engine, the plane tended to remain in whatever attitude or maneuver it happened to be in. If it was in a straight and level flight, the pilot who wanted to bank and turn first had to wrench his machine out of its straight flight path. Once in a turn, however, it would continue until wrenched once more into a straight flight pattern. During World War I, an attempt was made to overcome this gyroscopic characteristic, while at the same time preserving the rotary engine's excellent cooling abilities. The result was the Siemens-Halske engine, built in Germany, in which the crankshaft and propeller rotated in one direction while the cylinders spun the opposite way. On paper, the Siemens-Halske engine was feasible, but in practice it required too-frequent overhaul.

Horsepower for rumrunners

A 150-horsepower engine was considered a very beefy power plant at the beginning of World War I. The war brought demands for more speed, for higher altitude capability and greatly increased payloads. The key to all this was more power. Among the new engines developed was the American Liberty, whose two banks of six cylinders each arranged in

A LIGHT STEAM ENGINE, made by a skilled mechanic, John Stringfellow, was used in one of the first attempts to power a heavier-than-air craft, in 1848. Attached to a large model airplane, it did little more than keep running while the craft glided 120 feet.

THE FIRST GASOLINE ENGINE efficient enough to power a full-sized, man-carrying airplane was built by Charles Manly in 1901. A five-cylinder radial design, it put out 52 hp for its relatively light 125 pounds— a remarkable engineering feat for the time.

V-shape produced more than 400 horsepower. It came off production lines by the thousands. After the automobile industry was mobilized to turn them out, in fact, far more Liberty engines were made than planes, and lots of them were around to be put to other uses in the postwar years. The Liberty engine remained in service well into the 1930s. It was the power plant for the Navy's NC-4 seaplane, which made the first transatlantic flight in 1919, and for the Fokker T-2, in which Army Lieutenants John Macready and Oakley Kelly flew the first nonstop trip across the U.S., in 1923. In other uses, the Liberty lived up to its name during Prohibition. Bootleggers bought these light and powerful engines on the war-surplus market, adapted them to motorboats and outran the Coast Guard blockade against rumrunners.

Artificial respiration for a Wasp

In 1927 Pratt & Whitney Aircraft developed the air-cooled, 425-horsepower Wasp, the first fully successful large radial engine of the sort that became the primary type of airplane power plant. The first nine-cylinder Wasp featured aluminum cylinder heads; over the next 20 years, further improvements made the piston-driven engines increasingly powerful, culminating in 1948 with the Wasp Major, a 28-cylinder engine with four radial rows of seven cylinders each, providing a combined output of 3,500 horsepower.

A major innovation in the engines of the '20s was the supercharger, which did much to improve high-altitude performance. Since the piston engine is an air-breathing machine, any reduction in the intake of air results in a loss of power. As altitude increases and the air begins to thin out, the engine loses efficiency until it reaches the point where it is no longer able to make the airplane climb. The supercharger maintains an engine's power at higher altitudes by precompressing air. It does this by means of a compressor that, in effect, provides the cylinders with low-altitude air at great heights.

Throughout the long developmental cycle of the piston engine, designers and builders concentrated on improving reliability, perhaps the most important performance factor of all. Reliability means safety, first of all; to the airman it may mean life itself. To the airplane owner, it also means lower maintenance costs. In the early days of aviation, an engine required constant tuning up; in the post-World War II heyday of the piston engine, large and enormously complicated power plants were able to run more than 2,500 hours between overhauls. Without this great gain in reliability, the advent of low-cost commercial air transportation would have been considerably delayed.

The feeling of an airman for his engine, his dependence and gratitude, has rarely been more eloquently expressed than by Charles A. Lind-

AIRPLANE PISTON ENGINES, diagramed at right, have two different basic cylinder arrangements. The "in-line" engines have their cylinders positioned in straight rows, while the "radial" engines have theirs arranged in a circular pattern. Each type offers an advantage of its own: the small frontal area presented by the in-line design lowers wind resistance; the air-cooled radial style can deliver more power per pound of engine weight.

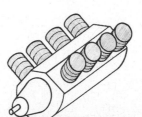

IN-LINE   V IN-LINE   HORIZONTALLY OPPOSED IN-LINE

bergh, describing the Wright Whirlwind engine that powered his *Spirit of St. Louis:*

"Here is the ultimate in lightness of weight and power—two hundred and twenty-three horses compressed into nine delicate, fin-covered cylinders of aluminum and steel. On this intricate perfection I'm to trust my life across the Atlantic Ocean.

"The inner organs of this engine—its connecting rods, cams, gears and bearings—will be turning over many hundred times each minute, sparks jumping, teeth meshing, pistons stopping and reversing at incomprehensible speeds. And I'm demanding that this procedure continue for forty hours if need be, for all of the 3,610 miles between New York and Paris. It seems beyond the ability of any mechanism to stand such a strain. . . ."

As engine performance advanced, it became necessary also to improve the thrusting device, the propeller, which had been a major source of trouble since the pioneer era of aviation. Until the 1920s, all propellers were made of wood. In wet weather they were likely to absorb water, and if one blade absorbed more than the other the propeller became unbalanced, setting up a tremendous vibration in the airplane. Propellers sometimes flew apart in the air. If one blade flew off and the other remained, the resulting imbalance could—and often did—tear the engine out of the plane.

The more powerful that engines became, the faster propellers had to turn. This produced very high tip speeds. As with any whirling mechanism—be it a propeller, automobile wheel or merry-go-round—speed increases with the distance from the hub, since the outer rim or tip must move a greater distance during each revolution. High tip speed brought on potentially destructive vibrations.

A perilous propeller

Hoping to avoid the defects of wooden propellers, planemakers tried aluminum. But metallurgy was in its infancy and aluminum propellers were subject to cracks and pitting, and occasionally one would shear off in flight. The first steel propellers, tested in the early 1920s, frequently caused trouble, sometimes before they left the ground. In 1921, Frank Caldwell, a propeller specialist, subjected an early steel propeller to twice its rated power on an electric testing device. It appeared to withstand the strain beautifully, so it was mounted on a stationary airplane engine in a laboratory. The propeller was revved up to its full power—at which point a blade broke off, sliced through an instrument control board, passed between the heads of two technicians, flew up a flight of stairs and out through the roof. The engine was reduced to rubble.

Years of testing and experimentation, particularly directed to reducing the vibration inherent in propellers turning at high speeds, led to

SINGLE-BANK RADIAL

MULTIPLE-BANK RADIAL

more reliable designs and manufacturing techniques. Propeller failure virtually ceased to be a serious problem.

But those who looked ahead to the day when aerodynamic research would make possible high subsonic and even supersonic velocities, concluded that even the best propeller had a limited future. They saw that the piston engine had a power potential of perhaps 5,000 horsepower, and this would increase the problem of tip speed.

Since tip speed is far faster than airplane speed, the propeller tips of most planes flying at 450 miles per hour would be moving at supersonic speeds. At such speeds the thrusting efficiency of the propeller is reduced. Clearly it was time to investigate a source of thrust free of the propeller's limitations.

A new power dimension

Such a source had already been under development since the early 1930s. It was a reaction engine, or the turbojet as it came to be called. Basically, a turbojet is a very simple mechanism: it is like a beer keg with both ends open. Great quantities of air are sucked into the leading end and mechanically compressed. In the center of the keg is a combustion chamber into which the compressed air and a constant spray of fuel are fed. As the mixture burns, its temperature and pressure rise sharply. It expands by rushing out the exhaust nozzles at the rear of the keg-shaped jet pod. (Part of its energy is used to spin a turbine that powers the compressor.) Since, according to Newton's third law of motion, for every action there must be an equal and opposite reaction, the reaction to the rearward thrust created by the hot gases is a forward thrust of exactly the same magnitude.

Jet propulsion for airplanes is generally considered a recent development, but its theory is almost as old as powered flight, having been proposed as early as 1908. In the '20s there was an attempt—an unsuccessful one—to build an aircraft gas turbine. But the real start of the jet age dates from 1930, the year a 23-year-old Royal Air Force flying officer named Frank Whittle filed a patent for a turbojet power plant.

Full of youthful enthusiasm, Whittle wanted to build his engine immediately but could not get financial support. He tried the British Air Ministry, and he tried a number of private firms. All he got were polite declarations from engineers that the principle seemed sound and might work—some day. "Scientific investigation into the possibilities," said the British Under Secretary of State for Air in 1934, "has given no indication that this method can be a serious competitor to the airscrew-engine combination."

During the next two years Whittle did additional turbine research and studied the latest advances in aviation. Armed with his new knowledge,

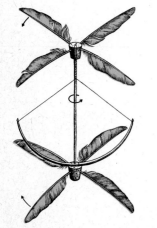

THE AIRSCREW appeared in Europe during the 1780s, partly due to experiments by two obscure Frenchmen, Launoy and Bienvenu, who invented this helicopter toy. Based on an ancient Chinese design, it employed two propellers, counter-rotated by an unwinding bowstring. Though crude, it was the direct ancestor of the helicopter rotor.

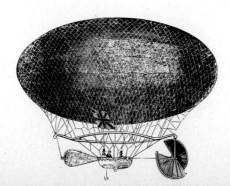

A LANDMARK in the evolution of the propeller came when Irish experimenter Monck Mason fitted a clockwork-driven airscrew onto a 44-foot model airship *(left)*. In 1843, the balloon flew down the hallway of London's Adelaide Gallery and became the first powered model dirigible in aviation history.

he revised his engine design, obtained new patents and once again sought financial help. The Government remained uninterested, but this time Whittle found backing from the investment banking firm of O. T. Falk and Partners.

Power Jets, Ltd., as Whittle's company was called, had its first engine ready for laboratory testing April 1937. The test was disappointing to Whittle; the engine developed considerably less than its 1,400-pound design thrust. To his associates, and even to the Air Ministry, however, such a partial success was a clear indication of the feasibility of this new type of aircraft power. The Air Ministry unbent to the extent of providing funds for future testing. The performance of the third version of the test engine, in July 1939, brought full Ministry approval. The Government agreed to underwrite the cost of future testing.

On May 15, 1941, with Britain already deep in the war, the W-1 engine first powered an airplane in flight. One witness to the flight was an RAF pilot, who sat that night in the officers' mess with a puzzled expression on his face. There had been something peculiar in what he had seen, but exactly what eluded him. Then suddenly he jumped up. "My God, chaps," he said, "I must be going round the bend—it hadn't got a propeller!" Whittle's flight, however, was not the first powered by a jet engine. In Germany another group of engineers had started later but moved faster. In 1935 a physics student named Hans von Ohain patented an engine design similar in concept to Whittle's but different in internal arrangement. Within a year the Heinkel aircraft company had hired Von Ohain to develop his engine, and by March 1937 he had built a small, 550-pound-thrust demonstration model of the power plant which led impressed Heinkel officials to order construction of a flight version. The first Von Ohain engine, designed for about 1,850 pounds thrust, fell far short of its rating. Heinkel and Von Ohain then developed a modified version of 1,100 pounds thrust which met all expectations. The engine was installed in a Heinkel He 178 fighter, and history's first turbojet flight took place on August 27, 1939, five days before Hitler's armies invaded Poland.

A revived design

From these beginnings, the jet engine progressed rapidly under the impetus of wartime crash-program research. By the summer of 1944, the Gloster Meteor was put into service by the RAF, and shortly after the German ME-262 fighter plane was also in action.

Commercially, the pure jet engine was slow to catch on in the postwar years. Because of the turbojet's high fuel consumption, airline companies regarded it as uneconomical. And so aircraft engineers resurrected a hybrid design of the 1930s, the turboprop engine, in which a propeller

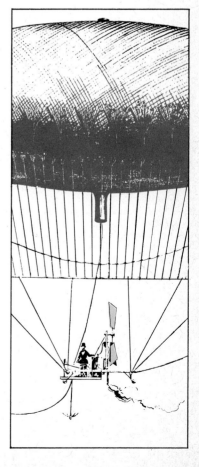

ANOTHER EVENTFUL STEP in the propeller's progress took place when Henri Giffard attached a large, steam-driven airscrew to a full-sized flying balloon *(right)*. The 1852 flight of this dirigible in Paris marked the first time that a propeller was used on a mechanically powered, man-carrying aircraft.

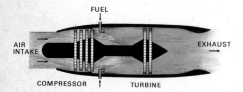

THE TURBOJET ENGINE obtains its power from the escape of expanding gases. Air sucked in the front is first compressed, then forced back into a combustion chamber where it mixes with fuel. The ignition of the mixture produces a rearward rush of expanding gases which, as they escape, propel the aircraft forward and also drive the compressor's turbine.

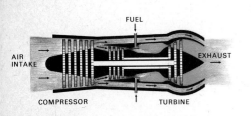

THE TURBOFAN, or bypass engine, processes greater quantities of air than the engine from which it derives—the turbojet. A substantial portion of the incoming air is shunted around to the rear of the turbine, where it merges with the heated gases. The cooler bypass air combines with the heated gases to improve the engine's efficiency.

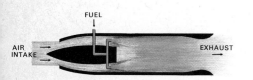

THE RAMJET is, paradoxically, both the most advanced and the most simple of all the jet engines: powerful enough to thrust an airplane at and beyond twice the speed of sound, it actually has no moving parts. Since in-rushing air is naturally compressed upon entering the carefully designed intake, the need for a compressor and turbine is eliminated.

is driven by a turbine rather than a piston engine. As a major power plant for commercial aircraft, the turboprop engine was in production for only about a decade—until continued research and development of turbojet engines overcame the turboprop's initial economic advantage. Turboprop airliners are still in service on short-haul flights, and the turboprop engine is finding application in vertical-takeoff airplanes and some advance helicopter designs.

A glutton for air

In the turbojet, or so-called "pure jet," the turbofan engine is perhaps the most significant innovation that has appeared thus far. The force or thrust produced by both the turbojet and turbofan engine is not only an example of Newton's third law of motion, it is also controlled by Newton's second law, which states that a given acceleration of a given mass (in this case, air) produces a predictable force. A larger force can be achieved either by increasing the acceleration of the air, or by moving a larger amount of it.

In the turbofan, also called the bypass engine, the exhaust gases actually are expelled from the rear nozzles at a slower velocity than in a turbojet engine. By itself, this decreased velocity would provide less thrust. But the amount of air passing through a turbofan engine is much larger than that passing through a turbojet, and results in a much greater push. Though the turbofan engine sucks in vastly greater quantities of air, only about half of it is pumped into the combustion chamber, while the remainder is ducted around it. Thus, the turbofan engine achieves greater thrust, actually with a lower fuel consumption, than the turbojet engine.

The jet is a natural fuel gobbler, but this negative feature is compensated for by the high thrust it provides. Most of the early jets burned somewhere in the neighborhood of a pound of fuel to produce a pound of thrust for an hour; continual improvement of all the engine's component parts has since cut the figure in half, and fuel consumption per pound of thrust is still on the way down.

Since its inception, the turbojet has offered a good thrust-to-weight ratio because it is a relatively simple engine of inherently light weight. The first jet produced about 1.2 pounds of thrust for a pound of engine weight; but today, even though the engines are considerably larger and have lost a lot of their basic simplicity, they operate at ratios of better than 5 to 1. From the thrust of the Whittle and Von Ohain engines, which was on the order of 1,000 pounds, ratings have climbed above 40,000 pounds in engines already in use and to 60,000 pounds in engines being tested for the future.

Paradoxically, the great speeds of which the turbojet engine is capable impose certain limitations on its use. As a jet plane begins to travel at increasingly high speeds, the great quantity of air being thrust into the intake ducts creates an ever-mounting "ram" pressure. This compression of the air being rammed into the intake is accompanied by a considerable increase in the temperatures of the air. At Mach 3, three times the speed of sound, the ram effect at stratospheric heights heats up the air entering a jet engine to about 635° F. At Mach 4, the ram-pressure temperature jumps to nearly 1,200° .

If, as is the case in an ordinary turbojet engine, this heated air is further compressed by the engine's compressors, the temperature of the air is raised even higher. By the time it reaches the combustion chamber, the air may be so hot that any further heating will endanger the metal turbine which drives the compressors. This upper limit on exhaust temperature can mean a loss of power. Since the thrust which powers the plane is based upon the difference—the contrast—in temperature between the air entering the combustion chamber and the burned exhaust gases, thrust drops off markedly whenever the temperature contrast is reduced. Less contrast means less expansion of gases, and without expansion there can be no thrust.

And so at speeds in the range of Mach 3 to 4, with present-day fuels and present-day engine materials, a new type of power plant and design is needed. This most modern of designs is, curiously, the simplest kind of aircraft engine known, for it has no moving parts.

Supersonic simplicity

It is called the ramjet, and is frequently described as a "stovepipe," because of the basic simplicity of its operation. It is like a turbojet engine without any compressor or turbine. Instead, a ramjet is a specially shaped open tube containing a combustion chamber and a fuel-injection system. Compression is achieved entirely by ram pressure, thus eliminating both the compressor system and the need for a turbine which might overheat.

Since the ram effect occurs only when considerable speed has been attained, ramjet engines cannot start from rest or function well at low speeds. Since any airplane must be able to operate at both low and high speeds, a hybrid power plant, called the turboramjet, has been proposed as a solution. For low and intermediate speeds, it would function as a normal turbojet. When the airplane reaches the range of ramjet efficiency, airflow to the compressor would be blocked off mechanically; bypassing the compressors, the air would be burned in the rearward ramjet section of the engine.

Another type of power plant under consideration is the rocket engine, to be used in airplanes rather than missiles. Like the turbojet and ramjet, the rocket produces thrust by means of the expansion of exhaust gases resulting from the combustion of fuel.

However, the rocket does not depend on oxygen in the atmosphere to burn its fuel. It must therefore carry its own oxidizer to mix with the fuel in order to get combustion. The rocket engine is capable of producing extremely high thrust; but where the jet is a fuel gobbler, the rocket is a fuel glutton, and expends its propellants at an enormous rate. The amount of propellants which can be carried on board the airplane sharply limit the operating engine time, and 10 minutes is the maximum any rocket-powered airplane has achieved to date.

The enormous concentration of research funds and talent on space exploration has accelerated development of the rocket engine, and continuing work on this form of propulsion may hasten its application to extended-duration airplane flight. For the immediate future, however, the turbojet engine will be the primary power plant for all large aircraft and possibly for many smaller types. The air-breathing jet has by no means reached the apex of its development cycle. It has powered military aircraft close to Mach 3, but aeronautical theorists now look upon such speeds in much the same way a World War I pilot looked back on the days of the Wright brothers. Already there is talk of aircraft operating in the stratosphere at velocities approaching Mach 25—about 16,500 mph.

Designs for Flight: Studies in Compromise

The first airplanes were designed to perform two simple tasks: getting off the ground and getting down again without cracking up. But as the airplane's capabilities increased, designers were able to demand more of their creations. They quickly found that a successful design involved continual compromise among various performance characteristics. Higher speed or longer range meant less payload; greater payload meant less maneuverability; a highly maneuverable plane would not necessarily be fast. Sixty years of development have merely confirmed this fundamental principle. Today, the designer employs computers to predict performance, structural materials combining unprecedented strength and lightness, power plants whose thrust could lift a score of 1910 airframes. The particular compromises he must make are not always the same ones that dogged his predecessors, but the necessity for compromise is still with him.

A COMPROMISE THAT CRASHED

In 1919, when the first commercial airliners were carrying only four passengers, Italian designer Gianni Caproni built his Model 60. Its nine wings and eight 400-horsepower engines were intend- ed to lift a 15-ton plane and 100 passengers. But Caproni's ambition outstripped his know-how. After two trial flights over Lake Maggiore, the Model 60 broke up and was never rebuilt.

SPEED

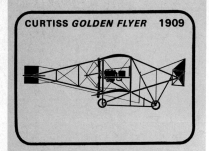

CURTISS *GOLDEN FLYER*   1909

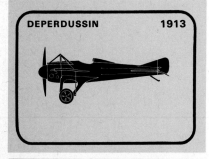

DEPERDUSSIN   1913

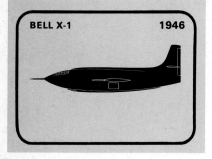

GEE BEE   1932

BELL X-1   1946

FIRST AIR RACE

Glenn Curtiss, piloting his *Golden Flyer,* rounds the final pylon at an air meet at Reims, France, in 1909. The struts and wires that held the biplane together were a potential source of crippling drag—but not at Curtiss' near-record speed of slightly more than 47 miles an hour.

ENGINE WITH WINGS

Sacrificing everything for speed, the designers of the Gee Bee R-1 wrapped a wood and fabric 18-foot airframe around a 730-horsepower engine. With Jimmy Doolittle as pilot, the R-1 set the 1932 world's record of 296.3 miles per hour at the National Air Races in Cleveland.

Faster than the Winds

Speed and ever more speed was one of the obsessions of the early fliers. By 1909, a scant six years after the Wright brothers' flight, more than 35 planes were entered at the first air meet at Reims, France, and nearly half the events were speed contests.

Two factors were soon recognized as important qualities in a fast airplane: a high-powered engine and an airframe with minimal drag. Engines improved apace. Engineers debated the merits of air-cooled versus liquid-cooled power plants, but meanwhile developed more and more powerful engines. Airframe designers had a harder time. Biplanes intrinsically possess greater drag than single-winged craft, but early monoplanes tended to be unwieldy fliers. Until the mid-1920s, biplanes made nearly all speed records. But by the 1930s, monoplanes, with many of their design problems overcome, were winning the trophies.

On the facing page, and throughout this essay, are silhouettes of planes showing some major steps in achieving particular characteristics, with the dates they were introduced.

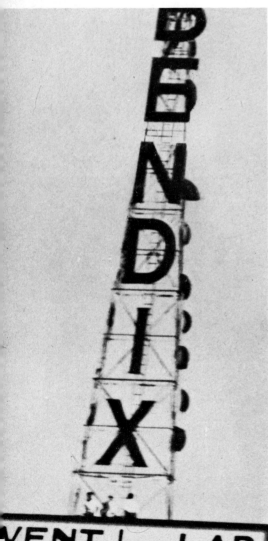

15 YEARS BEFORE ITS TIME
The Deperdussin (above), a French plane piloted by Maurice Prévost, set a 1913 record of 127 miles per hour, thanks to an advanced engine and streamlining. Planes of equal sophistication were not common until the late 1920s.

BEYOND THE SONIC BARRIER
In October 1947 the Bell X-1, piloted by Captain Chuck Yeager, became the first plane to exceed the speed of sound, racking up a record-breaking 670 miles an hour. The U.S. Air Force experimental plane was rocket-powered.

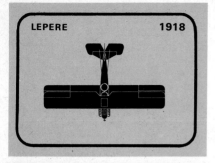

LEPERE 1918

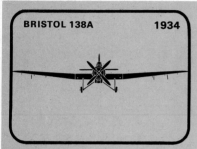

BRISTOL 138A 1934

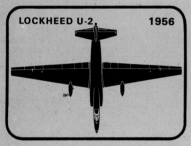

LOCKHEED U-2 1956

A GIANT STEP UP

Though this Lepère was of rather conventional design, its engine was not. Attached to the power plant was the first supercharger to be installed on an aircraft engine specifically for high-altitude flying. In February 1920, U.S. Army Major Rudolph William Schroeder flew the plane 33,000 feet over Dayton, Ohio, beating the official record by almost two miles.

More Air for High Fliers

The specifications for a high-altitude airplane are quite different from those of a low-level speedster. Drag-reduction is less important, especially at extreme altitudes where the thin air offers little resistance to the plane's passage. But thinner air also provides less lift, and consequently creates a need for large wings. Piston engines had to be coupled with a supercharger, a compressor that could pull in enough of the rarefied air to ensure proper fuel combustion. Pilots, too, found that they had to be "supercharged," with oxygen masks. Later fliers, soaring to even greater heights, required the further protection of pressurized suits or cabins.

NEARING THE 10-MILE MARK

In the mid-1930s, high-altitude records became a matter of national pride. Governments took an active part in financing and building airplanes that might break a record. Great Britain developed the Bristol 138A, whose large wings and supercharged engine carried it to a record 49,945 feet. Oxygen mask, pressurized suit and enclosed cockpit enabled its pilot, Squadron Leader F.R.D. Swain, to survive.

HIGH SPY IN THE SKY

The Lockheed U-2 was developed for the U.S. Central Intelligence Agency. Its long-range secret reconnaissance flights had to be made at extreme altitudes. Its top speed—less than 600 miles an hour—was low for a jet, but long wings and evaporation-resistant fuel gave it a ceiling of 100,000 feet, a range of 4,500 miles.

RANGE

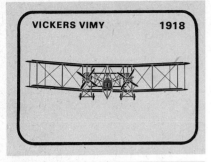

VICKERS VIMY · 1918

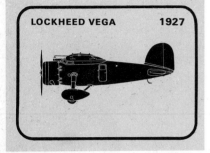

LOCKHEED VEGA · 1927

LOCKHEED P2V NEPTUNE · 1945

NORTHROP X-21A · 1963

OVER THE SEA AND INTO THE MUD
Its nose buried in an Irish bog, this Vickers Vimy rests after completing the first nonstop transatlantic flight. In June 1919 the converted World War I British bomber, piloted by Captain John Alcock, made the 1,960-mile trip from Newfoundland in just over 16 hours.

A GLOBAL FORERUNNER
In July 1933 Wiley Post, piloting a modified Lockheed Vega monoplane named the *Winnie Mae*, completed the first solo flight around the world. Landing only 11 times, he completed the 15,596-mile trip, starting and finishing at New York, in just over seven and one half days.

Beyond the
Far Horizon

One of the first attempts at long-range flight was made in 1911 by the American sportsman Calbraith Rodgers in a specially built Wright biplane. He crossed the United States in 49 days, including about 70 stops—and 15 crashes. Today, designers are testing planes that promise nonstop flights around the world. Though all long-range aircraft must be fairly large, they have few other common features; these depend on the plane's other functions. The annals of aviation record many long-range flights by stripped-down planes. But to be useful, a plane must carry something.

THE TURTLE THAT FLEW—AND FLEW
In 1946 the *Truculent Turtle*, a U.S. Navy P2V-1, flew nonstop from Perth, Australia, to Columbus, Ohio—nearly halfway around the world. But the stripped-down plane had a fuel load one and one half times the weight of the craft itself. Its payload was one kangaroo.

AROUND THE WORLD NONSTOP—IF
Cut lengthwise into the wings of this Northrop X-21A are rows of razor-thin slots. Based on a principle called laminar-flow control, they are intended to reduce drag radically. If successful, LFC could increase an airplane's range by 50 per cent and its payload by 75 per cent.

PAYLOAD

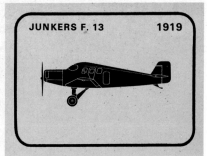

JUNKERS F. 13   1919

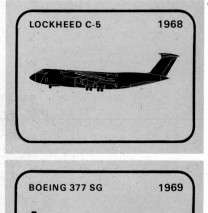

LOCKHEED C-5   1968

BOEING 377 SG   1969

Making the Airplane Pay Its Way

At the end of World War I the Allies forbade Germany to manufacture military aircraft, and German designers concentrated on the problems of cargo and passenger planes. Their work gave the Germans a 10-year lead in the development of commercial aircraft; not until the 1930s did other nations catch up.

The basic problem in designing a plane to carry a large payload was (and is) weight. Pounds had to be pared in every way possible. Metallurgists developed lighter yet stronger materials for airframes and engines. Aerodynamicists improved the wings to provide more lift with less area. Chemists found fuels that gave greater horsepower per pound. As materials improved, so did planes.

THE GRANDFATHER OF THE AIRLINER
The first plane designed specifically as a commercial airliner was the German-built Junkers F.13. Its body was of light, strong corrugated steel, its wings were cantilevered to eliminate external bracing. Introduced in 1919, the F.13 ferried mining and oil-drilling equipment over South American jungles, and for nearly 10 years formed the backbone of European airlines.

THE BIGGEST OF THEM ALL

The world's largest plane, Lockheed's C-5 Galaxy, which needs 28 clustered wheels to land, is a structure one half of a city block long weighing 350 tons. Powered by four mighty turbofan engines producing a total of 165,000 pounds of thrust, it can carry 265,000-pound loads 2,875 miles nonstop at 530 miles per hour and yet makes use of short runways.

CARRIER FOR A SPACE BOOSTER

Its shape suggesting a fat fish, the Super Guppy has a cargo compartment of such exceptional capacity that it has transported components of the 36-story-tall Saturn V moon rocket. The giant cargo hauler is an outsized descendant of one of the last of the big propeller-driven planes, the Boeing 377. Sections from four 377s are needed to make one Super Guppy.

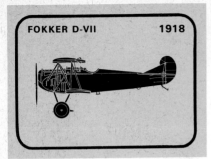

FOKKER D-VII   1918

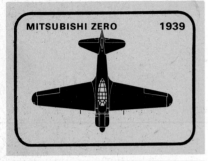

MITSUBISHI ZERO   1939

McDONNELL PHANTOM   1961
F-4

The Airplane Learns to Fight

When World War I fighters began to carry fixed, forward-firing machine guns, a prime requisite for victory was the ability to turn in tight circles, to "get on the enemy's tail."

To increase maneuverability, designers increased wing area. Though this entailed an increase in drag, other characteristics of the fighter plane offered design compensation. It could be lightly built and, operating over short distances, did not need a large fuel load. Instead its cargo consisted of armament, ammunition, armor and a crew of one or two. During World War II, maneuverability was still at a premium. But the development of jets brought a basic change in fighter planes, for tight turns are impossible at high speeds. The appearance of less maneuverable planes was paralleled, however, by the evolution of more maneuverable weapons. Instead of machine guns, today's fighter planes often carry small, air-to-air missiles which, launched in the general direction of an enemy aircraft, can seek out and destroy it.

THE NEW BREED
The McDonnell F-4 Phantom II *(above)* can carry more than six tons of bombs, rockets or missiles over a ground target, plus its complement of up to eight air-to-air missiles for attacking other planes. At 48,000 feet it streaks along at more than twice the speed of sound.

TOP DOG IN WORLD WAR I
The Fokker D-VII *(left)*, named by most experts as the best fighter plane of World War I, was slower than many of its adversaries. But as compensation it was highly responsive to its controls, could outclimb attackers, and could stay in the air at speeds as low as 30 miles an hour.

ZERO PLUS ZERO EQUALS TROUBLE
During the early years of World War II, U.S. pilots found the Japanese Zero *(right)* a dangerously superior airplane. Although a lack of armor made it exceptionally light, it was not as speedy as American fighters. But in aerial dogfights its maneuverability gave it the edge.

FAIRCHILD HILLER PORTER 1964

LING-TEMCO-VOUGHT XC-142A 1965

A Compromise That Works

A perennial problem for the aircraft designer has been combining high air-speed with short takeoff and landing runs. The faster a plane flies, the faster it must take off and land—and the longer must be its runway. Twenty years ago, 5,000-foot runways were standard; today, big jets require 10,000 feet. Small wonder, then, that the idea of a plane that can fly fast yet land on a dime fascinates the experts. The first practical helicopter, a partial realization of this dream, appeared in 1942; it could "land on a dime," but could not fly very fast. Even today, after decades of development, the fastest helicopters are limited to about 300 miles per hour.

In the 1950s, designers took a new tack—the Vertical TakeOff and Landing (VTOL) plane. Its power plants exert thrust in two directions: upward for takeoff and landing, forward for cruising. A less radical variation of the VTOL is the Short TakeOff and Landing (STOL) plane, well suited to the short and medium range flights that make up 80 per cent of all air travel. Such planes, already in use, bring fast air service to small towns.

A RUGGED CLIMBER
Leaping off the runway, the Porter, a Short TakeOff and Landing (STOL) cargo-passenger plane, climbs at a sharp angle with the help of its large wings, its flaps and a powerful turboprop engine. The rugged craft, designed to lift a ton of cargo off runways less than ten times the length of its 35-foot fuselage, has served in the mountainous terrain of Venezuela, Panama and Vietnam.

A TILT-WINGED MARVEL
Its four propellers pointed skyward (opposite, above), the XC-142A pulls itself nearly straight up. A few moments later, looking more like an airplane, the craft speeds along at more than 400 miles an hour (opposite). In addition, the 142A can carry a payload up to four tons.

5
The Making of
a New Airplane

IN MAY 1952 aviation reached a major milestone when British Overseas Airways Corporation introduced jet transportation to commercial air routes. Now civilian passengers could fly at speeds attainable hitherto only by military aircraft. The plane was the De Havilland Comet; and for some 20 months, while American jet designs languished on the drawing boards, it reigned as the only commercial jet transport in operation. Then, on the morning of January 10, 1954, disaster struck.

With 29 passengers and a crew of six on board, a Comet took off from Rome's Ciampino Airport. It climbed through thin broken clouds and headed for London. Less than an hour after takeoff, the plane plunged into the sea near the island of Elba. All on board perished.

The tragedy stunned the world. BOAC grounded all its Comets. The Royal Aircraft Establishment immediately started a thoroughgoing investigation, including reconstruction of as much of the airplane as could be brought up by divers working in water 70 to 100 fathoms deep, but no cause for the crash could be found. Service was resumed. Then, on April 8, a second tragedy occurred under remarkably similar circumstances.

This involved a Comet with 21 on board, bound from Rome to Cairo. The jetliner made a routine check with Cairo 33 minutes after takeoff. About five minutes later, it crashed into the Mediterranean southeast of Naples. Again, no one survived the accident. The British Ministry of Transport and Civil Aviation announced the withdrawal of the Comet's certificate of airworthiness.

Investigation of the accidents was long and detailed. It was more than a year after the first crash before the Ministry published the findings. The verdict: "The cause of the accident was the structural failure of the pressure cabin brought about by fatigue." Wreckage of the second plane was more than 500 fathoms deep in the Mediterranean, so the investigators could not be too specific. However, the circumstances and the available evidence were "consistent with the accident being due to the failure of the cabin structure owing to metal fatigue."

Fatigue, in aircraft structural parlance, means the same as it does with reference to living things. Repeated exertion or stress can "tire out" an airplane material. When metal fatigues, its microscopic structure is changed and it develops small cracks which, if undetected, can enlarge, and eventually bring about failure of an airplane section. In the Comet, the fatigue was brought on by repeated pressurization and depressurization of the main cabin—the system whereby airliners operating at high altitudes increase cabin pressure to simulate air conditions at lower altitudes.

This increased pressure exerts an outward force on the fuselage skin. The skin stretches, then contracts again when the pressure is reduced

A SHOCKING DISCOVERY
Tiny cracks caused by the shrieking wail of a siren appear in a sheet of new alloy, and are studied by a Convair engineer, his ears protected by special headphones. Vibrations similar to those produced by the siren menace the structures of high-speed jets. Scientists constantly seek to discover new materials capable of withstanding such dangerous stress and strain.

during descent. Repeatedly "loading" and "unloading" the skin may eventually cause metal fatigue, a fact which was not fully appreciated when the Comet was designed.

But cabin pressurization is only one of many types of loading to which an airplane is subjected. Consider only a few: lift, gravity, drag, engine thrust, air turbulence, violent maneuvers and landing impacts. And consider that these loads and stresses are acting upon a vehicle that may weigh upward of 150 tons and travel at perhaps 600 mph. From only these basic considerations, some appreciation of the task faced by an airplane designer may begin to emerge.

Today, when one thinks of an airplane, a rather standardized picture comes to mind. To begin with, it will be a monoplane and, except for some light private planes, it will be made of metal. Its wings will be self-supporting, with no external struts or braces for additional strength.

This more or less standardized type of airplane was long in coming; it took some 30 years to evolve. In the pre-Wright era, and for many years after the first powered flight, most gliders and engine-driven planes were biplanes with the wing frames covered with cloth to provide lifting area. Though the extra wing provided additional lifting surface, the biplane design was favored mainly for the structural strength it gave. First, it permitted a shorter wing span, and a short wing is inherently stronger than a long one. The Wright Flyer, for instance, had a wing area of 510 square feet with a span of only slightly more than 40 feet. Had the Wrights attempted to build a monoplane wing with the same wing area, such a wing would have needed a span of about 60 feet. To maintain strength in a span that long would have been a major problem. Furthermore, in a biplane the vertical struts and the diagonal wires which fastened the wings together resembled a simple trussed bridge and provided great strength.

But for its sturdiness, the biplane paid a price in aerodynamic disadvantages. The extra wing was an extra source of drag, as were the struts and wires. However, in the heyday of the biplane, speeds in general were so low that the drag penalty was an acceptable price for greater strength.

A persistent profile

For more than 30 years after the first powered flight, the fabric-covered, strut-braced biplane, with an internal (and thus birdlike) skeleton, remained the dominant configuration. During this period there were major design advances, but like most innovations they were very slow unseating the tried and accepted traditional concepts.

First came the monoplane. Long before aerodynamics was canonized as a science, the pilot-inventors of aviation's childhood had recognized

BIPLANES, such as Boeing's 40-A, were still much in evidence in 1927, even though monoplanes embodying such basic construction principles as the cantilever wing had proved practical 12 years earlier. Well into the 1930s, conservative engineers backed the biplane on grounds of its sturdiness and lift, and the misconception that it was more efficient. The 40-A, which inaugurated transcontinental air travel, could carry two passengers and handle 1,200 pounds of mail.

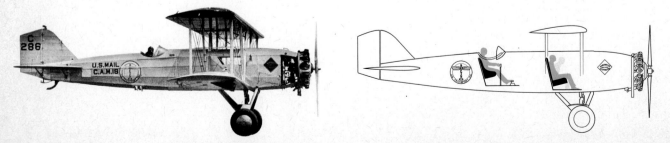

the problems the biplane presented. True enough, it was strong, but in addition to the drag it created, the dual-wing configuration set up a "smothering" effect. In this condition, airflow through the gap between the wings reduces their lift, with a sizable loss in efficiency.

The universally acknowledged apostle of the monoplane was one of aviation's greats, the Frenchman Louis Blériot. Presumably inspired by the work of the Hungarian designer Trajan Vuia, who had built an unsuccessful monoplane in 1906, Blériot became enraptured with this type of design and dedicated his life to its development.

He made several attempts to produce a flyable monoplane, and finally succeeded late in 1907 when he turned out his *Number VII*, which made four successful flights before it crashed. Blériot, uninjured, abandoned that particular design. He built and tested two more monoplanes with limited success; then, in 1908, he produced *Number XI*.

In *Number XI*, Blériot made a flight which electrified the civilized world. On July 25, 1909, he took off from Les Baraques, near Calais, and flew 23½ miles across the choppy waters of the English Channel to the English coast. Thirty-seven minutes after takeoff, he landed near Dover Castle.

A visionary repudiated

The Channel crossing was not the longest flight of that period; but never before had an aviator chanced a flight with no land underneath. The conquest of the Channel brought Blériot resounding acclaim and more than 100 orders for his monoplane. Aircraft design, however, was not noticeably influenced by Blériot's achievement, or by his prophetic dedication to the monoplane as the aircraft of the future.

In 1910, a year after Blériot's Channel flight, a German engineer named Hugo Junkers patented a "flying wing"—a monoplane with no fuselage. Though the plane never became operational, its design embodied the first cantilever wing. It was rigidly supported internally, with a "main spar," a lightweight girder running down its center, and thus required no external bracing.

Virtually all modern airplanes bear witness to the fact that Junkers' cantilever principle of wing design has become universally accepted. In 1919, almost a decade after Junkers first presented his design, another German designer, Dr. Adolph Rohrbach, offered an improvement by introducing the box-spar. Instead of a solid, girder-type main spar, Rohrbach employed four metal sheets welded together to form what resembled an elongated shoe box, very light and extremely strong.

Yet a further improvement, though one no longer used, was contributed in 1928 by one of the greatest American aircraft designers, John K. Northrop. Northrop called his invention "nested-channel construction."

Basically, it was a modification of Rohrbach's design, with one side of the shoe box open. Northrop employed a series of these small troughs, one behind the other, and running the length of the wing.

A self-taught engineer, Northrop used the nested-channel design on the Alpha, the first airplane produced by his company. In 1929, after the crash of an experimental Alpha, Northrop inspected the craft's wing and decided it was beyond repair. A road-paving crew was working nearby, so Northrop asked the operator of the road roller to run over the wing to flatten it and make it easier to convert to scrap. While a number of spectators watched in astonishment, the roller not only failed to crush the wing on several attempts, but hardly dented it.

In the matter of fuselages, most of the early structures were simply kitelike frames designed to hold together the various components of the airplane. By 1912, however, engine power was increasing, along with speeds, altitudes and maneuverability—all creating greater loads on the fuselage. In that year a great innovation appeared—the so-called monocoque structure. "Monocoque," from the Greek *monos* and the French *coque*, means "single shell." In the pure monocoque structure, there is no internal bracing; the shell bears all the loads and, because it is in the basic shape of a tube, it has enormous strength. In later years this approach was modified to the semimonocoque design, which had stiffeners running the length of the fuselage. Engineers also use the term "stressed-skin" construction, because even though there is internal bracing, the skin bears most of the flight loads.

Monocoque and metal

The first application of monocoque construction came from the drawing board of a French designer, M. L. Béchereau; the airplane itself was built of molded wood by the aircraft works of Jules Deperdussin, a famous plane maker of the time. The fuselage was molded in two halves, which were fitted together. In addition to structural strength, the rounded, streamlined shape provided an aerodynamic bonus in lower drag, and in Chicago on September 9, 1912, the Deperdussin monoplane set a new world's speed record of 108 miles per hour. In 1915, Hugo Junkers introduced another innovation: metal construction. However, the German Government, for which the iron and steel plane was intended, arbitrarily decided that it was too heavy for efficient flight, so the plane was never put into production. In 1917, Junkers built a two-seat monoplane, the J.4, this time using as his prime material lightweight Duralumin, an aluminum alloy. The J.4 was ordered into quantity production as a fighter in World War I.

Thus, as early as 1915, the basic elements of modern aircraft construction—the monoplane configuration, the use of metal, the cantilevered

A PRECOCIOUS FAILURE, the little *Vuia I* never flew more than 26 yards, but entered aviation annals as the first full-sized monoplane. Trajan Vuia piloted the craft on its longest run, at Montesson, France, in August of 1906. His design probably influenced the more successful Louis Blériot to continue the development of monoplanes.

wing and stressed-skin structure—had been applied and tested in flight, but it was to be another 20 years before all four principles became standard. Throughout the '20s and into the mid-'30s, the wooden-framed, cloth-covered biplane remained predominant. There were also monoplanes, metal planes, cantilever and stressed-skin designs, but few aircraft combined all four principles. For example, Lindbergh's *Spirit of St. Louis* was a monoplane with a tubular steel fuselage framework, but the wing spars and ribs were wooden, and both wing and fuselage were fabric-covered. It is impossible to set a precise date at which the all-metal, cantilever-winged, stressed-skin monoplane gained ascendancy, but by the late 1930s it was the rule rather than the exception.

Today such basic structural features are almost universally employed, and aircraft design and testing is more concerned with other areas, though it must still tackle such subtle structural problems as those which caused the two Comets to crash, as well as complexities resulting from high speeds.

Design for strength

The design of a typical modern jetliner, like the Boeing 727 or the Douglas DC-9, begins with some rather straightforward computations concerning the general specifications of the airplane to carry a given load at the desired speeds and altitudes under normal conditions. But the structure designer must make provision for abnormal as well as normal flight loads. In straight and level flight, an airplane experiences a load of one gravitational force, or one g. A sharp maneuver, like a steep diving turn, increases the load markedly, perhaps to several g. The procedure is for the structures team to compute the load which might be encountered in the most violent maneuver expected during an operational flight of the airplane. This is known as the *limit load.* A pilot, however, might inadvertently exceed the limit load; so the designer, then, must allow a comfortable margin of safety. He builds in what is called the *ultimate load factor,* which enables the airplane to withstand forces well beyond the limit load. Generally, the ultimate load is one and a half to two times the limit load. A typical jet transport, which rarely exceeds two g in normal operation, is built to take at least four. In short, these jetliners, as they developed on the designers' desks and as their vital statistics poured out of computers, were engineered to withstand more than twice the load to which they might be subjected in the most violent situation they would be likely to encounter.

Such is the big picture. But within the overall canopy termed ultimate load factor, there are thousands of minor and individualistic considerations. An airplane in flight is a machine in stress, and at various times the wings may bend; the fuselage may twist, bend, bulge or shrink. The

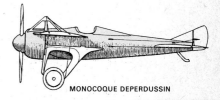

MONOCOQUE DEPERDUSSIN

THE MONOCOQUE FUSELAGE permitted the fuselage's skin, or shell, rather than the aircraft's frame, to carry the loads and stresses of flight. It was tested on Deperdussins, such as the 1913 model shown above. Eventually it became universally accepted as a standard principle of aircraft construction.

A PAIR OF PRECEDENTS—metal skin and cantilevered wings—were incorporated into a Junkers 1915 monoplane. Known as the "Tin Donkey," the Junkers J.1 was the first practical all-metal aircraft. Although the German authorities were skeptical of the design, Hugo Junkers' far-reaching innovations proved vital to the evolution of aviation.

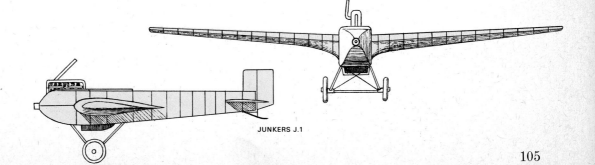

JUNKERS J.1

tail surfaces may wiggle, vibrate or bounce up and down.

This constant flexing may be very large and is measured in feet at the tips of the wings. Even in normal flight, the wing tips of a Boeing 707 may describe an arc of three feet. Contrariwise, this flexing may be almost invisible, e.g., under the force of full pressurization, the fuselage of a DC-9 swells one sixteenth of an inch.

As a result, some parts of a structure are "lightly loaded"; that is, the forces they encounter in flight are minor and not continual. Here the designer has some latitude in the selection of materials. But other parts, such as the wing, must have the longest possible fatigue life consonant with the strength-to-weight ratio. In addition, designers apply lessons learned through long experience to minimize fatigue.

Such experience, along with the aid of computers digesting reams of data on metallurgy, aerodynamics, propulsion and a host of other scientific disciplines, is ample to produce the design of a reliably flyable airplane. It is enough, in fact, to proceed with the physical building of the airplane. But the opinions of a computer are no substitute for actual testing; and in the building of an airplane like the Boeing 727 or the DC-9, the amount and variety of tests to which the emerging craft is subjected are every bit as imaginative as they are exhaustive.

As tragically illustrated by the Comet crashes, cabin pressurization and depressurization subjects the fuselage to fatigue. In fact the method by which some airplanes are tested for pressurization fatigue grew out of the Comet crashes. In an effort to simulate the stresses through which the downed Comets had gone in flight, a working Comet was taken out of service and its fuselage was lowered into a specially constructed tank of water. The fuselage, sealed as it would be in flight, was pumped full of water which was brought to the same pressure the plane would maintain in flight. A minute later the pressure was reduced. In this way, the cycle of flight pressurization could be simulated every two minutes, meaning that in the course of three months a test fuselage could be subjected to the same stress it would have to go through in 50 years of actual flight. This method, called hydrofatigue testing, determined the cause of the Comet crashes, and has since come into use for preflight testing of new types of airplanes under development.

Cannonading chickens

Equally unique tests have been dreamed up for the windows in the fuselage. Strain gauges, which electronically measure the tiniest amount of give, are attached to the window frames while the cabin is pressurized to a degree far in excess of operational loads. In addition to these pressurization tests, The Boeing Company, in the course of testing the 707 and the newer, short-haul 727, aimed a compressed-air gun

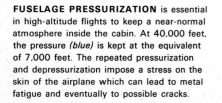

FUSELAGE PRESSURIZATION is essential in high-altitude flights to keep a near-normal atmosphere inside the cabin. At 40,000 feet, the pressure *(blue)* is kept at the equivalent of 7,000 feet. The repeated pressurization and depressurization impose a stress on the skin of the airplane which can lead to metal fatigue and eventually to possible cracks.

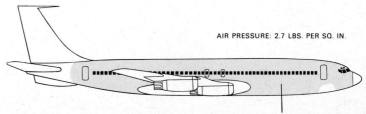

AIR PRESSURE: 2.7 LBS. PER SQ. IN.

CABIN PRESSURE: 11.3 LBS. PER SQ. IN.

at the passengers' windows and fired balls of ice one and one eighth of an inch in diameter at the windows to simulate a violent hailstorm. And the pilot cabin windows, which face forward and are therefore subject to much stronger impacts, were given proportionately tougher tests. Again a compressed-air gun was aimed at the window and the body of a four-pound dead chicken was fired at the glass at speeds ranging from 380 to 460 mph. Such far-out testing pays dividends. In the spring of 1960, a full-grown eagle hit the pilot's window of a 707 traveling 400 mph. The glass crazed but did not shatter.

Torture for a wing

In testing, special attention of course is paid to the wings. Almost every conceivable sort of test is conducted. Small sections of the wings are purposely cut with a saw, and then the section is artificially "aged" on machines which apply and release pressure in just the way it would occur in flight. Whole wings are taken into the laboratory and bent up and down, up and down. When the Boeing 707 was undergoing such tests, a prototype of its wing was bent upward nine feet without breaking, and a lift of 425,000 pounds was required actually to buckle the wing.

Testing techniques in the aircraft industry have in fact reached the stage where it is at least theoretically possible to guarantee that an airplane, rolling off the end of a production line, will take off and fly for its entire life without any significant failure. This, however, would assume a Utopian state of affairs of faultless materials in the airplane's construction along with impeccable maintenance and use.

Testing does not end when a jetliner is delivered to an airline. The Federal Aviation Administration, from the results of earlier tests, certifies that it will not require major airframe overhaul until the plane has amassed 6,000 flying hours, though during that period the structure is frequently given a visual "twice-over" by airline maintenance men. When it reaches the 6,000-hour mark, however, the plane is sent to the company's overhaul base for a complete examination.

The aircraft is first inspected visually and by X-ray machines similar to those used by a physician. In another test, ultrasonic generators send high-frequency sound waves flowing through a section under inspection and the wave pattern is displayed on an oscilloscope, like a test pattern on a television screen. If a flaw is present, it will show up as a deviation in the pattern.

Still another inspection technique is the dye check. Structural metal is first treated with a penetrating, liquid red dye, then covered with a white liquid which dries into a powder. If there are subsurface cracks, the red dye will bleed through the powder along the length of the crack. If a detected flaw is minor, it is repaired; if major, the whole structural

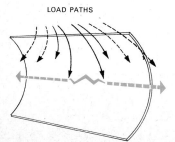

LOAD PATHS

THE FAIL-SAFE DEVICE known as the strap is designed to contain in-flight cracks which may appear in a plane's skin. Such a crack will normally continue to tear at either end *(dotted line at left)*. But with the use of a strap *(right)*, now a common reinforcement on jets, the tear is diverted and rendered at least temporarily harmless.

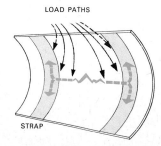

LOAD PATHS

STRAP

section—a wing panel, for instance—is replaced.

The sum total of all this—computerized design, followed by static tests, flight test and sharp-eyed maintenance—means that some remarkably reliable pieces of machinery are in the air, which sometimes even exceed the limits they are engineered to withstand. One of the most dramatic examples occurred in February 1959, and involved a Boeing 707 only a few months after the model had been introduced to commercial service. Pan American Airways Flight 115, bound from Paris for New York, was approaching Gander, Newfoundland. The 707, flying at 35,000 feet, was under the automatic guidance of the autopilot.

Suddenly the plane went into a steep diving turn to the right. Unknown to the copilot, the automatic pilot had cut out, as they sometimes do, and the plane was not under any sort of control. The pilot, however, managed to reach the throttles and ease them back to idle. By then the craft was approaching the speed of sound. The plane was now down to 6,000 feet, having lost 29,000 feet of altitude. With a crash only seconds away, the pilot pulled back on his wheel, and leveled off.

Later investigation showed that the airplane, designed for an ultimate load limit of 3.75 g, had actually survived, without damage, a load estimated to have been 5 g.

The Cockpit:
A Crowded
Command Post

Perched high in the nose of a giant 138-foot fuselage, the cockpit of a modern jetliner looks incongruously small. The crew members who man the cockpit can see none of the tail assembly of their craft and only part of the wings. But they do not need to. Crowded into the cockpit—not much larger than the inside of the average family sedan—are all the intricate instruments and precise control systems required to guide the huge plane's operation from takeoff to landing. From throttles and control column to radio compass and radar screen, everything is instantly available or readable in a layout carefully designed for maximum efficiency. The modern cockpit is a functional outgrowth of decades of development which began with little more than a seat, joy stick and rudder bar in the earliest planes. The fruits of this evolution are illustrated on the following pages, which present a guided tour of the cockpit of the Boeing 707 jetliner.

CHECKING IT OUT
During preparations for a night flight, the cockpit of an American Airlines Boeing 707 is a bright island of activity. Checking controls and instruments for takeoff are the first officer, or copilot *(left)*, the captain and the flight engineer. Though 707s may be operated with four men in the cockpit—for example, on intercontinental trips— a crew of three is standard for American Airlines.

CLOSE QUARTERS

A display of more than 200 controls and instruments confronts the captain *(left)* and first officer, sitting at their working stations. The 707's cockpit, seen here as from the flight engineer's position behind the central pedestal (his chair and logbook are in the foreground), is only 8½ feet long, 8⅔ feet at its widest point, and has only five feet of headroom at the pilot's seat.

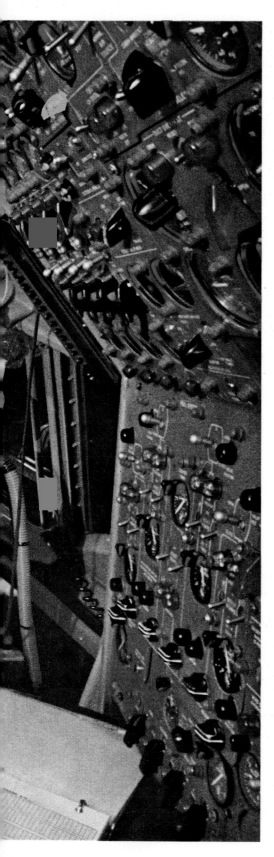

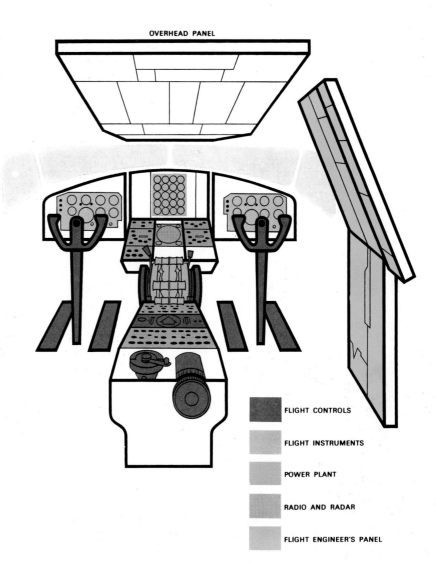

■ FLIGHT CONTROLS

▨ FLIGHT INSTRUMENTS

▨ POWER PLANT

▨ RADIO AND RADAR

▨ FLIGHT ENGINEER'S PANEL

Familiar Order of a Busy Nerve Center

Looking into the cockpit of a 707 air-liner, the layman sees an apparently chaotic jumble of dials, switches, lights and cryptic labels. But crew members get a different picture: to them, every dial reports a precise message and every wheel, handle and switch commands a specific re-sponse somewhere in the plane. With all the fixtures set in a familiar pat-tern, the crewmen know where to look, where to reach and what to do.

The diagram above outlines the orderliness of the cockpit's arrange-ments. Showing the same forward-looking view as in the picture at left, the drawing indicates in different colors the five major groups of in-struments and controls. The flight controls, for example, which handle the aircraft in the air, are outlined in red; the flight instruments, which guide the pilot, in orange; the power-plant section, which governs the en-gines, is shown in green. All these will be discussed separately on the following pages.

Over the crew's heads are instru-ments and switches that do not need constant attention during flight. A "Here's How" graph reminds the pi-lot of the airspeeds he must main-tain at various weight loads to keep his plane flying. Buttons and switches activate such auxiliary mechanisms as the windshield wipers, turn on the "No Smoking" and "Fasten Seat Belt" signs, and call the stewardess.

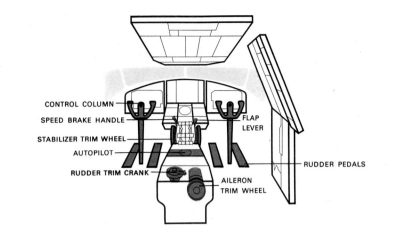

CONTROL COLUMN
SPEED BRAKE HANDLE
STABILIZER TRIM WHEEL
AUTOPILOT
RUDDER TRIM CRANK
FLAP LEVER
RUDDER PEDALS
AILERON TRIM WHEEL

The Agents of Control

Though a World War I flier would scarcely recognize the flight deck of a 707 as the cockpit of an airplane, certain aspects would seem familiar as soon as he settled into the pilot's seat. Basically unchanged in 50 years —though considerably refined—are the controls the pilot uses to take off, fly and land his craft. These fixtures, outlined in red at top left, control the movable surfaces of wings and tail shown on the opposite page. The stick, or control column, activates the elevators, which force the plane's nose up or down. The half wheel, governing the ailerons, banks the wings; the pedals control the rudder, helping the craft to turn. Modern refinements are trim wheels for ailerons, stabilizer and rudder, permitting fine adjustments in flight. New, too, are flap and speed brake handles, governing those vital mechanisms that increase lift and slow the aircraft's speed during takeoff and landing.

All of the flight controls operate through hydraulic, electrical or mechanical systems that power-assist the pilot's hands and feet. Should power fail, the combined strength of pilot and copilot could still fly the airplane, through a back-up manual system.

Once in the air, however, the pilot may not touch the controls for hours: an autopilot does the flying for him. A computer keeps the plane on its course at a preset altitude, leaving the pilot free to keep a watchful eye on other traffic and his instruments.

FINGERTIP CONTROL
Not much different from those of any modern plane, big or small, a 707's flight controls are grouped within comfortable reach of the pilot, seen at left with his hand on the rudder trim wheel. Rudder pedals, control column and half-wheel aileron control are duplicated for the copilot; all others are on the pedestal between. Should the pilot need to take over from the autopilot when in flight, he can do so instantly by pressing the red button by his left hand.

UP, DOWN AND SIDEWAYS

The tail assembly, 43 feet in span and 30 feet tall, has a rudder on the vertical fin and elevators on each side of the horizontal stabilizer. Wire cables a quarter inch in diameter connect these movable surfaces with the power-assisted flight controls 40 yards away in the cockpit. An aerial juts forward from the top of the fin.

A MANY-SURFACED WING

The wing of a landing 707, with all its moving parts extended, looks as if it were falling apart. This passenger's-eye view shows the flaps in the full down position and the speed brakes, or spoilers, up. Ailerons are straight for level flight as the airplane glides in to a landing.

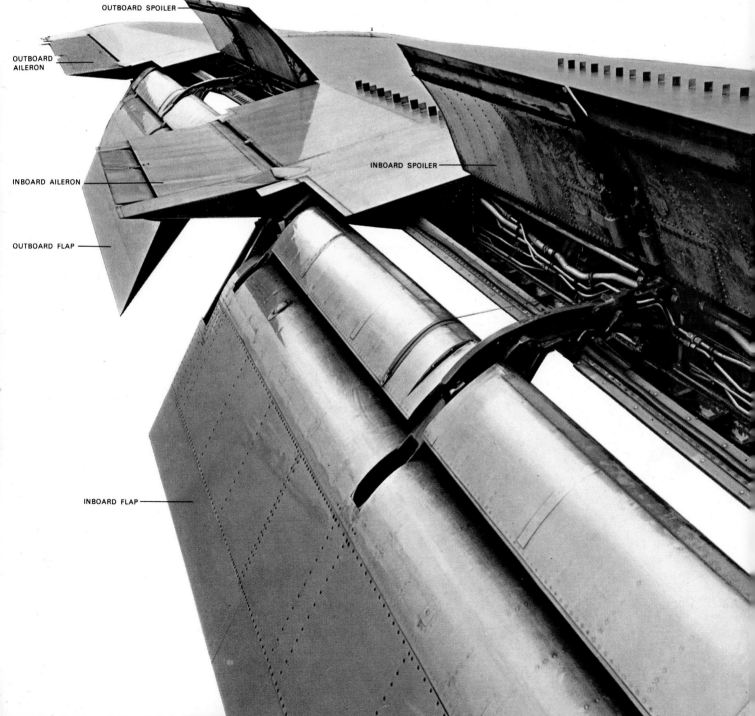

OUTBOARD SPOILER

OUTBOARD AILERON

INBOARD SPOILER

INBOARD AILERON

OUTBOARD FLAP

INBOARD FLAP

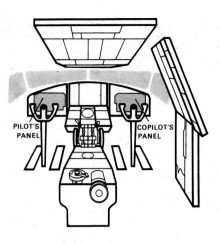

Instruments to Fly By

A modern airliner in flight may spend hours in a world of its own, suspended in clouds that obscure both earth and horizon. But though pilot and copilot perhaps cannot see beyond their windshield wipers, they have a host of sensitive instruments to show them their plane's precise position and attitude in the air. A glance at the banks of dials directly in front of them *(colored orange at left)* tells them everything they need to know about their flight path—their speed and altitude, whether they are on course, their progress in terms of Greenwich, local and elapsed time.

Of these instruments, the four most important (three are discussed in detail opposite) are arranged in a "basic T" configuration that is now standard in all airliner cockpits. Long experience has shown that this arrangement, which gives airspeed, attitude, altitude and course, presents the pilot with the information he most needs in the shortest time.

ALL IN ONE GLANCE

Over his control column *(foreground, above)*, the pilot has a clear view of his primary flight instruments. The "basic T" begins with the airspeed dial *(top row, left)*, with the next two dials forming the crossbar of the T. The Course Deviation Indicator *(next row down)* forms the leg. The dial at top right shows the rate of climb or descent; under that is a clock and to its left a magnetic compass. The two lower instruments at far left are a turn-and-bank indicator and a Machmeter, which measures the plane's speed relative to the speed of sound.

THE HORIZON DIRECTOR INDICATOR
Central dial of the T's crossbar, this shows the plane's attitude in the air. The white face represents the horizon; the bar across it changes attitude with the plane. The model at right is here climbing 15° and banked in a 30° left turn; thus the horizon seems to tilt right.

COURSE DEVIATION INDICATOR
The compass of this navigation aid shows the plane to be heading 315° *(dotted line, right)*, but the pilot has just set its radio-directed pointer to 270°, the course he wants to fly next. A 45° left turn will line him up on the radio beam; the pointer will indicate deviations.

THE ALTIMETER
This instrument, activated by barometric pressure, shows the airplane's height. The window records altitude in thousands of feet, the pointer in hundreds. The plane is here at 35,000 feet, the altimeter set at 29.92 inches of mercury—standard for planes above 18,000 feet.

FINDING THE STRAIGHT AND LEVEL

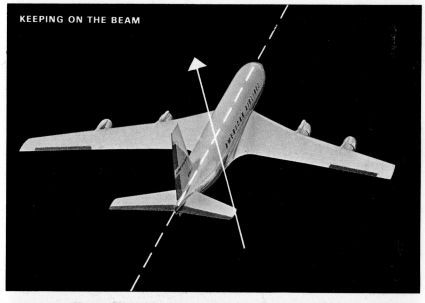

KEEPING ON THE BEAM

KEEPING TABS ON HEIGHT

Powerhouse with Fingertip Control

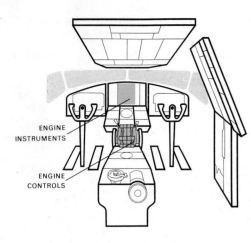

ENGINE INSTRUMENTS

ENGINE CONTROLS

The pilot and copilot of a 707 have fingertip control over four jet engines, the most potent but also the simplest power plants yet devised to carry passengers around the sky. The four pods projecting gracefully from the wings of the plane (below) can deliver 72,000 pounds of thrust—enough to generate electricity for all the homes in Delaware. Yet for all their thunder, jet engines are veritable models of simplicity compared to their piston predecessors. Gone are the cylinders, valves, ignition systems and other intricacies that complicate big piston engines.

The jet's simplicity is reflected in the cockpit. A 707 has close to 100 fewer dials and switches than its piston-engined counterpart, largely because of the simplified engine instrumentation (opposite, right). Five dials for each engine, clustered on a single panel (in green, left) tell the pilot all he needs to know about his power plant.

Thrusting up from the central pedestal are the four numbered throttles (opposite, left) that control this powerhouse of energy. Each controls one engine by regulating the amount of jet fuel spurted into the combustion chamber. When necessary the pilot can summon the total thrust of all four engines with a smooth push of one hand.

Directly forward of the throttles, and linked with them, are the thrust reversers used to brake the airplane on the runway after landing. They act to deflect the full power of the jet blast forward, slowing the aircraft with a roar from the engines until the wheel brakes can take hold.

(4)

(3)

ORDERS TO THE ENGINES

The 707's four throttles, each numbered for the engine it controls, are seen at left in the off position. Hidden just forward of them are the thrust reverser knobs. Beneath the throttles are the four start levers, which, when raised by the pilot, initiate combustion in each engine.

(1)   (2)   (3)   (4)

REPORTS FROM THE ENGINES

The four columns of instruments above, numbered to match the engines below, show identical sets of dials. The top row records each engine's exhaust pressure, or thrust. The second and fourth rows monitor the revolutions of the two air compressors in each engine. The third row indicates exhaust temperatures; the last row shows fuel flow in pounds per hour.

(1)

(2)

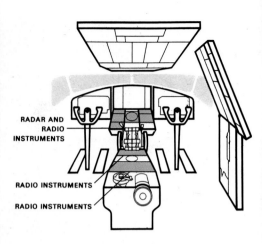

RADAR AND RADIO INSTRUMENTS

RADIO INSTRUMENTS

RADIO INSTRUMENTS

COCKPIT LISTENING POST
Using his hand microphone, the pilot requests taxi instructions from an airport control tower. He leaves one ear uncovered so he can also listen to his crew members. Pilot and copilot share communications duties, depending on which one is handling the airplane at the time.

Keeping in Touch with the World

Despite their seeming isolation, the crew members of a 707, thanks to an elaborate complex of radio and radar equipment *(purple in diagram)*, are in constant touch with their airplane and the world beyond. At the flip of a switch they can talk by radio to the traffic-control centers below, to other planes in the air, among themselves and to the passengers behind them. They can even relay messages to telephone services on the ground.

Just as vital as communications is the navigational function served by the cockpit's electronic array. The key instrument is the Visual Omni Receiver. When the VOR is tuned to one of 906 stations, an indicator shows the station's direction. Many stations also provide an additional signal, which the plane's Distance Measur-

ing Equipment (DME) translates into distance from the station. The Automatic Direction Finder Receiver (ADF RCVR) is used for landings.

The Air Traffic Control Transponder operates with only occasional attention from the crew. Its special radio beam can transmit, at the push of a button, a signal that is recognizable to receivers below, thus providing a surefire way of identifying the plane in Air Traffic Control centers along the path of flight.

Another radar unit *(center of top picture, opposite)* serves a unique safety function. Scanning the skies as far as 150 miles ahead, it provides a constant picture of the weather along the route. Thus the pilot can be forewarned of storms or clouds which might bump his passengers around.

WEATHER AND NAVIGATION

Like a round, yellow eye, the weather radar screen dominates the panel of communications equipment *(above)* located between pilot and copilot. Its controls are at top left; opposite are those for the ATC Transponder. The two middle panels have a navigational function, operating the two ADF Receiver systems. At bottom left and center is a SELCAL unit (from SELective CALling), which monitors a special radio frequency: when a message from the airline company is directed at this particular airplane, the crew is alerted by a warning chime to tune in.

RADIO COMMAND STATION

Two pairs of panels separated by the autopilot *(left)* control the airplane's very-high-frequency navigation and communications equipment. They are duplicated left and right for the pilot and first officer. The top panels combine the VOR controls, used for navigation, and VHF, the voice communications system. The bottom panels have switches with which the crew selects various channels for communicating with ground stations or with other aircraft aloft.

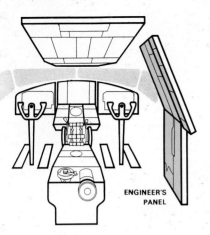

ENGINEER'S
PANEL

The Vital
Third Man

The flight engineer is the 707's main-tenance officer and general handy-man. In flight his province is the big board in front of him *(blue at left)*, but actually the whole plane is his responsibility, from before takeoff until after landing. He is the first crew-man at the airplane, checking everything from tires to tail fin. Aloft he watches over the dials and lights *(right)* that report on the plane's vital systems: fuel, electrical power, air conditioning, pressurization and oxygen. One of his most important duties is to record in a logbook everything from fuel-flow data to minor or major malfunctions, providing a meticulous diary of the life of a 707.

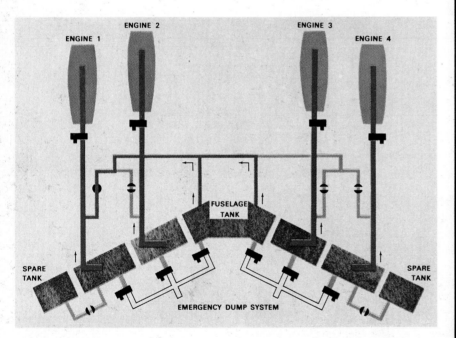

ENGINE 1   ENGINE 2   ENGINE 3   ENGINE 4

FUSELAGE TANK

SPARE TANK   SPARE TANK

EMERGENCY DUMP SYSTEM

HOW THE FUEL FLOWS
The 23,855-gallon, 159,828-pound fuel load of a 707 is carried in seven tanks: one in the fuselage, and in the wings one for each engine, with two spares. The flight engineer regulates fuel flow by control valves. The drawing above shows No. 1 engine being fed fuel *(dark red)* from the center tank as well as its own. The emergency dump system jettisons fuel in flight.

HOW THE SYSTEMS GO
With his hand on a fuel-flow control and his logbook in front of him, the flight engineer monitors his board in the rear of the cockpit. Controls for the electrical system are at upper left, for pressurization and oxygen supply at upper right, and for the fuel system at bottom.

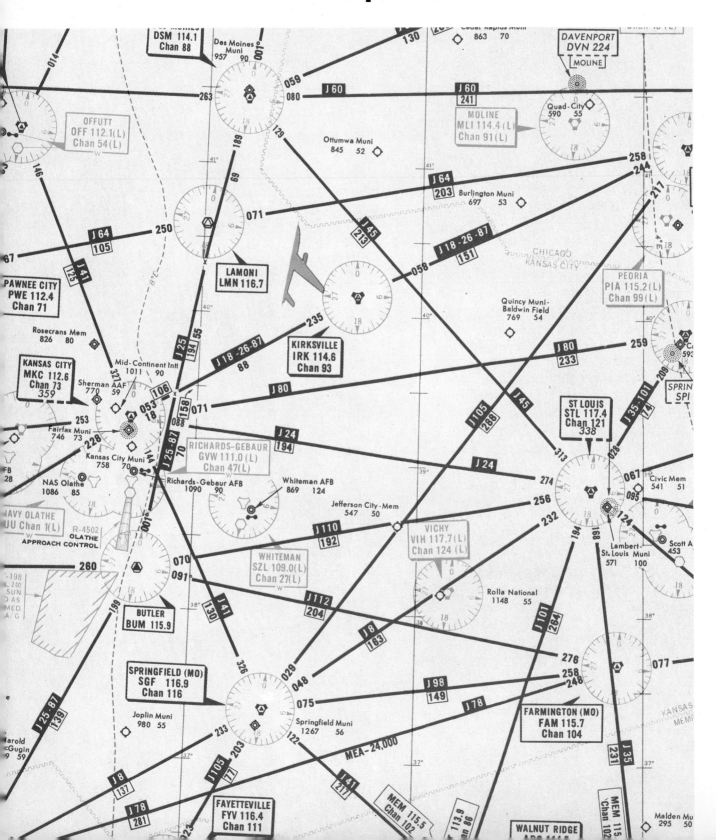

6

EVERY DAY OF THE YEAR, 2,500 commercial flights fill the skies above the United States, each headed for a specific destination on an exact timetable at speeds ranging from 200 to 600 miles per hour. Many airliners, flying by night or above the clouds, are never in sight of the ground from takeoff to landing. Yet, barring severe weather conditions or mechanical failure, each arrives close to schedule. In every cockpit navigation is entrusted to a battery of alert and precise instruments which have virtually eliminated what was once the most formidable obstacle to long-distance aviation. Today's pilot can fly a perfect nonstop course from coast to coast, instantly pinpointing his position at any time without so much as a glance out the window.

Airliners fly from city to city along clearly defined airways, numbered aerial highways complete with directional signs, speed limits and traffic patrols. Invisible to the passengers, the airways are marked by interlocking radio signals constantly beamed into the sky by ground transmitters along the route. Receivers in the plane pick up these signals and immediately indicate the direction and distance of the station. By checking these with an airways chart, the pilot can fix his exact position with more ease and certainty than a motorist reading a roadside sign.

This, however, is only the primary navigation system. It is backed by a complex of other cockpit gadgets: direction, altitude and airspeed indicators; as many as eight radios; lights which flash on automatically to indicate that the plane is passing over a radio beacon; and airborne radar for detecting and steering around storms.

Although navigation is taken for granted today, it posed a major problem in the early days of powered flight. Long after Kitty Hawk, getting from one point to another was more a matter of luck than science. On October 30, 1908, Henri Farman flew the first cross-country trip, a 16½-mile course from Bouy to Reims, France. Just nine months later, Louis Blériot made his notable flight across the English Channel. Neither Farman's nor Blériot's plane was equipped with navigation aids of any kind. After 1910, cross-country flights became more frequent but navigation remained primitive. Pilots relied on their eyes, a clock or watch, and an ordinary ground map. The pilot drew on the map a line to his destination and noted various landmarks—towns, bends in rivers, railroad tracks —over which he would fly. As the flight progressed, he would look for the landmarks, correcting his heading if necessary. By jotting down the elapsed time between two landmarks, he could compute his speed by simple arithmetic and estimate the time he should see the next checkpoint. This simple navigation was known as pilotage, or contact flying.

The railroad track was the "iron compass" of the early airmen, who followed it from city to city. But this type of navigation was only as accurate as the flyer was alert. When Calbraith Perry Rodgers was plan-

A HIGH-ALTITUDE ROAD MAP
To a pilot, this maze of lines and numbers, a high-altitude map published by the Air Force, indicates the normal traffic patterns for all planes flying at or above 18,000 feet in the Kansas City-St. Louis area. The circles show the location of ground stations that constantly transmit radio signals to give directions and distance information to the pilot during flight.

ning the first U.S. transcontinental trip in 1911, he mapped a route from Sheepshead Bay, New York, to Long Beach, California, in a series of short hops, following railroad tracks wherever possible. He used the iron compass to fly a precise first leg from Sheepshead Bay to Middletown, New York. His second scheduled stop was Elmira, New York, but somehow Rodgers missed a switch. Reaching a fair-sized city that he assumed could only be Elmira, Rodgers landed and prepared to accept the congratulations of the city fathers—only to discover he was in Scranton, Pennsylvania.

The birth of dead reckoning

The first mechanical aircraft instruments were being introduced at about the time of Rodgers' odyssey. Their history is somewhat hazy, but it is known that a Frenchman, A. Etévé, invented an airspeed indicator as early as 1910, and that in the following year a Captain Creagh-Osborne of the British Navy designed the first workable aircraft compass. These two basic cockpit instruments, together with an ordinary clock, permitted an elementary form of navigation by dead reckoning. The pilot fixed his position by calculating his course, speed and elapsed time rather than by ground observation. But the position plotted was strictly guesswork because the instruments were so unreliable.

The magnetic compasses wobbled erratically with plane vibration and movement. The airspeed indicator, a device which translated the impact pressure of air into miles per hour, did not take into consideration the varying density of the air due to altitude and weather. The pilot had nothing but his eyes and instincts to determine wind speed and direction, and this handicap was not overcome until 1914, when the driftmeter was invented by Elmer Sperry Sr. This instrument was a circular glass set in the floor of the cockpit, through which the pilot could sight on a convenient surface object. By rotating the glass to align the object's path with a set of parallel lines, he could then read his degree of drift from a scaled ring around the glass, at least during the day.

Navigating at night was extremely haphazard until 1919, when an aeronautical version of the mariner's sextant was designed. Equipped with a sextant and a precise chronometer to note the exact time of observation, the nocturnal navigator could use the technique of celestial navigation to sight, or "shoot," a star, measuring the star's angle above the horizon. From tables showing the position of the star at the time the sight was taken, he plotted a segment of a circle on his chart. He then sighted on a second star and drew a new segment. The point at which the two arcs intersected was his exact position.

The driftmeter and sextant, however, were limited by visibility conditions, and the sextant required more attention than the average pilot

CROSS-COUNTRY FLIGHT was inaugurated on October 30, 1908, by Henri Farman, piloting his Voisin-Farman biplane, the first equipped with practical ailerons. He flew 16½ miles from Bouy to Reims. This famous photo of the takeoff at Bouy shows a scene summed up by Farman as "the joy of soaring high above the heads of people."

could spare. Right up to the 1930s navigation was still mostly dead reckoning backed by pilotage and whatever wind information was available on the ground. Pilots still found themselves very much "up in the air" when it came to relatively simple navigation. The first air-mail flight between Washington and Philadelphia in 1918 was a navigational fiasco. After President Woodrow Wilson, Postmaster General Albert S. Burleson and other members of the Cabinet had gathered near the Washington Monument to witness the takeoff on a perfectly clear day, the pilot somehow ended up near Waldorf, Maryland, some 20 miles southeast of Washington—and a good hundred air miles from Philadelphia. The mail was unceremoniously removed and sent on by train.

Despite such embarrassments the Post Office gradually expanded air-mail service to the Western states and finally set up a coast-to-coast operation. By 1921 the Post Office Department felt confident enough to test round-the-clock service. The pilot who flew the first night run from North Platte, Nebraska to Chicago was, appropriately, Jack Knight. Knight successfully navigated by dead reckoning plus pilotage checks on prearranged bonfires, the locations of which were marked on a road map. On later flights, runway lighting of a sort was occasionally provided by the simple but effective expedient of flagging down passing motorists. With headlights on, their cars were spotted along the runway to give the pilot a landing target. In the mid-'20s, the Government installed electric runway and airport boundary lights at major airports, and rotating light beacons replaced the bonfires.

Without proper navigational equipment, however, the early air-mail service was undependable. Weather information was spotty and the planes had no instruments for flying above the weather. Often a pilot would take off in clear weather and run into a storm en route. Of the first 40 airmen hired to fly the mail, 31 were killed.

Fifteen hours without a checkpoint

A surviving mail pilot, Charles A. Lindbergh, used his hard-earned experience to achieve one of the most remarkable navigational triumphs of all time when he made his momentous New York-to-Paris flight in 1927. Lindbergh could have included a two-way radio, which at that time was being successfully used by pilots seeking position or weather information. Lindbergh, however, carried neither radio nor sextant. They were too heavy, he argued, and radios "cut out when you need them the most." So Lindbergh groped his way across the ocean by dead reckoning, using pilotage checks wherever possible.

On the 27th hour of his flight, he began to worry about his location. It had been 15 hours since his last pilotage check, in Newfoundland. According to his calculated position, he should have been nearing Ire-

A LUSTROUS FIRST for heavier-than-air craft was scored by Louis Blériot on July 25, 1909, when he flew his frail monoplane across the English Channel *(above)*. A map in his own hand *(below)* indicates the route from takeoff near Calais to landing near Dover. Lacking even a compass, he navigated by what he could see below. Notes show where he spotted a ship, where he was lost for 10 minutes, and the point at which he saw England.

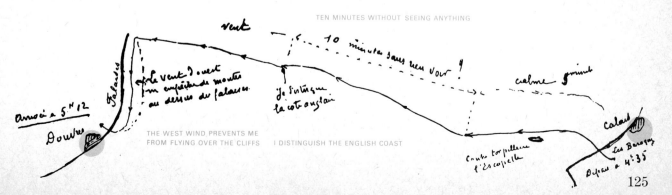

TEN MINUTES WITHOUT SEEING ANYTHING

THE WEST WIND PREVENTS ME FROM FLYING OVER THE CLIFFS   I DISTINGUISH THE ENGLISH COAST

land but there was no way to confirm it. Suddenly he sighted a fishing boat, an indication that land was close—but what land? Cutting his engine and gliding down to within 50 feet of the water, he leaned out the window and shouted, "Which way is Ireland?" But the boat's crew was either too startled to reply or could not hear him. Lindbergh flew on for another hour and then the monotonous vista of sea and sky was broken by the vague outline of wonderful, comforting land. Soon he was able to identify the town of Valentia on the southwestern coast of Ireland; after 16 hours of overwater navigation, he was almost exactly on course—and two hours ahead of schedule.

Navigation on the beam

In the same year the U.S. Government began installing the first radio navigation system, the LF/MF Four Course Radio Range. (LF/MF referred to Low Frequency-Medium Frequency, a radio wave band just below the broadcast band.) A transmitter sent out a set of signals forming a cross pattern, with the transmitter in the center. The pilot could tune his receiver to a station in the general neighborhood of his flight position, the frequency and location of which were marked on his chart. A steady hum in his earphones meant he was "on the beam," flying along one of the four arms of the cross pattern. If the hum increased in intensity, he was headed toward the station; if it faded he was going away. If the hum changed to a Morse code "A" (dot dash) or "N" (dash dot) he was off the beam to one side or the other, depending on the direction of his approach. The simplest form of exact position-fixing was to fly directly over the transmitter. There the hum would cease altogether; silence was the checkpoint.

The system had some flaws, the most glaring of which was the band's high susceptibility to static. The pilot often could not hear the signals during periods of bad weather when he most needed navigational information. But the LF/MF beam was the best that technology could provide at the time and, coupled with dead reckoning, it was a great aid to navigation above the clouds, where contact flying was impossible.

Flying *in* the clouds was another matter, however. An early airman, unable to see the ground or horizon, might feel that he was flying straight and level while the airplane was actually in a steep bank. Pioneer pilots, suddenly trapped in cloud or fog, all too frequently became confused and permitted their planes to slip into a spiral from which they could not recover. "Flying blind" with precision required far more sophisticated instruments than any that existed even in the 1920s.

J. H. ("Jimmy") Doolittle was the man who demanded and got them. Doolittle is best known for his World War II exploits, including the bombing of Tokyo from an aircraft carrier in 1942, but he had already

A LANDMARK IN AIR NAVIGATION
Lindbergh's 3,610-mile, 33 1/2-hour, solo flight from New York to Paris in 1927 was guided by this instrument panel. Set close to his face, it was probably the most advanced instrument panel then in existence. Later he noted: "All instruments functioned perfectly . . . I was less than five miles off course." Considering the fledgling instruments of the time, this was a remarkable performance.

1 MIRROR
2 VOLTMETER INDICATOR FOR EARTH INDUCTOR COMPASS
3 INSTRUMENT LIGHTS
4 ALTIMETER
5 AIRSPEED INDICATOR
6 COMPASS CORRECTION CHART
7 EIGHT-DAY CLOCK
8 PRIMER OPERATING KNOB
9 LATERAL LEVEL
10 LONGITUDINAL LEVEL
11 OIL-TEMPERATURE GAUGE
12 FUEL GAUGE
13 OIL-PRESSURE GAUGE
14 MIXTURE CONTROL
15 MAGNETO SWITCH
16 TACHOMETER
17 TURN AND BANK INDICATOR
18 PERISCOPE
19 PERISCOPE HANDLE

earned an important place in aviation as the first man to successfully fly blind on instruments alone. In 1928 the Daniel Guggenheim Fund for the Promotion of Aeronautics set up a laboratory at Mitchel Field, Long Island, for the development of blind flying. Harry Guggenheim, president of the Fund, managed to borrow Lieutenant Doolittle from the Army Air Corps to head the project.

Doolittle had available to him two radio beacons, one of which gave the pilot directional guidance to the landing runway. But these were inadequate without precise instruments in the cockpit to provide exact information on direction, height and attitude of the airplane. The wobbly magnetic compass was no good for low-altitude flight near obstacles, nor was the barometric altimeter, which might be off as much as 100 feet. Doolittle also wanted something better than the existing bank-and-turn indicator, in which a ball rolled to one side or another when the wings dipped, for the important job of keeping the wings level during the approach and touchdown on the runway.

Doolittle went to work on the altimeter problem first. He sought out instrument maker Paul Kollsman, who had built a barometric altimeter that he claimed would indicate height to within an accuracy of no more than 10 feet. Kollsman's altimeter was far more sensitive than those in standard use. Its secret was a precision gear created by a Swiss watchmaking firm to Kollsman's order: "I want you to cut me a better gear for this altimeter than you ever cut for a watch." On its first flight test the altimeter worked perfectly.

Gyroscopes in the cockpit

The Sperrys, Elmer Sr. and Elmer Jr., meanwhile had begun work on instruments to replace both the existing compass and bank-and-turn indicator. The Sperry Company was already the world's leading manufacturer of the gyroscope, a device which is based on the principle that a body spinning rapidly around an axis opposes any variation in the direction of that axis. The Sperrys now applied the gyroscope to Doolittle's needs by creating the Sperry Artificial Horizon. The key element was a wheel spinning at several thousand revolutions per minute, whose axis was set horizontally. An indicator in the cockpit had a fixed horizon line and a movable bar, which represented the wings of the aircraft. As the plane climbed or dived, the bar would move above or below the horizon line. When the plane banked, the bar would dip accordingly as the gyro reacted to each change from true horizontal. Thus the pilot was provided with a constant picture of his plane's attitude. To replace the magnetic compass, the Sperrys devised the directional gyro, which was also built around a horizontally spinning gyroscope. This instrument could be set to a compass heading and would remain "dead on" course despite all movements of the plane.

On September 24, 1929, Doolittle put his new instruments and his radio techniques to the ultimate test. Early that day a heavy fog rolled in and smothered Mitchel Field, but the fog was meaningless for all it mattered to Doolittle. His cockpit was covered by a hood which sealed off all outside view. Using the radio beacon to line himself up with the runway, Doolittle took off, climbed to a thousand feet and flew several miles along two different headings, using the directional gyro and the LF/MF beam. Then he flew back to the field, homed on the radio beacon, glued his eyes on the instruments and came in for a bumpy landing. A new era of navigation had begun.

By the late '30s, commercial airplanes were flying routinely on instruments. The ingenious automatic pilot could, in fact, free the human pilot from the controls. The autopilot uses two gyroscopes to detect any horizontal or vertical deviation from a set heading. Any change of course activates small motors which make the necessary corrections by adjusting the plane's controls.

A new electronic alphabet

The electronics industry perfected two systems during World War II which speeded the process of automation and laid the foundation for modern navigation. The first was the Very High Frequency Omnidirectional Range, or VOR, successor to the LF/MF system. The VHF band fits into the radio spectrum just above the frequency band of the home FM radio and is virtually free of static, even in severe thunderstorms. The "omni" transmitter superposes two signals over a full 360°, the combination varying with the direction. A receiver immediately identifies the combination and a needle on the instrument panel indicates the direction, but not the distance, of the station. By tuning to a second station to get another bearing, the pilot can accurately chart his position. Airliners have added a device which eliminates the need for the second bearing. This is the Distance Measuring Equipment, or DME, and consists of transmitter/receiver units in the plane and at the various ground stations. The transmitter in the airplane, called the "interrogator," asks the ground unit for information by sending a radio signal to a specific station. The signal triggers an immediate reply from the "transponder," which is picked up by the receiver in the aircraft. An electronic device precisely measures the time lapse between the two signals and promptly displays before the pilot's eyes the distance between plane and station. VOR/DME, combined with the military's similar TACAN (Tactical Air Navigation), which uses a single signal for both distance and bearing, forms the system called VORTAC. This is the basic element of today's worldwide navigation network.

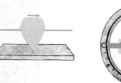

THE ARTIFICIAL HORIZON, used to indicate an airplane's position in relation to the actual horizon, operates on the same principle as a top *(left)*. So long as the top spins fast enough, it remains fixed in space, even if the position of its base is changed.

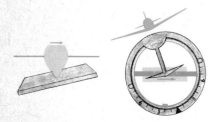

A LEFT-HAND BANK shows up on the artificial horizon indicator *(right)* exactly the way the plane would appear against the actual horizon. The gyroscope, the heart of the instrument, holds a fixed attitude in relation to the earth regardless of the plane's movements.

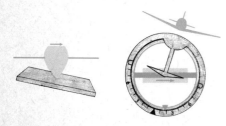

A RIGHT-HAND BANK registers in the opposite direction. In 1929, with the aid of the first artificial horizon indicator, Lieutenant James Doolittle accomplished the first successful blind takeoff and landing, in a plane with a hooded cockpit.

The second important wartime development was the refinement of radar. A radar transmitter sends out a beam, usually a pulse-type wave with a ten-thousandth of a second between pulses. The beam moves through space until it strikes something solid in its passage, then bounces back to a receiver at the point of origin. As with the DME, distance can be accurately measured by time lapse. A ground operator sees an airplane's position as a blip of light on a viewing screen. The radar altimeter employs the principle in reverse, sending a beam to the ground to determine the plane's exact height above the terrain rather than above sea level, as indicated by the barometric altimeter. Airborne radar can also be beamed forward to locate storms.

A skyful of airplanes

An even bigger problem than point-to-point navigation is control of air traffic in a period of snowballing aviation growth. At air terminals and 21 en route control centers, controllers monitor and guide airplanes with the help of long-range radar displaying an electronic picture of the airspace on screens, and computers relaying flight information among the centers. But there are now some 110,000 airplanes in the United States, more than five times as many as at the end of World War II.

Since about 1965 flight volume has been outstripping the air traffic network's ability to control it. The system is still safe, but not even its staunchest defenders would call it efficient. Saturation of the airways and air terminals is causing ever more frequent flight delays and cancellations. The old jibe "If you've time to spare, go by air" has become more painful for its aptness.

The trouble starts at the airport, particularly in the large centers of population known as "hubs." Any airport is a funnel that can accept only a given number of airplanes during a given period. When traffic volume exceeds capacity, the flow backs up behind the funnelneck; aircraft en route to the funnel must be directed into holding patterns to wait their turns, others are held on the ground at points of departure, clogging other funnels. Congestion spreads in a chain reaction that slows down the whole system, costing the airlines millions and jarring the nervous systems of thousands of irate travelers. Bad weather makes everything worse. It may knock out a radar, necessitate routing airplanes around storms or require an increase in the separation between aircraft in flight.

The traffic jam has at times reached crisis proportions. Stop-gap measures—training more controllers, temporarily restricting the number of arrivals and departures at the most congested terminals, rescheduling flights to avoid peak traffic loads—have helped. But much more is needed before air traffic can once again flow smoothly and efficiently.

The primary requirement is more concrete—more airports and more runways at existing airports. Even New York, which already has three major passenger terminals, needs at least one, perhaps several more, depending on how far you look into the future. Its John F. Kennedy International Airport is handling close to 500,000 take-offs and landings a year—nearly double its rated capacity for "delay-free" operations.

A comparable situation exists at other hubs. The Federal Aviation Administration sees a need, by 1973, for 900 additional airports and major improvements at perhaps half the nearly 4,000 publicly owned airports in the U.S. The FAA also looks ahead to installation of a computer-directed all-weather landing system that will eliminate delays caused by zero-zero visibility and to considerably increased automation at terminals and en route centers.

But even this $6 to $7 billion program is no cure-all, for traffic continues to mount. By 1979 there will be 1,500 more airliners and U.S. airports will be handling a staggering 167,000,000 annual operations, over three times the recent volume. To meet this monumental demand, the government must develop and install new, supersophisticated equipment that can make maximum use of airspace at no sacrifice of safety or reduce air travel, with severe penalties to the national economy and public convenience. For years to come, much of aviation's huge research program will continue to be aimed at the old and unfinished work of getting planes safely and surely from one place to another.

Controlling the Aerial Highways

"United 348 standing by for clearance." These words from the cockpit to the control tower, shown here, initiate a routine flight from Chicago to New York aboard a four-engine, 600-mile-an-hour United Airlines jet. The crew of 348—pilot, co-pilot and flight engineer—shares the hard-won skills of millions of flight miles. But in today's overcrowded skies, the men in the cockpit cannot by themselves guarantee a safe, on-time arrival. For every crew of every airliner aloft, there are teams on the ground working for the plane's safe passage. In the U.S., these are the Air Traffic Controllers of the Federal Aviation Administration. Using radar, radio, telephones, Teletypes and computers, they control or assist every flight throughout the United States. With this equipment—and their own good judgment—some 35 controllers will guide Flight 348 from the loading gate at Chicago's O'Hare Field to the arrival ramp at New York's Kennedy International Airport.

THE WATCHTOWER
In their many-windowed room atop the control tower at O'Hare Field, airport controllers keep their vigil. Every airplane taxiing on the ground, taking off or landing, is in their charge. Day and night the place crackles with the radio dialogues between tower and plane—a stream of talk between men who never see each other, but who work together in the airport's never-ending drama.

From Ramp to Runway

To keep air traffic separate and orderly, control is divided into three main areas: ground and local control at the airport; departure and arrival control within about 30 miles of the airport; and area control en route. For United 348, control begins at least a half hour before departure time, when the pilot files his flight plan with the Chicago Air Route Traffic Control Center. The plan includes his proposed departure time, route, desired altitude, destination and flight time from takeoff to arrival.

When he is ready to go, the pilot receives his first instructions from the ground controller: "United 348 cleared to runway 32 left, taxi via the inner circular taxiway." When the pilot reaches the runway, the local controller takes him over. With a final check to ensure the runway is clear, he announces: "United 348 cleared for takeoff," and the jet starts to roll.

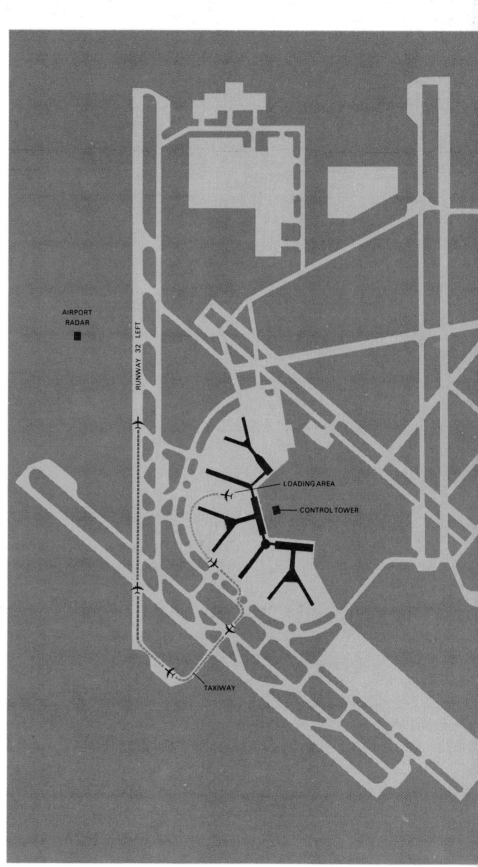

THE ROOM AT THE TOP

In the O'Hare tower, a glassed in aerie seven stories above the field, seven busy men are responsible for all air traffic within a ten-mile radius of the airport. Watching from the big windows and observing small radars that resemble TV sets, they clear planes onto and off the runways.

THE MAZE ON THE GROUND

On this map of O'Hare, United 348's path to the runway is indicated by a dotted line. Because traffic on the ground is as heavy as in the air, its control is shared: ground control supervises taxiways and aprons, while local control watches over the runways and the air above.

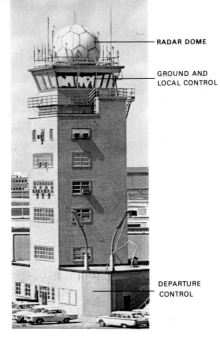

RADAR DOME

GROUND AND
LOCAL CONTROL

DEPARTURE
CONTROL

THROUGH RADAR EYES

From this darkened ground floor office, O'Hare Field's departure control, staffed by a complement of up to 15 men, governs the outbound flight paths of as many as 1,300 planes a day. Signals from a radar transmitter at the edge of the runways *(below)* cover a radius of 60 miles, sending back a steady stream of information on planes entering O'Hare's jurisdiction.

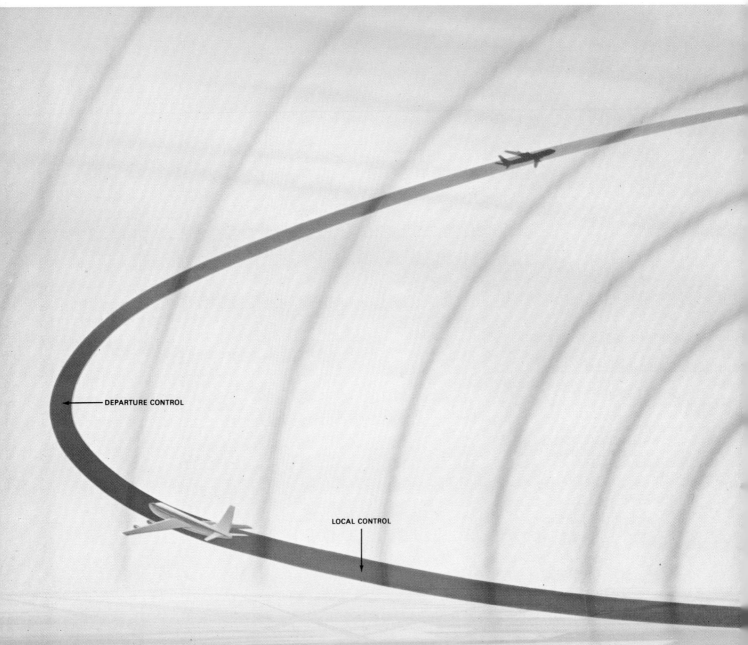

DEPARTURE CONTROL

LOCAL CONTROL

Up from
the Ground

Some 6,000 feet down the runway, United 348 lifts off and begins a curving climb. A half mile from the runway's end, the copilot tunes the airplane's radio to departure control, whose jurisdiction covers a 30-mile radius of the airport—an area through which funnel the many airplanes leaving or converging on the busy field.

The men of departure control never see the skies surrounding O'Hare, but their control is far more precise than it ever could be visually. Every aircraft, regardless of type or altitude, shows up on their two-dimensional radar screen as a white blip, identical to all other blips. Positive identification of United 348 can be made by asking the pilot to activate his transponder, an electronic device in the cockpit that brightens and enlarges the radar blip made by the airplane.

About five minutes after starting its takeoff, United 348 has climbed to 12,000 feet and reached the limit of departure control's surveillance. Responsibility now passes to the Chicago Air Route Traffic Control Center.

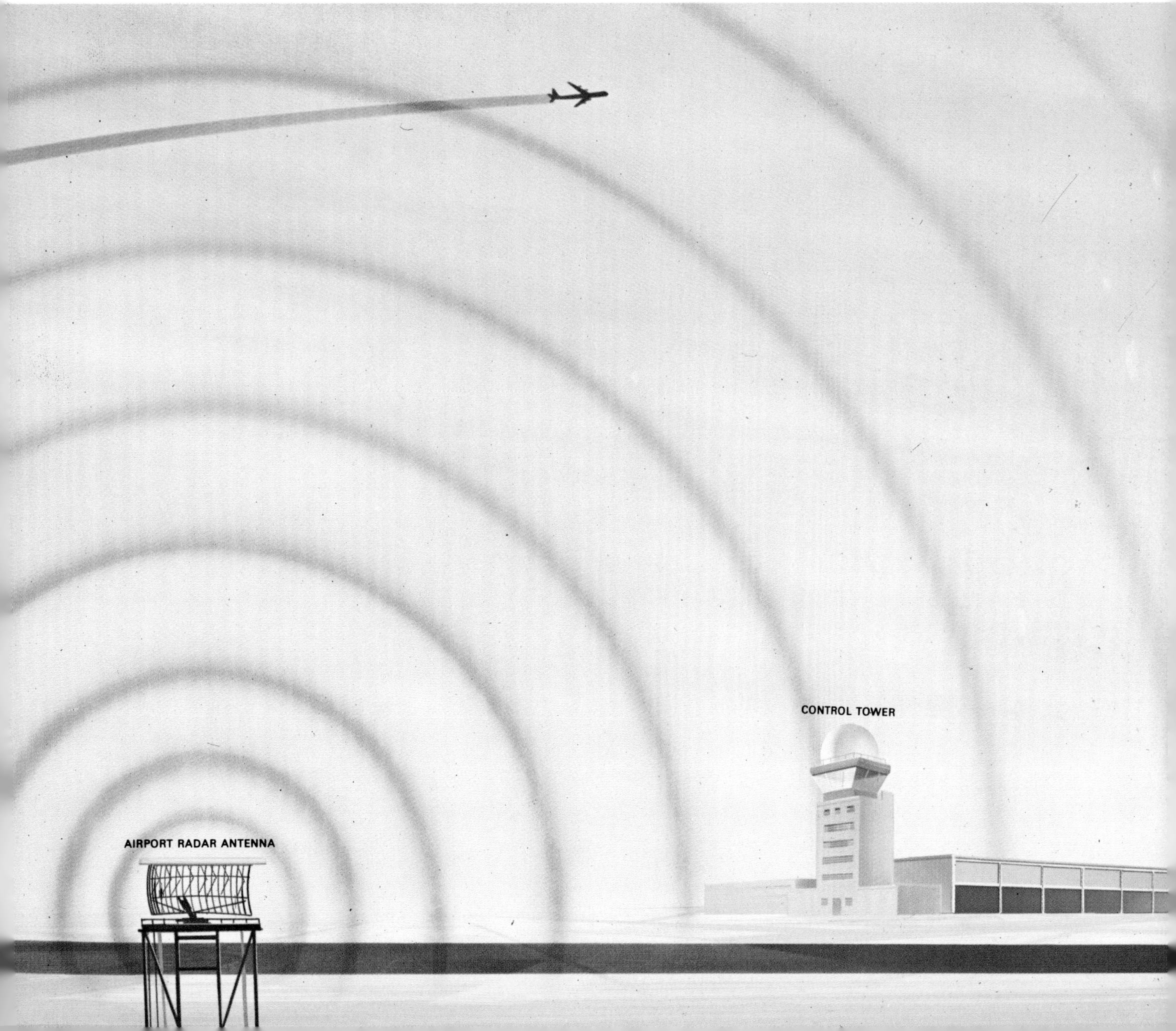

CONTROL TOWER

AIRPORT RADAR ANTENNA

The Radar Hand-off

"Chicago Center, this is United 348 . . . leaving one two thousand, over."

"United 348—Chicago Center, radar contact, change to transponder code two zero. . . ."

This simple exchange heralds a routine but important part of air-traffic control, the radar hand-off. Essentially, this is a transfer of jurisdiction over a plane from the radar control of one area to that of another. In practical terms, it means that the blip of United 348 is about to reach the limit of departure control's area of jurisdiction and must now be identified and tracked by the Chicago Air Route Traffic Control Center, which handles traffic over an area of 163,000 square miles on all the airways leading into and out of Chicago. Thus the aircraft is never beyond the reach of at least one radar controller: the pilot has only to identify himself to the watchers below and stand by for further instructions as to route and altitude.

To make doubly certain that they are tracking the right airplane, the controllers at Chicago center now ask for a transponder identification. Thus positively tagged on radar screens, United 348 is guided by Chicago center at a predetermined rate of climb along the access route to the aerial highway it will follow to New York.

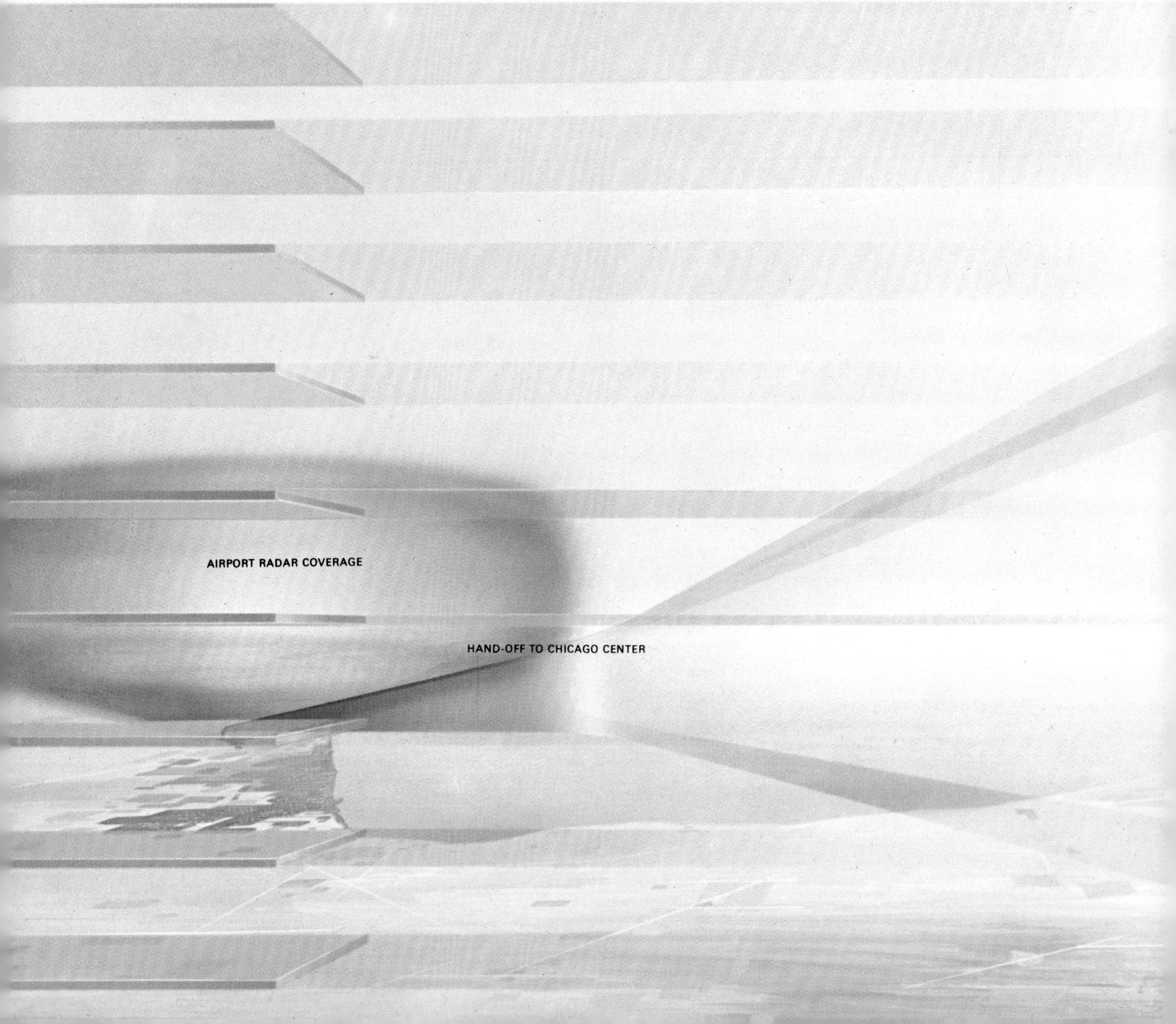

AIRPORT RADAR COVERAGE

HAND-OFF TO CHICAGO CENTER

FROM AIRPORT TO AIR ROUTE

The most delicate part of any flight for both pilot and controller is flying the access route *(below)* to or from an aerial highway. The airplane, constantly gaining speed and altitude, must cross the paths of diverse types of aircraft in the crowded layers of sky. At Chicago center *(left)*, controllers refer constantly to racks of "flight strips"—abbreviated flight plans of every controlled aircraft on their radar screens.

ACCESS ROUTE

The Many Highways of the Sky

Like a multilayered network of highways and superhighways, air routes crisscross the skies of the eastern U.S. Below 18,000 feet are the low-level routes, and above the high-level routes of jets. The layers of these airways are 1,000 feet apart (2,000 feet above the 29,000-foot level). In addition, each plane is protected on all sides by five miles of airspace.

United 348 is flying route J-60, an airway marked electronically by VORTACs—ground radio transmitters which, together with a cockpit instrument, keep the pilot on his course. United 348 has three such markers—at Joliet, Illinois, Cleveland, Ohio, and Philipsburg, Pennsylvania—to guide it until controllers bring it down to Kennedy airport.

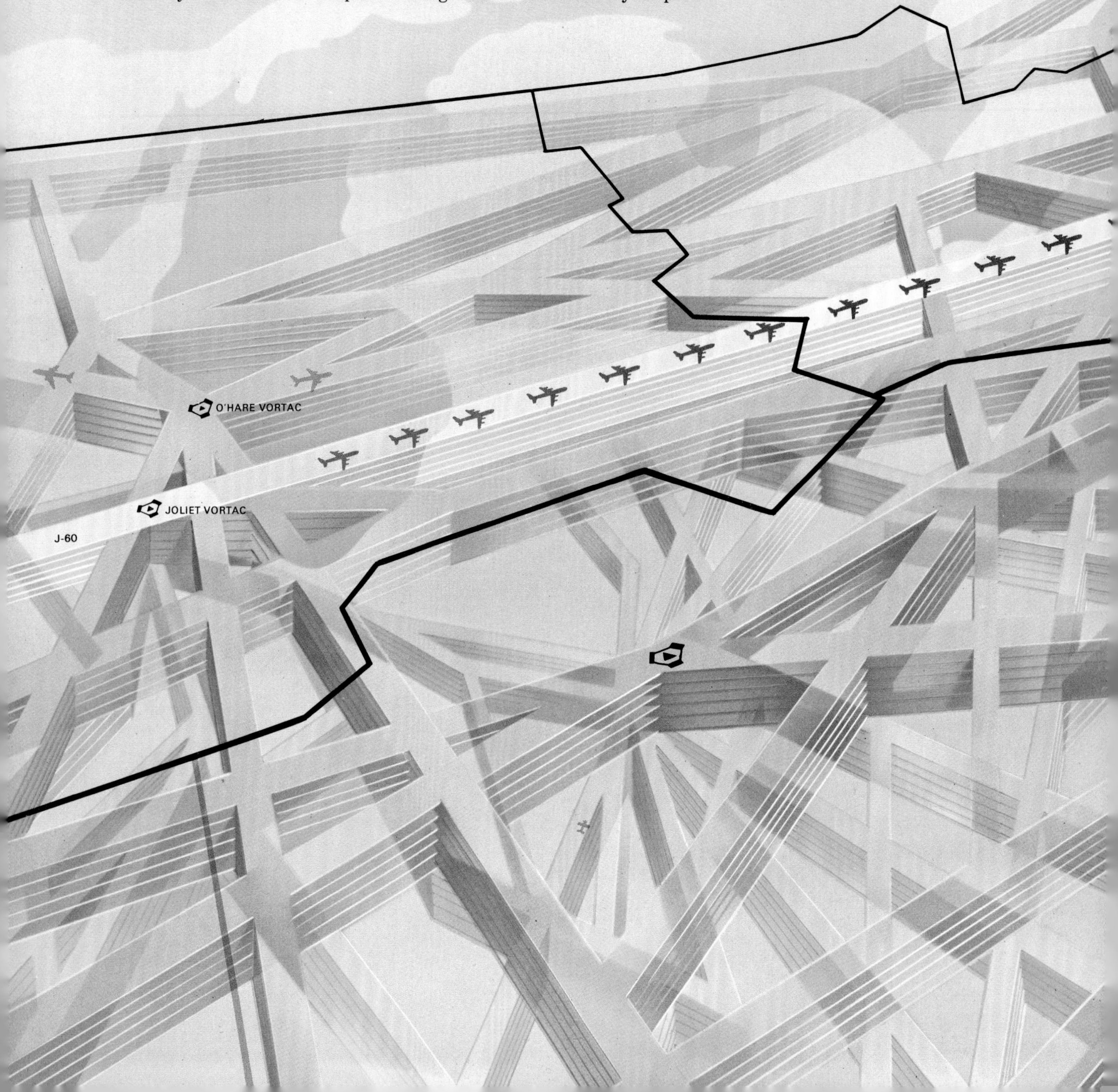

O'HARE VORTAC

JOLIET VORTAC

J-60

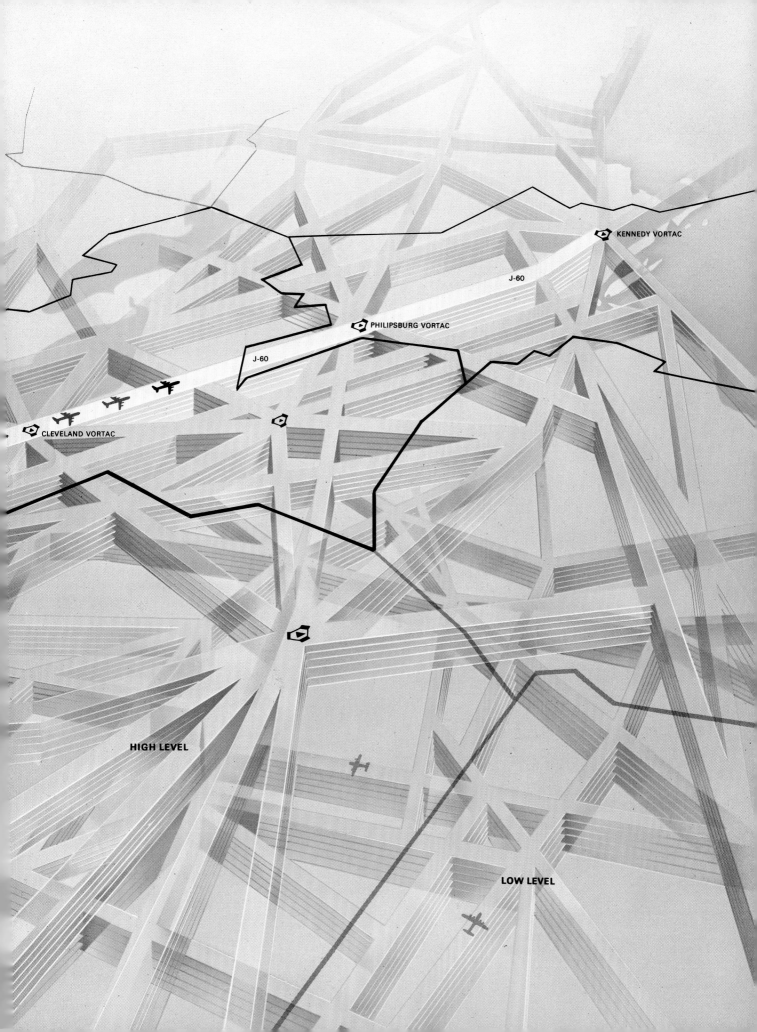

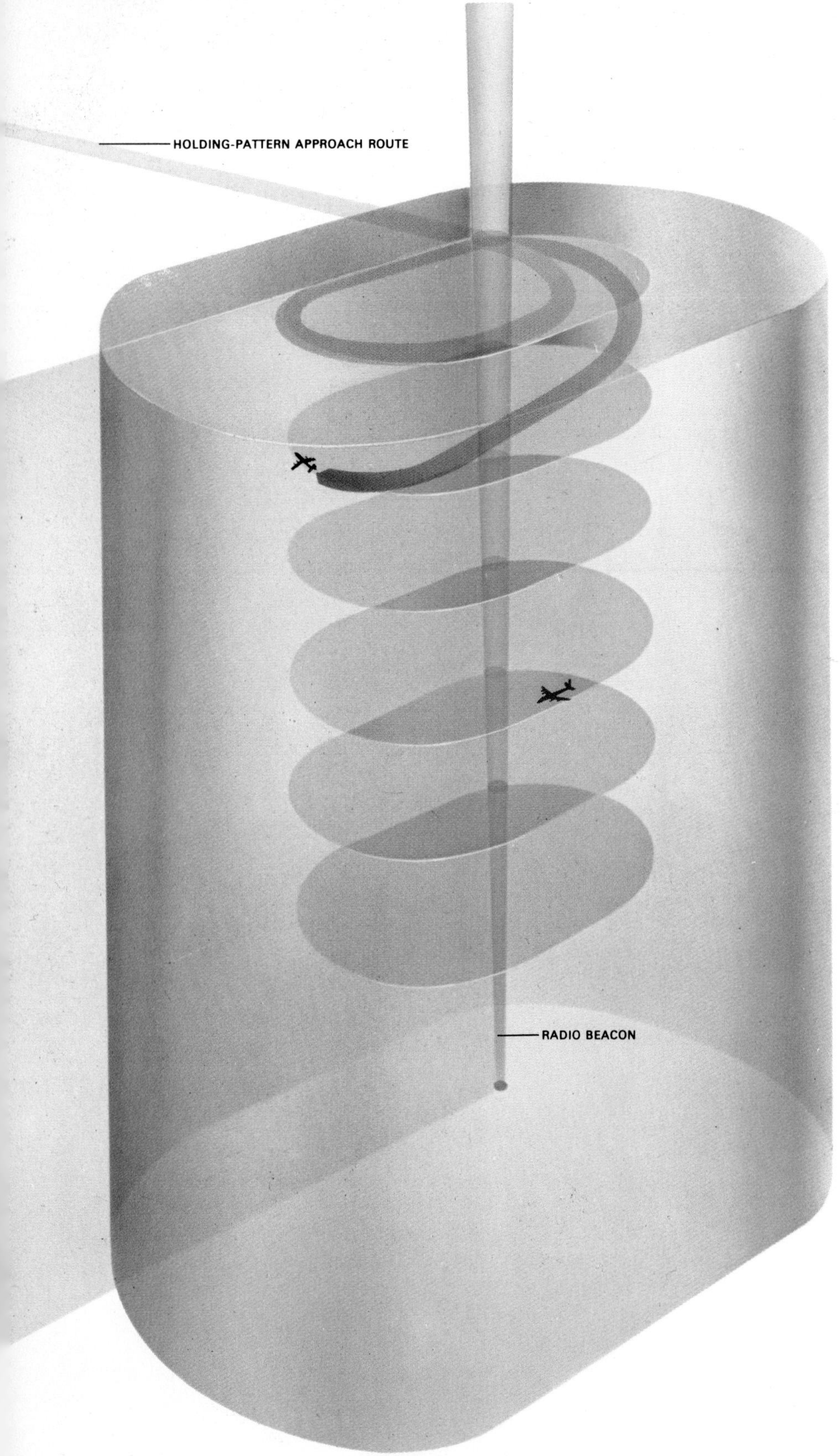

— RADIO BEACON

Aerial Stacks to Cope with Traffic

Approaching New York, United 348 flies into one of the most congested aerial traffic systems in the world. With only four major airports to handle the city's passenger, cargo and business flights, an efficient method of regulating the flow down onto the runways is imperative. To this end, Air Traffic Control has devised the holding pattern, a clearly defined loop marked by a radio beacon, where planes can circle until there is a free runway (*left*). There are 15 such holding patterns (*opposite, below*) in the metropolitan sector covered by the New York Air Route Traffic Control Center, and at times there may be more than 10 planes stacked in a pattern. Following the instructions from New York center, United 348 takes its place at the 23,000-foot rung of the Colts Neck, New Jersey, stack. As the big jet turns its regular, four-minute loops around the beacon, earlier arrivals periodically peel off from the bottom rung as they are cleared to land. Thus United 348 drops steadily down, in 1,000-foot steps, until it has reached the bottom rung some 45 minutes later and is cleared for its landing approach.

DOWN THE LADDER

From top to bottom the stack at Colts Neck, New Jersey, a standard jet holding pattern for Kennedy field, is more than two and one half miles high. Its highest rung is at 23,000 feet, its lowest at 11,000; the oval it forms is some nine miles long and four miles wide. Surrounding the stack is a protected airspace considerably greater than that normally used by the stacked aircraft. No plane may enter this space without orders from the Air Traffic Controller.

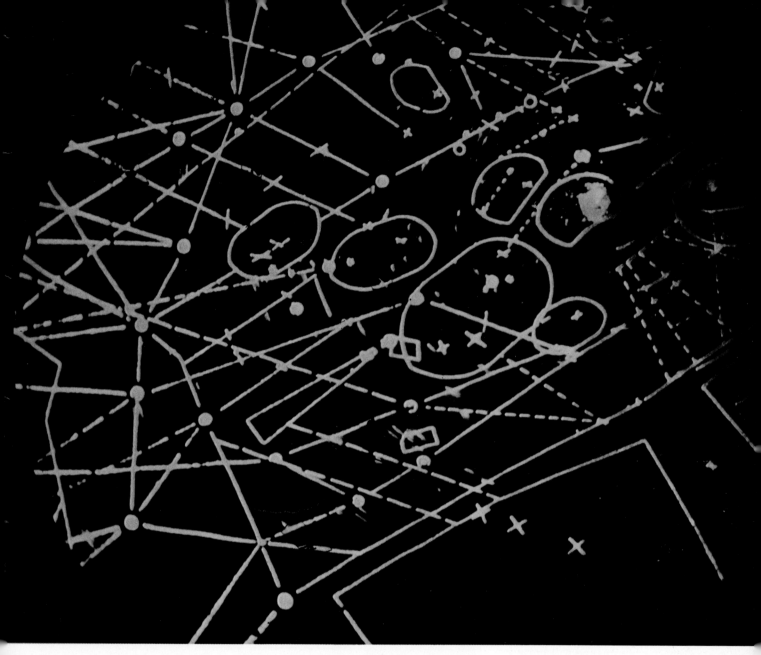

A CONTROLLER'S SKY

Etched on this radar screen at the New York Air Route Traffic Control Center are the air routes and holding patterns covering an area which stretches some 180 miles to the south and west of Kennedy field. The location of the airport is indicated by the bright green patch in the upper right. With this picture as a guide, a controller can easily pinpoint the exact location of all airplanes in his sector around Kennedy.

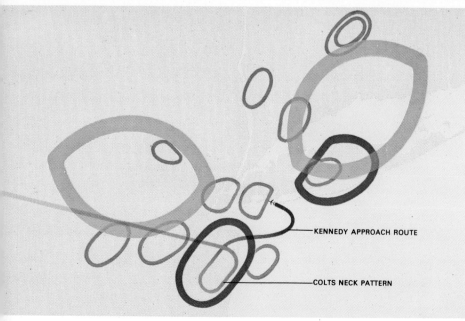

KENNEDY APPROACH ROUTE

COLTS NECK PATTERN

LOOPS AT MANY LEVELS

This map shows the major holding patterns in the New York area, color-coded by altitude. The very-high-level orange patterns, for jets, are used only when heavy traffic overloads other stacks. The two outlined in brown, including the one assigned to United 348 at Colts Neck, are high-level stacks normally used by Kennedy-bound jets. At lower altitudes are the patterns in purple, used chiefly by piston-powered craft.

Coming In on Radio Beams

Very often, incoming airliners find New York hidden under a blanket of clouds, but as United 348 slips into the gray layer, pilot and crew are unconcerned. As long as the ceiling, or bottom of the cloud layer, is no lower than 200 feet, and visibility on the ground no less than a half mile, they can plan a routine landing.

Called the Instrument Landing System, or ILS, the procedure that makes this possible utilizes a combination of three radio systems (right). One is the glide slope beam, which guides the pilot on his angle of descent; the second, intersecting the glide slope beam vertically, is the localizer beam, which leads the aircraft straight to the runway. Both glide slope and localizer activate a cockpit instrument with intersecting crossbars: when these are centered, the aircraft is descending toward the center of the runway at an angle of 2.5° to 3°. The third component of ILS comprises two vertical radio marker beams, which tell the pilot his distance from the runway. Generally, the first marker is set five miles out, the second one half mile from the runway.

At the second marker, the airplane will be about 200 feet up, 20 seconds from touchdown, and will break into the clear below the clouds. United 348's flight is nearly over; all that remains is for the pilot to land, reverse his engine's thrust, apply the brakes and, following the local controller's directions, turn off the runway and taxi slowly to the terminal.

A CONTROLLED DESCENT
Guided by instruments and instructions from the approach controller, the pilot of United 348 positions his jet on the glide path. The approach is observed on a precision radar screen, which shows bearing, distance and altitude, giving the controller a three-dimensional view. If the craft is off the beam, control will alert the pilot and instruct him how to get back on again.

LOCALIZER BEAM TRANSMITTER

GLIDE SLOPE BEAM TRANSMITTER

SECOND MARKER

APPROACH
ROUTE

GLIDE PATH

FIRST MARKER

7
Theory Today, in Flight Tomorrow

FERTILIZER, of the common farm and garden variety, is hardly a product ordinarily associated with aviation research. Yet in the near future you may see airport runways coated with artificial manure as an aid to bad-weather landings—it promises to help keep aircraft from skidding on icy runways. The substance being examined is urea, a commercial fertilizer that also acts as an antifreeze. Early investigations showed that urea, sprinkled on a runway before or during a snowfall or freezing rain, can prevent ice formation, but long-term tests are needed to determine the effects of the chemicals on airframes and engines and to show what form of urea—powder, pellets or liquid—will prove most efficient.

The fertilizer program exemplifies the simplest form of aviation research, the application of existing materials or techniques to the solution of contemporary problems. At the other end of the spectrum are studies that look far into the future and explore flight concepts and phenomena about which little or nothing is known. In between there are thousands of separate projects covering all types of aircraft in speed ranges from zero to hypersonic, myriad airplane components and many items of ground equipment.

Today's aviation research effort is so vast in scope that it requires, in the United States alone, expenditures of more than $1.5 billion annually. Most of this money is spent by the military services, which operate a number of research facilities aimed primarily at the special requirements of defense. The greatest concentration of these is at Wright-Patterson Air Force Base near Dayton, Ohio, where the Research and Technology Division of the U.S. Air Force Systems Command runs four major laboratories —Flight Dynamics, Aero Propulsion, Materials and Avionics (Aviation Electronics). The focal point for civil aviation research is NASA, which also has four laboratories engaged in aeronautical work in addition to its many space research facilities. Foremost among these installations is Langley Research Center, where there are groups working on aerodynamics, propulsion, structures and operating problems, applicable to military as well as civil aircraft.

Both Wright-Patterson and Langley are concentrating on high-speed research, their goals the same, their focuses slightly different. In the supersonic field, the military center seeks mainly to improve the efficiency of supersonic types now flying, and to develop new fighters and bombers capable of sustained flight at Mach 3 and above. Langley is heavily concerned with advanced concepts for supersonic flight and also conducts hypersonic research. But much additional and valuable research is being carried on by other organizations as well. At Atlantic City, the FAA's National Aviation Facilities Experimental Center concentrates on the problems of navigation aids, air traffic control and all-weather operation, of the greatest importance in view of today's crowded skies. FAA addition-

A RESEARCH TOOL
A scale model of the SCAT 15F, one of the research planes used by NASA to obtain basic information for the design of SSTs, is shown before testing. During tests, a balance mounted inside the model records such forces as lift and drag. This information is then fed into a computer and the results are translated into adjustments to improve supersonic performance.

ally supervises the national program for development of an American SST, with the assistance of NASA and the military services. Aircraft manufacturers conduct both their own and Government-contracted research, while vital areas of aeronautical investigation are explored by the airlines, a number of private groups and a great many colleges and universities.

Tools of the trade

The type of work being done by all of these organizations can be classified in four categories. First, there is basic research, the general acquisition of aeronautical knowledge without regard for its immediate application. Basic research may involve the work of only one man in a specialized field, working out theories on paper and studying the endless flow of scientific literature to absorb the knowledge of others who have experimented in the same field. Or it may involve a team of many scientists working in an elaborate facility, testing and modifying existing theories and exploring new phenomena on which no theories have been developed.

The next category is applied research, where scientists attempt to apply the results of basic research to actual use. Such work might involve experiments to improve structural strength by creating new metal alloys or to increase the combustion efficiency of an engine. A step further is developmental research, the actual construction and flight-testing of an airplane, its propulsion system and its equipment. Finally, there is operational research, the ironing-out of problems encountered by planes already in service.

Aeronautical research is primarily a ground-based function requiring a wide variety of research tools, some of which are as complex and costly as the airplanes they are helping to build. The most widely used tools are the wind tunnel and the electronic computer. The wind tunnel actually predates powered flight by more than 30 years. In 1871, a pair of British engineers, F. H. Wenham and John Browning, designed an apparatus consisting of a steam-driven fan which blew air over a model mounted in a tunnel, creating an effect comparable to the movement of an airplane through the atmosphere. Modern wind tunnels still employ the same basic principle, but with a great deal more sophistication. Where the Wenham-Browning tunnel operated at low airflow speed and constant sea-level pressure, today's tunnels can reproduce a variety of temperature, density and other atmospheric conditions, while generating air velocities up to 20,000 miles an hour.

The versatile computer is employed in a number of ways. It performs the millions of mathematical calculations required in aeronautical research, providing in minutes accurate answers that might have required months or even years of human effort. It stores and analyzes data from research instruments and, coupled with an automatic plotter, it draws graphs to give researchers a visual presentation. Fed the characteristics of a hypothetical airplane, the computer can actually simulate a flight and evaluate the machine's aerodynamic efficiency, stability and a number of other factors that determine aircraft design.

Other tools are specialized for specific research. There is available such equipment as vacuum chambers for duplicating extreme altitude conditions, acoustic rooms for studying the effect of high-frequency jet noise on structures, "ovens" for applying high temperatures to materials, vibration machines to provide the flutter of a wing panel in flight, high-speed cameras to record test observations and huge hydraulic rigs for measuring landing impacts. But for all the capabilities of the laboratories and their equipment, there is one indispensable tool of research—the airplane. The theories born in the laboratories must be validated by actual flight test, either of the new design itself or of a component installed in a test plane. In some areas, such as atmospheric research, the desired information can be obtained only in flight. Because there are still conditions that cannot be duplicated in a ground facility, the military and civil research organizations employ a multitude of experimental and operational test planes in every attainable speed range.

The biggest research projects involve all the technologies and most of the tools, and often developments in one area will have a profound effect on work being done in other areas as well. An example of this overlapping research is the accelerating investigation into hypersonic flight by both the Air Force and NASA. The ultimate goal is to create a vehicle capable of taking off from earth, attaining velocities up to 25 times the speed of sound, flying into orbit and returning under its own power and control. As an intermediate goal, researchers are focusing on more modest but nonetheless incredible targets—airplanes capable of operating in the Mach 6 to 12 range. The Air Force is thinking in terms of fighter and reconnaissance aircraft for tomorrow's operational squadrons. NASA, looking beyond the still-unbuilt supersonic transport, has selected as its target a hypersonic passenger-carrying plane.

To fly at eight times the speed of sound

For this airplane, NASA researchers have "thrown away the book" and taken a brand-new approach. All the effort that has gone into determining the shape of the supersonic airliner is of little use in the hypersonic transport, which probably will be most efficient in the Mach 6 to 8 speed range, or 4,000 to 5,000 miles per hour. The combined aerodynamic, propulsion and structural requirements for a hypersonic transport will make it much larger than the huge SST, even with similar range and payload. Says John Becker of Langley's Aero-Physics Division, and head of NASA's basic research team: "At first it looked as though the hypersonic trans-

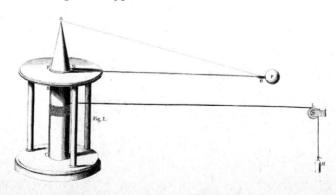

AIR RESISTANCE was proved to be a vital factor in the flight of projectiles by the British mathematician Benjamin Robins in 1746. In Robins' machine *(right),* weight (M) turns a drum and rotates shape (P), representing a projectile. After measuring the speed of rotation of the arm (GH), Robins removed P and found that he could move GH at the same speed with less weight at M. Robins realized that the difference in the weights at M corresponds to the air resistance offered by P.

port would have to be a four-to-five-million-pound airplane. Now, though, it seems possible to get it down to something less than a million pounds." A million-pound plane, once inconceivable, is no longer even breath-taking; aircraft with gross weights in the neighborhood of three quarters of a million pounds are already flying.

The basic design of the hypersonic transport is still in doubt, but theoretical, computer and wind-tunnel research have produced a shape that is at least a departure point—a flat, triangular wing bisecting a long, cone-shaped fuselage. The final design, however, will depend in large part on the requirements of propulsion and structure.

Nourishing the ravenous ramjet

Since the conventional turbojet engine cannot supply the vast power needed for hypersonic flight, a new propulsion system is needed. Independent studies at Langley and Wright-Patterson point to the ramjet engine as the most promising. As a preliminary step, NASA is building an 18-inch-diameter ramjet, a miniature version of the huge power plant a hypersonic transport would require; it will be wind-tunnel tested in the Mach 5 to 7 range. In a separate project, NASA is constructing part of a hypersonic wing containing an engine and nacelle. The aim of this investigation is not ramjet combustion research but a study of external aerodynamics—how the fast-moving air reacts with the engine inlet—and structural cooling requirements. Working along similar lines, the Air Force Aero Propulsion Laboratory has built a "boilerplate"—nonflyable —model of what it calls a "scramjet," a contraction of "supersonic combustion ramjet" (the hypersonic airflow is slowed in the engine inlet to supersonic speed before it enters the combustion chamber). The 30-inch model is now undergoing tunnel tests at Mach 6 and above. The Air Force laboratory has also contracted for construction of a regular ramjet for hypersonic studies.

Reflecting its never-before-realized, very advanced concepts, hypersonic flight demands not only entirely new engines but also completely new, high-energy fuels. Today's hydrocarbon fuels, derived from petroleum, simply do not generate enough energy per pound of fuel for the voracious ramjet. There is general agreement among experts that liquid hydrogen, which propels some of the rocket-launched vehicles used in space research, seems to be the answer. In a rocket engine, liquid hydrogen is mixed with an oxidizer, like liquid oxygen, and burned. In a ramjet, the high-velocity air serves as the oxidizer. In addition to its high energy per pound, nearly three times as great as conventional jet fuel, it offers a bonus in its cooling ability. Carried aloft at a temperature of about −423° Fahrenheit, liquid hydrogen also serves as a refrigerant that can cool the engine before being consumed in the form of gas.

AIRFOIL TESTING in a wind tunnel was first accomplished in the 1880s by an English aerodynamicist, Horatio Phillips. He constructed a wind tunnel *(right)* which used steam pressure forced through jets (into Tube B) to suck air through Box A. This provided an airflow of 60 feet per second and avoided the wobbly airstream produced by fan-powered wind tunnels. Inside the box Phillips placed an apparatus which held airfoils of various shapes *(left)* in the airflow and which, by a sensitive system of weights, measured the lift and drag forces generated by the foils.

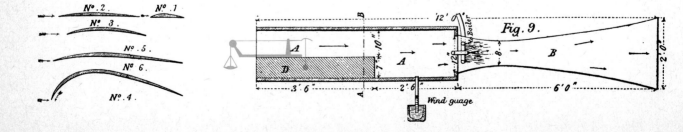

But, as is so often the case, a plus in one area means a minus in another. Liquid hydrogen has a very low density, about one tenth that of jet fuel, requiring 10 times as much space for the same fuel weight. This means that the design of the hypersonic plane must include an enormous fuel tank, greatly complicating the task of the aerodynamicist who must contend with this great bulk while seeking ways of reducing the tremendous amount of drag at hypersonic speeds.

At Langley and Wright-Patterson, the structures researchers are tackling another problem stemming from the spiraling temperatures of outer surfaces—up to 2,500° Fahrenheit above Mach 5. New materials are needed and the structures teams are investigating such metals as columbium and tantalum, which retain their strength up to about 3,000° Fahrenheit, and molybdenum, which can withstand even higher temperatures. They are also conducting research on coatings, such as silicides that form a wall to protect the skin against oxidation—which at hypersonic speed would literally vaporize the metal. Someday there may be an iridium-coated airplane, for iridium, similar to platinum and very costly, will not readily combine with oxygen. An approach being pursued at Langley is "refurbishable" components for such parts as the wing leading edges, which are subject to the highest temperatures. The metals of these parts can withstand great temperatures for only a few flights, but it may be possible to replace entire sections whenever examination reveals signs of metal deterioration.

These are examples of research applied to the basic problem involved in building a structure that can withstand hypersonic speeds, a problem that can be compared to creating a super Thermos bottle capable of keeping a liquid cold in a furnace. Instead of liquid, however, the hypersonic structure must protect human cargo, sensitive flight instruments and other internal equipment. And it must keep heat from penetrating to the liquid-hydrogen tank, where it would cause vaporization, a situation that could bring about truly disastrous consequences. The vaporized hydrogen could build up pressure on the walls of the tank until it finally burst.

A hypersonic Thermos bottle

One promising approach being explored by NASA is the "hot monocoque" structure. This is actually two separate structures, the inner composed of a conventional material like aluminum, covered by fibrous insulation, and the outer of a superalloy, probably coated for greater oxidation protection. Between the two structures is a space through which carbon dioxide gas is circulated. The hot-monocoque concept prevents air from reaching the inner structure where it would liquefy and freeze in contact with the liquid-hydrogen tanks, adding weight to the aircraft.

MAKING AIRFLOW VISIBLE was the next logical step after experimenters had learned how to measure the aerodynamic forces on objects in a wind tunnel. In 1899 a French physiologist, Etienne Marey, constructed a vertical wind tunnel fitted with tubes that released threads of smoke into the airstream. He was then able to see and photograph the behavior of airflow around various shapes placed in its path *(above)*.

Also, some of the carbon dioxide forms a frost that absorbs friction heat.

The hypersonic plane is a long way from operational research, but considerable data have already been gathered from flights of the X-15, which reached Mach 6 before it was retired in 1969. Scientists are now studying the possibility of building an even faster test plane, one which can operate for longer periods at Mach 8 and attain speeds as high as Mach 12. The cost and design problems are monumental, but it probably will be built because man still has a lot to learn about hypersonic flight within the atmosphere.

At the other end of the speed spectrum is an area of equal interest to both NASA and the Air Force researchers: the VTOL (Vertical Take-Off and Landing plane). The VTOL combines the vertical lift feature of the helicopter with cruising speeds that will eventually be in the supersonic range. Such planes have wide applicability in military operations, their potential uses ranging from short-haul personnel and cargo transport within a combat zone to interception and bombing by high-speed VTOLs capable of operating from small fields. They also offer great advantages in commercial air transportation, with their ability to operate from mid-city locations.

Accent on the vertical

At Wright-Patterson, all four Air Force laboratories are heavily engaged in VTOL studies. Aerodynamicists are working on new designs, the structures experts are looking into new lightweight materials and the Avionics Laboratory is investigating the type of information and instruments a pilot needs to fly straight up and down. The greatest concentration of research is in the Aero Propulsion Laboratory, which is exploring a variety of engine designs in its attempt to develop a VTOL power plant with a thrust-to-weight ratio of 20 to 1, or an output equal to 20 times the weight of the propulsion system.

At present, there are about a score of VTOLs in the development stage in the U.S., England, France, Germany and the Soviet Union. In the United States one of the most heavily tested is the XC-142, a "tilt-wing" design that is considered one of the better approaches for a medium-speed VTOL. It has four turbine engines mounted on a conventional wing, driving large propellers. A mechanism in the fuselage permits the pilot to rotate the entire wing through an arc of 100°. For takeoff and hovering, the wing is positioned vertically so that the propellers spin in a horizontal plane, like the rotor of a helicopter. Once airborne, the pilot moves the wing so that the propellers swing forward to drive the XC-142 to speeds up to 430 miles an hour. The propulsion system has 11,400 horsepower to provide vertical lift for the 35,000-pound weight of the plane and its payload.

For higher speeds, NASA favors the "vertifan" approach, exemplified by the XV-5B, which started test flights in 1968. In each wing and in the nose are outlets which look like downward-aimed large electric fans. For takeoff and landing, the jet exhaust is channeled into the rapidly spinning blades of the fans, which force it downward for vertical thrust. Aloft, the pilot can block off the flow to the fans and divert it rearward for horizontal thrust, accelerating the plane to forward speeds up to 500 miles an hour.

France has developed a third type of VTOL, designed primarily for fighter aircraft operating at supersonic speed. The Dassault Mirage III-V has a conventional high-thrust jet engine for forward flight and a separate system of eight lifting engines for takeoff and landing. Each lift engine, which weighs only 250 pounds, produces 4,000 pounds of thrust for a thrust-to-weight ratio of 16 to 1. Their combined thrust of 32,000 pounds gives them a vertical lift capability 20 per cent greater than the normal weight of the airplane.

Basic and applied research have established the feasibility of these and other VTOL designs, but large informational gaps are still being filled in by flight-test programs. Of particular importance are stability and control during vertical flight and the period of transition, when the VTOLs convert from one form of flight to another.

The creation of a completely new aircraft, like a hypersonic or VTOL plane, provides a glamorous and dramatic aspect of aviation research that is often ballyhooed while equally important, but less exciting, work in other areas tends to be overlooked by the general public. A vital project that commands the attention of virtually every level of research organization today is not the development of any aircraft, but the problem of all-weather flying.

A seeing-eye landing device

All of the military services, NASA, FAA, the airlines and a number of manufacturing concerns are currently engaged in a great many individual projects in this field. One that represents an important step forward is AWLS (for All Weather Landing System), which is designed to permit completely automatic landings in absolute zero-zero weather.

With AWLS, the pilot aligns his plane with the runway, puts it on autopilot and turns the controls over to a battery of small but complex computers, each about the size of a shoe box, which fly the airplane the rest of the way to the runway. Although he can override the system if necessary, the pilot normally serves only as a monitor while the computers make the decisions and actuate the controls to keep the aircraft on course at the proper speed and rate of descent.

The computers get most of their input from the Instrument Landing

"THERMOS" DESIGN—a container-within-a-container called "hot-monocoque" construction—is one way the interior of the hypersonic plane of the future could be protected from the 1,500°- to 2,500°- temperatures caused by air friction. Carbon dioxide circulates between the walls and some of it is frozen into an insulating layer of dry ice by the −450°F. liquid hydrogen in the fuel tank. A disadvantage of hot-monocoque construction is the additional weight burden it imposes on the aircraft.

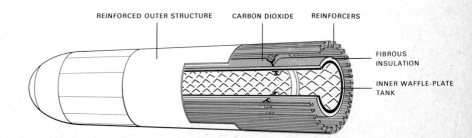

REINFORCED OUTER STRUCTURE   CARBON DIOXIDE   REINFORCERS

FIBROUS INSULATION

INNER WAFFLE-PLATE TANK

System long in use at air terminals. By radio beam, the ILS sends the computers an electronic picture of the desired glide path to the ground and constantly informs them of the plane's deviation from the runway center line. The aircraft's own radar altimeter keeps the computers posted as to the plane's precise height above the runway. The automatic system makes appropriate corrections in the flight path until a special "flare computer" decides it is time to level off and touch the wheels to the concrete.

At the National Aviation Facilities Experimental Center, FAA pilots have monitored hundreds of hands-off landings under a variety of simulated weather conditions. The results of initial flights prompted FAA to approve AWLS for landings under what the agency calls Category II conditions, i.e., ceiling of 100 feet or more and visibility permitting the pilot to see 1,200 feet of runway. Years of testing and refinement remain before AWLS can qualify for the ultimate Category IIIc: "Ceiling zero, runway visual range zero." But the success of early experiments holds out hope that, sometime in the 1970s, AWLS may provide the solution to one of aviation's oldest and most pressing problems—*all*-weather flying.

The 'groovy' runway

Even moderately bad weather can pose serious dangers to airline operations, and much research effort is devoted to such problems as hydroplaning, a difficulty often experienced by airline pilots during landings in heavy rain. Their planes seem to float on the wet runways, with landing rolls much longer than normal; use of reverse thrust from the engines, the usual runway braking procedure, sometimes causes a skid.

NASA has a facility at Langley for just this type of research. It is a walled runway 2,200 feet long which can be filled with water, ice or snow, or used as a normal landing strip. A large test rig, driven by a stream of high-pressure water, rolls down the runway at speeds of up to 130 miles an hour, approximately those of a landing airliner. In the center of the rig is a multiwheeled aircraft main landing gear, which can be dropped and raised. For the hydroplaning research, engineers put about an inch of water on the runway and photographed the action of the wheels as they struck the wet surface. It was found that the wheels tended to skim the top of the water like hydroplanes and failed to grip the concrete until the rig was slowed considerably. Langley made the test results available to aircraft manufacturers and operators, and offered a simple solution: install small air jets on each landing gear truck. High-pressure air, diverted from the engine and ducted to the wheel jets, could be blown downward ahead of the wheels. The airstream would part the water and permit the wheels to get a grip on the concrete.

The solution, though sound, had its drawbacks: the additional weight, complexity and maintenance requirements of the engine diversion sys-

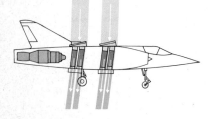

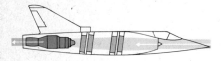

VTOL PLANES—the initials stand for Vertical TakeOff and Landing—are expected to be of great military and commercial value. The French Mirage III-V shown here is lifted straight up by four small turbojet engines placed on each side of the fuselage. A larger engine (aft) provides forward thrust.

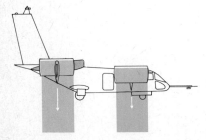

PROPELLERS IN DUCTS power one U.S. VTOL under development: the Bell X-22A. The ducts, which increase thrust during vertical takeoff, also serve as lifting surfaces during forward flight. Because of the ducted propeller's greater payload potential per horsepower, this design may be used as a transport.

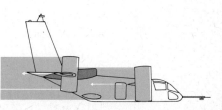

tem, the ducting and the air jets. So NASA took a second look at its data and reapproached the problem from a different direction—modifying the runway instead of the aircraft. Seeking to "give the water some place to go," researchers designed the "groovy runway," in which thin grooves are cut across the width of a runway at right angles to the path of a landing airplane. Even in heavy rain, the water settles in the grooves rather than puddling and eventually drains off.

At Langley's Wallops Island substation, NASA grooved a section of runway with slots a quarter inch deep and built dams along the edges of the runway to hold the water at prescribed depths. In repeated flight tests of both a jet transport and a Navy fighter, the investigators found that the aircraft hydroplaned as usual on the unaltered portion of the runway but slowed rapidly as the wheels gained traction on the grooved area. Further study confirmed that the grooves had no ill effect on landing gear. The FAA, the airlines and some airport operators joined the program and modified a number of runways at regular air terminals. After a year's operational evaluation, an Air Transport Association survey found that grooving reduced wet runway landings by an average of 1,000 feet, a margin that may save many lives.

Another landing problem may eventually be solved by flat tires. Planes continue to get bigger and heavier, necessitating an increase in "footprint," the amount of rubber that comes in contact with a runway; a broader footprint better distributes the weight of a landing aircraft and reduces impact shock. The mammoth C-5a military transport, for example, has 28 wheels in five landing gear trucks.

The question is: where do you put this massive gear when it is retracted? Modern high-speed wings are too thin to accommodate the tremendous bulk and even the fuselages do not have enough space for it. One way of making room in large aircraft is to widen the fuselage underneath for a "wheel well pod." But this creates drag, cutting down on range and payload. Smaller aircraft, such as fighters, do not need multiple-truck landing gear, but they carry ever-increasing amounts of special-purpose equipment and space—even inches—is always at a premium. Valuable gains could be realized if landing gear and wheel wells could be made smaller.

Putting flat tires to good use

Searching for ways to achieve this, engineers of the Air Force Flight Dynamics Laboratory came up with the novel idea of flattening the tires. An airplane's tires must be inflated only during takeoff, landing and taxiing. But why couldn't they be deflated in flight, when they serve no useful function? The laboratory staff built test models of a tire with its own valve opener and pressurized-air bottle mounted on the wheel hub, per-

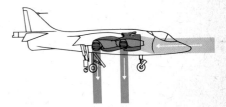

EXHAUST DEFLECTION enables the British P-1127 to rise and even drift in reverse. Instead of pouring from a single tail pipe, the exhaust of the turbofan engine is funneled through two nozzles on each side of the fuselage. A single control in the cockpit can rotate the nozzles 100° within a second.

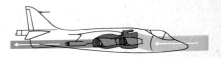

mitting rapid deflation and re-inflation as required. The system works automatically; when the pilot retracts his landing gear after takeoff, the valve opens and deflates the tire. The side walls then cave in toward the center of the tire and the circumference flattens around the rim, considerably reducing wheel diameter and permitting storage in a smaller wheel well. When the pilot lowers the gear for landing, the air bottle goes into action, expanding the tires.

In quest of quiet

No such bright technical gimmick as the flat landing-wheel tire seems likely to get around a major block to aviation progress: noise. It is an inescapable result of the production of energy in an engine and it increases in proportion to the amount of energy produced. The high-thrust jets of modern airliners have raised it to a level that is no longer tolerable to many people. Citizen groups all over the nation are demanding relief. The FAA is attempting to ease the din by regulating landing and departure patterns. The airlines are cooperating by installing on their aircraft such noise suppression devices as are available (the plumber's nightmare of pipes protruding from the rear of an engine is a suppressor nozzle designed to cut down on exhaust roar). NASA, in concert with several airframe and engine builders, is looking farther ahead and tackling the research job not only from the standpoint of today's problem but of the potentially bigger one that will come with tomorrow's still higher energy engines.

There are a number of sources of aircraft engine noise and not all of them have been identified. Among those known are the intake that admits air to the engine, the turbine that creates the jet of fast gases, the compressor that squeezes air before combustion, the fan that by-passes cool air around the combustion chamber, and the high-velocity exhaust. As a first step, NASA is treating the areas around these components with an advanced type of soundproofing, an acoustical padding made of woven metal to withstand high engine temperatures.

A potentially more effective measure is reducing noise at its source, and NASA has instituted a "Quiet Engine" program to reduce noise by design methods rather than by soundproofing. It focuses on the two primary racket-producers: the fan and the interaction of the high-velocity jet exhaust with the outside air. Fan noise can be reduced by such steps as redesigning the system to operate efficiently at a lower rotating speed, using only one instead of multiple fan stages and changing the shape of the fan blades. NASA hopes to lower exhaust noise by reducing the velocity of the jet stream. This can be accomplished by higher "bypass ratios," which means channeling a greater amount of air around the combustion chamber. The slower-moving bypass air merges with the gas exhaust at the rear of the engine, producing a net reduction in velocity.

Under the Quiet Engine program, NASA is assigning several contractors to make extensive studies of these and other design techniques. NASA, meanwhile, is conducting its own fan research in a special facility. Agency officials forecast a substantial reduction of noise; the next generation of jets will be quieter by 15 to 20 decibels, a difference that should be apparent not only to a decibel meter but also to the human ear.

In the meantime, manufacturers continue to develop more powerful engines. Power plants of more than 40,000 pounds thrust are already flying, 50,000-pounders are only a step behind and designers can see 100,000-pound-thrust engines on the horizon. To cope with the noise problem in the face of these advances, something more than Quiet Engine technology is needed. The fundamentals of jet noise are not well understood and a much more comprehensive program of basic research is required. NASA has proposed establishment of an Aircraft Noise Reduction Laboratory; surprisingly, no such facility exists in the United States.

A booming sky trail

The noise produced by subsonic jets is disturbing enough, but supersonic flight brings a completely new phenomenon. It is noise emanating not from the engine but from the shock waves produced by a machine moving through the air at high velocity—the sonic boom. Americans' introduction to it came from military airplanes, some of which are capable of speeds up to Mach 3. But most of these planes fly only a small portion of their missions at supersonic speed and most people have never heard a sonic boom or witnessed its house-shaking, window-breaking potential. Today, with the advent of the first supersonic transports the problem has become crucial. The boom is much more than a minor ache to be relieved with technological aspirin; its effects are so severe they threaten to restrict overland flights of the SST and thus seriously impair its utility.

In 1968, the President appointed a group of scientists to find out just how troublesome the boom can be. Sifting all the evidence, including data from flight tests of the largest supersonic airplane, the since-retired XB-70, the commission submitted a disturbing report: If SSTs are allowed to operate at supersonic speeds over the continental United States, they will subject "between 20,000,000 and 40,000,000 Americans under a path 12½ miles on either side of the expected flight tracks to five to 50 sonic booms per day." Each boom represents a noise equivalent to that of "a large truck traveling at 60 miles per hour at a distance of 30 feet" from the listener. In addition, the Government or the airplane operator could expect property damage claims of as much as $80,000,000 annually.

Bowing to pressures from anti-noise groups, the Department of Transportation has in effect prohibited supersonic travel until the boom problem is solved. Its official policy was set forth in a statement: "Commercial flights at supersonic speeds will not be permitted if the consequences of sonic booms generated by such flights are judged to exceed public acceptance or to threaten the natural environment." This puts it squarely to aviation researchers to find an answer if the SST is to realize its full potential for fast, economical transport.

The prognosis is less than optimistic. From theoretical studies and flight test experience with planes like the XB-70, researchers have hit upon design changes that could lessen the boom's impact. Not, however, to a degree acceptable to the public eardrum. "We've done all we can to lower boom effect by redesign of aircraft as we know them," says a NASA official. "Now we must go back to basic research." NASA plans to seek brand-new concepts, fashioning aircraft primarily for boom-lessening rather than performance. Once the goal of a boom-suppressing design has been achieved, engineers believe they can modify it to make it reasonably efficient without impairing its quiet operation.

These are but a few tiles in the vast mosaic that is aeronautical research today. At hundreds of facilities in the United States and abroad, research teams are exploring at all levels in such component fields as aerodynamics, propulsion, structures and avionics. Out of this vast body of research is already emerging a new generation of aircraft for the 1970s and the concepts of a more revolutionary generation for the 1980s.

"The True Face of the Earth"

"Our sight has been sharpened," wrote the French pilot and author Antoine de Saint-Exupéry in *Wind, Sand and Stars*. "The airplane has revealed to us the true face of the earth." From the mid-19th Century, when photographers first ascended in balloons to capture panoramic views of cities, to the space age, when whole continents are scanned by satellites, man's view of his planet has sharpened and expanded. Aerial photography has opened up beautiful perspectives; it has also proved itself a valuable tool of science. In striking vistas like the one shown on the opposite page, airborne cameras record such vast and gradual processes as the erosion of land by rivers and the sea, the ponderous movement of glaciers. They have also yielded new information, and even rediscovered traces of vanished cultures that men had heedlessly walked across for centuries, too close to the evidence spread out beneath their feet to notice it was there.

THE PATTERN OF EROSION
From an altitude of 14,000 feet, this water-riven tidal flat in Baja California resembles a great tree spreading its branches upward from the Colorado River *(bottom)*. Mosaics of such photographs, made every few years, aid the United States and Mexico in determining where the shifting river's channels must be dredged or where endangered banks must be shored up with protecting levees.

GEOMETRICAL 16TH CENTURY DEFENSES GIRD, PALMANOVA, ITALY.

ANCIENT CANALS OF SPINA, SHOWING UP AS LUXURIANT STRIPES OF VEGETATION, CRISSCROSS A MODERN DRAINAGE SYSTEM.

The Past Disclosed
—and Recorded

For the archeologist, aerial photography not only affords new insights into familiar treasures *(above)*, it has also turned up a wealth of evidence of life in ancient times. The Etruscan city of Spina, not far from present-day Venice, is one such discovery. A rich Sixth Century B.C. port, Spina was overrun and destroyed as Roman power grew. Its buildings and waterways sank back into the obscurity of the marshes. Its site remained a mystery until 1956, when an Italian archeologist, looking at aerial photographs of the coastal plain, saw the entire city plan laid out before him.

ON AN ALASKAN ISLAND ROOKERY, SEALS BLACKEN A BEACH.

A BLIZZARD OF SNOW GEESE COVERS A PLOWED FIELD.

ROCKY MOUNTAIN ELK ARE HERDED BY HELICOPTER TO BE TAGGED IN A CORRAL.

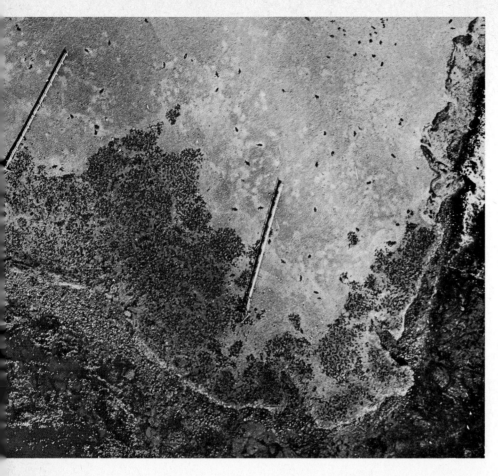

An Aerial Animal Inventory

Until aerial photography provided the tools, taking a census of animal populations was a guessing game for ground observers, whose job was made all but impossible by the sheer numbers of the restless populations to be counted. Who could say how many seals colonized an island, how many snow geese crowded a field? But a photo interpreter today can reliably state that the dark spots *(left)* represent an estimated 100,000 seals, the white dots *(below)* an estimated 8,500 geese. Aerial pictures made it possible to count 4.5 million ducks and 731,000 geese in California alone in 1965. Such inventories, especially when backed up by periodic ground studies as with the elk on the opposite page, provide valuable data on animal migration. They also help governments to establish hunting seasons and set bag limits, adjusted every year to the changing numbers of the various species of wildlife.

161

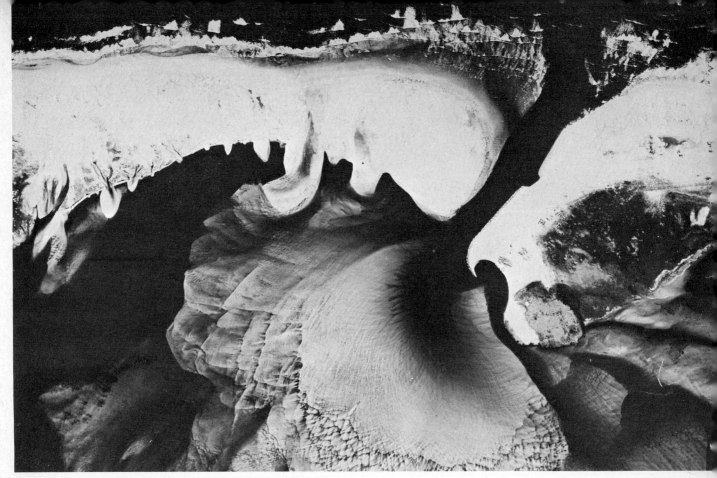

1950: MORICHES INLET, NARROW BUT STILL OPEN.

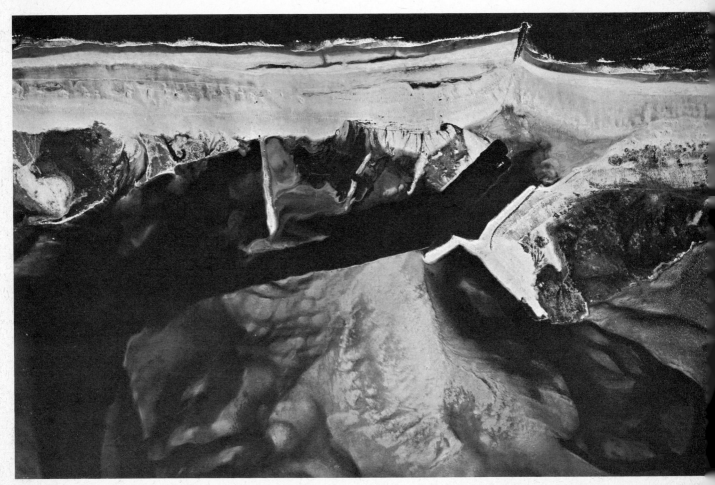

1953: THE INLET COMPLETELY CLOSED BY STORMS.

Charting
a Changing Shore

The erosive action of the sea, a menace to many coastlines, is nowhere more dramatically revealed than in aerial survey pictures like the ones shown here. Moriches Inlet, one of several linking the Atlantic with the great system of bays along the south side of Long Island, New York, illustrates how air surveys help engineers to protect a threatened shore. In 1950, the inlet was open *(opposite)*. Sand swept in by the sea formed a glistening underwater fan. Two years of severe Atlantic storms built up the bottom to the point where it finally choked the opening. Boats in the bay could no longer reach the open sea; stagnation endangered fish and shellfish. Dredging reopened the inlet, and to prevent a recurrence, existing jetties were extended. Today the inlet is continuously watched from the air, dredged when necessary, and the jetties kept in repair.

1957: OPEN ONCE MORE, THE INLET IS NOW REGULARLY SURVEYED.

DEEP BAY CRATER, SASKATCHEWAN: SIX MILES WIDE, 60 MILLION YEARS OLD.

HOLLEFORD CRATER, ONTARIO:
1.5 MILES WIDE, 500 MILLION YEARS OLD.

BRENT CRATER, ONTARIO: TWO MILES WIDE, 500 MILLION YEARS OLD.

Evidence of an Old Bombardment

In the 1950s, Canadian researchers scanning aerial-mapping photographs of Ontario came across a huge and almost perfectly round scar in the ground *(opposite, bottom)*. Intrigued by its size and shape, geologists made borings in the area. The samples brought up identified the scar as a "fossil crater"—a pit left by a gigantic meteor which exploded when it hit the earth some 500 million years ago. Further search among the more than 400,000 photographs in the aerial survey of Canada turned up a dozen more meteoritic scars. Investigators now suspect that aerial mapping of other regions of the world will show that bombardment from outer space, far from being rare, has pocked the earth with many more such craters, long since concealed by sediment or camouflaged by vegetation.

Surveying a River of Ice

When geologists began to study glacier movement a hundred years ago, investigators drove stakes into the ice and returned periodically to note how far they had been bent by the slow flow. The terrain was hazardous, the research arduous. Aided by aerial photography, glaciology today has become, according to one expert, "a pleasant blending of art, science and detective work." From the air, glaciers can be mapped with ease, their retreats or advances documented in detail. Alaska's Yanert Glacier (*right*), moving down from the 12,000-foot peaks in the background, is one whose advance is unusually swift— 25 to 30 feet a day. Increasing accumulations of snow and ice press it forward; a wide valley, carved out in the ice age, offers it a natural avenue. Advancing in the midst of a rugged region strewn with ice fields and other glaciers, Yanert Glacier is almost inaccessible on foot. From the air, however, its majestic progress is easily recorded and beautifully observed.

YANERT GLACIER NEAR McKINLEY PARK, ALASKA.

8
Plans
and Dreams

SIR GEORGE CAYLEY, a pioneer theorist of powered flight, visualized the modern airplane almost a century before Kitty Hawk: ". . . we shall be able to transport ourselves and families, and their goods and chattels, more securely by air than by water, and with a velocity of from 20 to 100 miles per hour."

Today it is difficult to find an airplane that cannot exceed Sir George's prophesied limit. Man's achievement in atmospheric flight is matched only by his plans for the future, and there appears to be no type of flying machine which can be termed absolutely impossible from the standpoint of science and technology. Technological feasibility, in fact, is no longer the paramount consideration in aircraft development. Even such advanced concepts as the hypersonic transport and the earth-to-orbit vehicle, where enormous problems loom, are considered definite possibilities. The chief barrier to getting them off the drawing board is the tremendous amount of research still to be done which, with developmental and production costs, will run into billions of dollars. There must be not merely a desire for such airplanes, but a requirement strong enough, in terms of military and commercial necessity, to justify the enormous expenditures of both research efforts and funds.

It is possible, however, to predict new types of aircraft that will be operational in the 1970s and beyond; some are already flying. One of the more exciting of the new breed is the commercial supersonic transport, or SST. Actually there are two types of SST, best identified as Mach 2 and Mach 3 airplanes, although these figures are only loose approximations of their speeds. The primary difference between them is structure. The Mach 2 SST can be built by conventional manufacturing techniques, employing aluminum as the principal structural material. The Mach 3 transport, however, must withstand higher temperatures generated by air friction, and it has to be made of titanium, entailing additional years of research not only on design but on fabrication methods as well. The aluminum-framed Mach 2 airplane has little "stretchability"; it is limited to speeds below Mach 2.5. The advanced SST, on the other hand, can be stretched beyond Mach 3 as engines and other components are improved.

European airplane manufacturers, challenging traditional U.S. domination of the airliner business, elected to accept the limitations inherent in the Mach 2 design in order to get their planes in the air earlier. One is the *Concorde*, produced by a sometimes stormy alliance of British and French firms. It has a relatively small capacity of 136 passengers, and an unusual delta wing that curves gracefully for most of the plane's 193-foot length. Beneath the wing are four 35,000-pound-thrust engines. The Soviet SST is of comparable design and even smaller. The Tupolev 144, or the "Concordski" as the Russians jokingly call it, has a similar curved delta wing, four turbofan engines also in the 35,000-pound-thrust range

THE FUTURE WITHOUT WINGS
An artist's rendering of two wingless flying machines envisions the design of craft that may someday return men to earth from distant orbiting satellites. These planes, Northrop's HL-10 *(top)* and M-2 *(bottom)*, are the forerunners of planes that will reenter the earth's atmosphere at many times the speed of sound and then, slowed by increasing drag, land at conventional speeds.

and 180-foot length—but its passenger capacity is limited to 121 persons.

These planes have ranges of 4,000 miles and cruising speeds slightly above Mach 2. "Block times," point-to-point flying times that take into consideration climb and descent at subsonic speeds, are approximately half those of the subsonic jetliners; a New York-to-London flight, for example, can be made in about three hours.

A one-day round trip to Europe

The American Boeing Supersonic is a Mach 3 design, but it will not fly passengers until after 1975. Much larger and faster than its European competitors, it has a straight delta wing and a long slender fuselage that stretches almost the length of a football field; the cabin will seat 234 passengers in the initial version, 300 or more in later models. At 750,000 pounds, the Boeing will weigh more than twice as much as the Mach 2 airplanes, but it will still be able to operate from existing airports.

Four mighty engines, each equipped with an afterburner to produce 63,-000 pounds of thrust, will propel the American SST at a cruising speed of Mach 2.7, or about 1,800 miles an hour. In terms of block time, this permits a two-hour transatlantic flight and offers to the business community the possibility of same-day round trips to Europe.

To passengers, SSTs of either variety will not seem much different from ordinary jetliners. There will be no more impression of speed than there is in a subsonic plane; although the SSTs move far more rapidly, they fly at much higher altitudes—above 60,000 feet. To compensate for the greater height, an advanced pressurization system maintains cabin air pressure at customary levels. The cabins are roughly the width of a DC-9 interior with seats arranged in the familiar way, five abreast. Outside the cabin airplane surfaces will be heated by air friction to high temperatures—above 400 degrees in the advanced SST—but a cooling system will keep the interior around 75 degrees. One difference—a pleasant one —will be the absence of noise as the SST travels so fast it leaves behind the sound of its engines. Another—not so pleasant—will be the cost of a ticket; operating costs of the SST may someday approach those of the subsonic jet, but at first, the passenger can expect to pay a premium fare.

SSTs are expected to carry only a small percentage of total air traffic. Throughout the 1970s and into the 1980s, the workhorses of air transportation will be the new family of subsonic aircraft known variously as "jumbo jets," "wide-bodied transports," "airbuses," and "advanced-technology jets." These planes herald even more far-reaching changes in commercial flight than did the transition from piston to turbojet power.

The jumbo jets stemmed from an advance in the design of turbofan engines. In a single giant step, thrust ratings were boosted from the 15,000-20,000 pound range to more than 40,000 pounds by providing a "high

OVER-THE-GROUND DISTANCE covered in an hour's flight has undergone a dramatic increase since the Wright brothers' airplane of 1909. While that early one-passenger biplane could cover 42 miles in one hour, the proposed supersonic transports will fly as far as 2,000 miles in the same time.

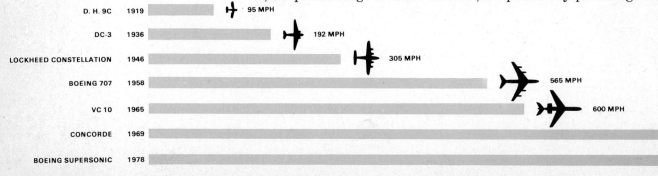

SIGNAL CORPS 1	1909	42 MPH
D. H. 9C	1919	95 MPH
DC-3	1936	192 MPH
LOCKHEED CONSTELLATION	1946	305 MPH
BOEING 707	1958	565 MPH
VC 10	1965	600 MPH
CONCORDE	1969	
BOEING SUPERSONIC	1978	

bypass ratio," which means the engine is built so that a great deal more air flows around the combustion chamber than goes through it. In earlier turbofans, the amount of air bypassing the combustion chamber was about one-and-a-half times as much as that being burned, a bypass ratio of 1.5 to 1. The new engines have bypass ratios of 5 or 6 to 1, which provide very high thrust, low fuel consumption and quieter operation. They gave airplane designers new latitude. Because the turbofans could overcome the increased drag of larger craft, it was possible to build huge planes with very wide fuselages and thus increase passenger capacity.

A race of giants in the air

The first of the jumbos, introduced in 1969, is the Boeing 747, a four-engine behemoth that weighs more than 700,000 pounds, or more than twice as much as the largest of its predecessors. Depending on how seats are arranged, the 747 carries from 300 to 500 passengers. Companion members of the jumbo family include the McDonnell Douglas DC-10 and the Lockheed L-1011, both "trijets," with two engines in wing mountings and a third in the rear. They are smaller than the 747—if "smaller" can be applied to aircraft weighing in the vicinity of 400,000 pounds—and they carry from 250 to 350 passengers. These jetliners are in part complementary, in part competitive. The 747, with a maximum range of 8,000 miles, was designed principally for long-distance transport, but a modified version may operate at short to medium distances. The DC-10 and L-1011, basically intended for short and intermediate length trips, will fly more than 5,000 miles in later "growth versions."

The jumbos will have great impact on air transportation. Carrying twice as many people on a single flight, they make for less congested airways and airports. They reduce operating costs 20 to 30 percent below those of first-generation jetliners and afford the traveler new comfort and convenience; seats and aisles are wider, and generous increases in cabin volume per passenger create a roomlike atmosphere.

For a time it seemed that the jumbos would bring sizable fare reductions. But the airlines have had to pay several billion dollars for the new planes and are faced with higher costs of everything from fuel to salaries. So fares must go up, not down. The only solace is that rates are lower than they would have been if the jumbos had not come along.

The huge passenger capacity of each of these planes initially raised fears of worsened congestion at airports. When Boeing first announced plans for the 747, the reaction was one of horror. "Can you imagine," asked one executive, "500 people waiting in line to check their baggage?" Replied Pan American World Airways chairman Harold E. Gray: "Any terminal that can handle two 707 or DC-8 aircraft within the same time span —say about 15 minutes—can equally well handle a 747." The trouble is

1,500 MPH

1,800 MPH

that at present few can, and the airlines must spend at least $2.5 billion in new terminals and ground equipment. They are planning not for 500 people per plane, but for greater numbers, because any new class of airplanes is "stretched" in size and payload over the decade after its introduction. Stretching the jumbos may send passenger capacities over the 700 mark by the end of the 1970s.

Their great volume makes the jumbos superb cargo carriers. But, big as they are, they will have to compete with something even bigger. Only three to five years behind in development is an airplane that comes within a whisker of meeting a long-time dream of the air freight lines: a superplane that can carry 100 cubic feet of cargo for two cents a mile. It is the Lockheed-Georgia L-500, an air giant that dwarfs even the 747.

Powered by four 45,000-pound-thrust turbofans, the L-500 is, at 833,000 pounds, the heaviest airplane ever contemplated. A commercial derivative of the military C-5, currently the world's largest airplane, it exceeds the C-5's gross weight by 100,000 pounds. In its enormous double-deck fuselage it can carry 300,000 pounds of cargo more than 3,000 miles at 545 miles an hour, and it is designed for use with an automated loading system that cuts down on the time the plane must spend on the ground.

A fleet of flying trucks

The huge payload—and lower shipping rates—promised by the L-500 makes practicable air delivery of an entirely new range of products. Bananas, for instance. To fruit growers the big freighter brings rapid transport directly to the best market instead of a slow series of transfers from ships to trains to trucks. A grower could leave his bananas on the tree longer, allowing them to gain extra weight and bring a higher price. Spoilage en route would become negligible. These advantages, plus the plane's ability to carry large loads, make the L-500 competitive with surface transportation that charges lower ton-per-mile rates.

Another potential cargo for the L-500 is luxury autos. General Motors, for example, ships Cadillacs from Detroit to the West Coast by rail. For five days to two weeks, the cars are exposed to weather, vandalism and damage inflicted by hoboes who like to travel first class. By L-500, it's a four-hour trip and there is no damage. To ship a car by air will cost an estimated $40 more, but that may be made up by the advantages of rapid, damage-free delivery. Again, a major attraction is capacity; even with luxury cars GM does a volume business and has no interest in shipping a few at a time. The mammoth L-500 can swallow 58 Cadillacs.

To the average person who does not ship freight, the L-500 holds promise of a new type of low-cost vacation. One version of the giant transport is the car ferry. In the lower hold it has room for 46 average-size autos; upstairs on the top deck are roomy accommodations for 200 passengers.

Pile the whole family into your auto, drive it up a ramp into the maw of the L-500, climb a flight of stairs to a comfortable seat and fly cross-country in five hours. When you arrive, you have your own car for inexpensive touring. No baggage problem—just load it in the trunk. Cost? One airline has already filed for authority to operate a car ferry at a coast-to-coast fare of $500 for the auto and all its occupants.

While major manufacturers concentrate on supersize aircraft, another group is building a family of small airplanes for a new and burgeoning air travel market—the commuter airline. Commuter operators provide scheduled service connecting large central cities with smaller towns. An example is Trans Central Airlines, which connects Denver with such places as Pueblo and Trinidad in Colorado and Raton in New Mexico.

The short haul by air

These airlines need special equipment. They must be able to take off and land in short spaces because many of the airports they serve have runways no longer than 4,000 feet. They must operate economically on extremely brief hops, some of them only 50 miles. And they must be convertible, jiffy-switched to any combination of seats and cargo space; a bustling business in light air freight permits the commuter lines to operate profitably even when passenger volume is slim. Typical of this new breed of aircraft is Trans Central's Metro, a 300-mile-an-hour plane jointly developed by Swearingen Aircraft and Fairchild Hiller Corporation. Powered by twin-turboprop engines, the Metro offers almost every one of its 20 passengers a window seat; they are positioned in two rows separated by an aisle. But in a matter of minutes, the seats can be folded and a movable bulkhead placed so that the Metro can carry both passengers and cargo. The Metro weighs only 12,500 pounds and takes off with a full load in only 2,500 feet. About a dozen types of planes like the Metro are being built in the U.S., Canada, England, France, Germany and Sweden, and already manufacturers are planning faster and more economical ones. They will probably be entirely jet-powered, as continuing development of the turbojet engine makes it efficient even for very short hops.

A quite different new type of plane is already in use by air taxi operators. This is the STOL, or Short TakeOff and Landing plane, well suited to relatively short, high density routes and wherever roomy airports are lacking. STOLs, which employ high thrust-to-weight-ratio engines and aerodynamic devices designed for exceptionally high lift, have a competitive advantage over medium-size jets in their ability to fly from short strips nearer to cities than jet ports. Separate STOLports, together with a low-altitude network of airways now planned expressly for STOL operations, can help ease the crowded-sky problem. An example of a big-city STOLport is included in New York City's master plan. It calls for a

1,500-foot strip and a multi-story building housing ticket offices, baggage facilities, a hotel, shops and surface transportation services—all to be elevated along a 10-block stretch of the Hudson River waterfront.

Airlines are also testing STOLs. One—Eastern Airlines—has drawn up specifications and declared readiness to place an order as soon as a manufacturer can deliver the right airplane at the right price. Eastern wants a plane that can carry 100 to 150 passengers as far as 500 miles. It must cruise at better than 400 miles an hour, land at 60 miles an hour and operate safely from a 1,500-foot runway.

Still on the horizon is the VTOL, which could go the STOL one better and operate from a compact airport the size of a city block in a convenient downtown location. The letters stand for Vertical TakeOff and Landing, and that's what VTOL does: rise straight up like a helicopter, fly horizontally like an airplane, then descend straight down like a helicopter again. VTOLs will make their operational debuts in military service, where their advantages are clear-cut; they promise great utility as short-haul cargo carriers in combat zones and as fighter-reconnaissance aircraft operating from small, unimproved fields. Although large subsonic jet VTOLs may someday carry airline passengers on the short- and medium-range routes, this job is more likely to be filled just by STOLs. The VTOLs earliest usefulness seems to be in very-short-haul duty, shuttling 30 to 50 passengers between major airports and midcity points and carrying commuters to and from the outer suburbs.

An airplane in every garage

Not forgotten in the picture of tomorrow's aviation is the small private plane, which may undergo radical changes in years to come. Today's private plane still looks and flies pretty much like its counterpart of the 1930s. The dream of "everyman's airplane," the low-cost, easy-to-fly automobile of the air, has never materialized. It still takes much skill and coordination to fly an airplane, and the smallest lightplane still costs more than a luxury auto. But the "airplane in every garage" could become a reality according to Charles W. Harper, NASA's director of aeronautical research, who proposes a drastic revision of lightplane design.

Harper's lightplane of the future would bear no resemblance to any flying today. Focal point of the new design approach is the control system, which, despite a number of improvements and refinements, is basically the same today as it was when Blériot flew across the English Channel. Conventional airplanes still use "acceleration control": if a pilot starts any movement of the plane, that movement will continue until he rectifies it with a countering movement. If a flyer wants to bank 10°, he uses his control stick to deflect the ailerons and the plane starts to rotate in the desired direction. It will tend to continue rotating at an increasing

AN ADAPTABLE CARRIER, the experimental Sikorsky S-64 *(below)* exemplifies one of the many flexible and fast helicopters that can make tomorrow's transportation by air more convenient. Capable of fastening onto a crate of cargo or a passenger vehicle *(below right),* the S-64 has successfully handled a van carrying 90 soldiers.

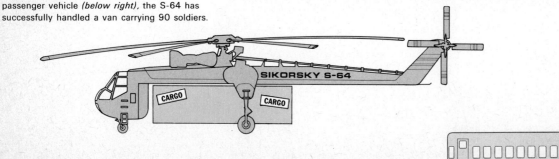

rate unless the pilot applies reverse control to stop the rotation and level off the plane even before the 10° bank has been attained. This technique requires considerable practice.

The "displacement control" system, which is now in limited use by the military, makes the job of maneuvering an airplane far easier. With displacement control, the pilot would move his control stick to an indicated 10° and the plane would bank to exactly 10° and remain in that position until the pilot initiated a new control movement. A relatively simple electronic system could provide this type of control for the lightplane and even stabilize it automatically, freeing the designer from the traditional long fuselage with its horizontal and vertical stabilizers.

The reborn lightplane might be a thumbnail-shaped craft, with wings, fuselage, engine and controls integrated in a compact shape that would lend itself to mass production, perhaps using advanced plastics. The plane would be turbine-powered, and could include a system of thrust diversion for short takeoff performance and even "surface" travel, hovering a few inches off the ground. It could operate from small fields, from flight strips, and conceivably even from highways. Mass-produced, tomorrow's easy-to-fly lightplane eventually might cost no more than a high-priced car.

Harper's lightplane research is in a very early stage, not because it presents any impossible problems but because development depends on a large-scale demand that does not yet exist. Harper feels the demand will come with a continuation of the "away from the city" trend, and that when homes, offices and plants begin to spread out a hundred or more miles from a city, the "flying auto" type of vehicle will find a market. Thus, while the new plane could be technologically feasible within six to eight years, it may take many more years for the demand to develop.

One hour to cross the Atlantic

Looking further beyond the horizon, there are some fantastic possibilities, the most extraordinary of which is the long-range hypersonic transport. Such a plane could be developed in about 15 years. Here again, demand becomes a major factor in view of the enormous expense required for development of a Mach 6 to 8 hypersonic airliner that could cross the Atlantic in an hour. The questions that must be answered affirmatively by the public—which supplies the money for development —and by the airlines are: Does man really need or want to fly that fast? Does the time-saving justify the tremendous expenditure? These are not new questions; they were being asked throughout the sixties in relation to the supersonic transport and are still being asked; they were asked in the early fifties when the first subsonic jetliners were being considered. They cannot be answered with any authority today, but there are many who feel that the requirement for greater airplane speed will continue.

If the demand for hypersonic transportation develops, science and technology will produce it. The groundwork has already been laid not only for the hypersonic airliner but for completely revolutionary aircraft which previously existed only in science fiction.

One that goes well beyond the hypersonic transport technology is the "aerospace" plane. To bridge the gap between atmospheric and orbital flight, researchers are considering a craft that will be able to take off from earth, fly into orbit at Mach 25 and return under its own power and controls. The aerospace plane represents a tremendous challenge, requiring years of concentrated research and staggering costs running into billions of dollars. Yet most experts feel it can and will be built, even though no possible civilian use of such a craft can be foreseen. Its futuristic role may be to defend against hostile satellites or to serve as an invaluable tool for even more advanced aeronautical research.

With science recognizing no absolute barrier to any type of flight within the atmosphere, it seems to be only a matter of time before these and even more radical designs actually take to the air. In the course of a single lifetime since the Wright brothers made powered flight a reality, aviation's pace has advanced from the 30 miles per hour at Kitty Hawk to the 4,000 miles per hour of the X-15. And the ultimate goal is still as far away as the eye can see into the heavens.

Faster than Sound

Like the four-minute mile, flying faster than sound was long thought to be beyond human achievement. The problem lay not in attaining sonic speed—around 760 miles per hour at sea level, considerably less in the cold air of high altitudes —but in overcoming the unexpected things that happened to planes as they approached that speed. The trusted laws of aerodynamics seemed suddenly to go haywire; planes experienced loss of control, severe shaking or buffeting and a tendency to nose over as if in a stall. The phrase "sound barrier" was coined to describe the problem, as though there were some invisible wall in the sky. Finding a way through that wall took aircraft designers deep into studies of the physics of sound and into unexplored aerodynamic realms. But so spectacularly have they succeeded that now the sound barrier is a mere threshold to an age beyond sound symbolized by the sleek craft of the future on the opposite page.

SHAPE OF THE FUTURE
The streamlined form on the opposite page is a scale model of the *Concorde*, a supersonic airliner developed by French and British designers that will soon carry transatlantic passengers at twice the speed of sound. Here it is getting a water-tunnel test to determine its airflow characteristics, traced by the confettilike streamers caused by dye released into the water stream.

What Happens at the Sound Barrier

Any plane in flight displaces the air through which it flies, and produces countless small disturbances. Called pressure waves, these radiate from various points on the plane's surface like ripples from a boat. All of them travel at the speed of sound.

At subsonic speeds, these waves are able to move harmlessly out ahead of a plane. At sonic speeds, the waves cannot move ahead: the aircraft is now traveling as fast as they are, and so they pile up, reinforcing one another to create a high-pressure shock wave (below).

The first shock waves always form on the wings, where the airflow is speeded up by the wing's curve; in effect, parts of the wing reach sonic speed before the rest of the plane. These shock waves can impair the effectiveness of control surfaces, but especially they create a heavy increase in drag.

Shock waves can rarely be seen on a plane in flight. But in a wind tunnel, they can be made dramatically visible by a special photographic technique, the schlieren process, which shows air-pressure variations in colors. At right and on the opposite page are visual records of how shock waves form at Mach 1, the speed of sound.

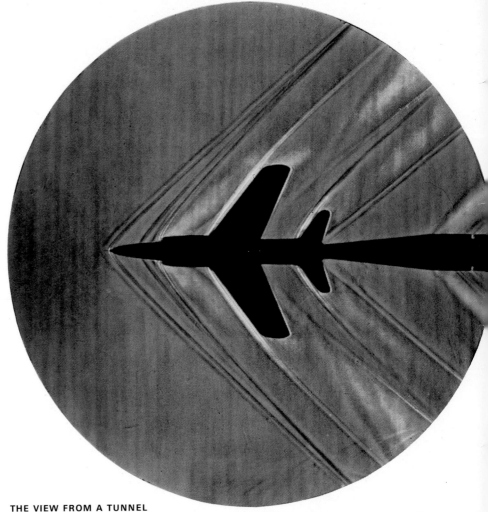

THE VIEW FROM A TUNNEL

This picture, using the schlieren technique, was taken in a wind tunnel where flight conditions can be accurately simulated. Air *(blue)* is flowing past the plane model at Mach 1.4, causing shock waves to form at different points on the model. The first waves occurred along the wings, where air speeds up the most. As in the diagram below, the shock waves bend back into a cone.

WHERE THE SHOCK WAVE COMES FROM

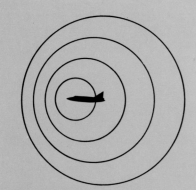

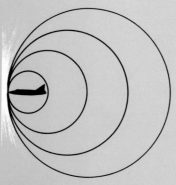

BELOW MACH 1
These diagrams show just one of the innumerable pressure waves sent out from various points on a plane. Here, at subsonic speed, the waves move out ahead of as well as behind the plane, which never catches up.

AT MACH 1
As sonic speed is reached, the waves can no longer move out ahead, since their point of origin is moving right along with them. The result: they build up into a shock wave that is perpendicular to the line of flight.

ABOVE MACH 1
As the plane exceeds sound speed, its pressure waves are left behind, and the shock wave bends back, still rooted to the plane. Austrian physicist Ernst Mach defined the shape of successive wave fronts as a cone.

ENTERING THE TRANSONIC RANGE

This series of schlieren photographs shows a wing cross section in wind-tunnel tests. The air moving through the tunnel shows up green; areas of low pressure are blue and high pressure shows red. Though the general airflow is still subsonic, about Mach .7, the airflow over the center of the wing has just reached Mach 1 and a perpendicular shock wave is beginning to form.

PICKING UP SPEED

As speed increases, the air under the wing also reaches Mach 1 and a shock wave forms there. Meanwhile, the wave above the wing gets bigger and stronger. Already the turbulence in the wake of this upper wave is affecting the airflow over the wing's rear surfaces: in an aircraft, this would impair control. A high-pressure area is also building up at the wing's leading edge.

HIGH IN THE TRANSONIC RANGE

Though the general airflow is still subsonic, at Mach .9, the flow over all but the leading edge of the wing is now supersonic. The upper and lower shock waves have moved back and joined together at the wing's trailing edge; in this situation, aileron control could be reduced. Ahead of the wing, pressure is still building in a small area as some sound waves continue to move out.

SUPERSONIC FLOW EVERYWHERE

Mach 1 has been reached and exceeded, and with dramatic suddenness a second shock wave has rooted itself to the leading edge. Both waves will stay with the wing as long as the airflow is supersonic. These waves, spreading out behind the plane, and somewhat weakened by traveling through air, eventually get to earth and are heard and felt as the now familiar sonic boom.

179

The B-47, a grizzled veteran by modern standards, having been launched in 1947, was a pioneer aircraft designed for near-sonic speed. It was the first big plane to have thin, flexible wings which were sharply swept back to inhibit the formation of shock waves. This enabled it to operate at speeds closer to Mach 1 than any conventional bomber was then able to attain.

Wings for Solving Sonic Problems

Since the primary shock waves are created by an airplane's wings, a key to solving sonic problems clearly lies in wing design. Shock waves cannot be prevented, but their ill effects can be reduced by three means: (1) making the wings thinner, with sharper leading edges; (2) designing them shorter and wider; and (3) sweeping them back in a V shape so the air passes over them at an angle, which lessens the speedup of wing airflow.

One or the other or a combination of these principles has been built into all modern high-speed aircraft (opposite). But all designs are at best compromises: some high-speed capabilities have to be sacrificed to enable the aircraft to operate at low speeds —e.g., for takeoff and landing. This difficulty is now being tackled with a variable-sweep wing that could combine the best of both worlds (right).

A CHANGING PROFILE
The wings of the new F-111A (formerly the TFX) stick out almost straight (right, above) for low-speed flight. But for high-speed operation, the wings can be angled back in mid-flight (right, bottom). A drawback of this system is the complex equipment needed to move the wings.

SHORT, THIN AND STRAIGHT
The deadly looking craft above, the F-104 Star-fighter, was designed to fly at Mach 2.2, about 1,450 miles an hour. An operational fighter, it has more flying hours at that speed to its credit than any other plane. Its wings are very thin and short to reduce supersonic drag, but are almost straight to provide low-speed maneuverability.

AN ARROW WITH NO TAIL
The delta wing of the F-106 Delta Dart at left combines the advantages of sweepback with those of a thin wing, and is structurally stronger and easier to build than either. It also entirely eliminates conventional tail surfaces. The Dart at one time held a world speed record of Mach 2.3, or 1,526 mph, but like all delta wings, it has to sacrifice some low-speed handling qualities.

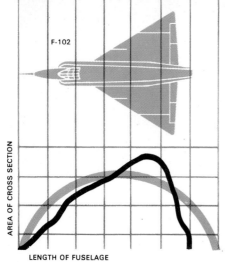

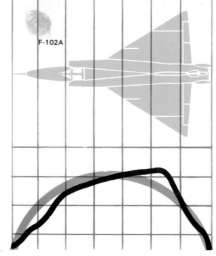

THE FLYING "COKE" BOTTLE

The pinched-in waist of the supersonic F-102A Delta Dagger is a hallmark of area-rule design: by reducing fuselage area, it compensates for the increase in cross-sectional area at the point where the wings are thickest. The original F-102, not designed to the area rule, could not even reach Mach 1 because of excessive drag.

SMOOTHING OUT THE CURVE

The graphs at left are plotted by measuring the areas of successive vertical slices from nose to tail of the F-102 and F-102A. Pink lines represent an ideally smooth progression, the black lines are the actual curves. They show how the F-102A's slim waist and bulged tail produced a smoother curve—and a lower wave drag.

Within the diagrams:

F-102

F-102A

AREA OF CROSS SECTION

LENGTH OF FUSELAGE

SPEED BEFORE BEAUTY

The experimental XB-70 owes its extraordinary shape and speed (Mach 3) to a design theory called the compression-lift rule. The basic idea here is that surfaces can be so arranged that shock waves will actually reinforce each other to provide lift, as in a planing speedboat. The delta wing is aft; the forward "canard" wings are actually stabilization surfaces.

Strange Shapes and New Materials

To reduce supersonic wave drag further, engineers studied wings and fuselage as a unit facing the onrushing air. It was important, they found, that the areas of consecutive cross sections of the plane, increasing from the nose and decreasing toward the tail, should add up to the smoothest possible curve. Under this theory, called the area rule, the perfect shape would be an egg—but the necessity for wings forced compromises. The results affected not only the performance but also the look of supersonic craft (*opposite*).

Research has produced other exotic supersonic creations. The weirdest is the XB-70 (*above*), a 500,000-pound test plane that has explored the far reaches of high-altitude flying. Used in its construction is a material that is so airy it can be seen through yet is as strong as a metal sheet (*right*).

STRENGTH WITHOUT WEIGHT

Strength, lightness and heat resistance are the three vital factors in supersonic aircraft materials, and the sheet of honeycomb aluminum shown screening a Northrop engineer above combines all three. A honeycomb, sandwiched between thin plates, weighs one fifth as much as a solid sheet. The equivalent of half an acre of this material was built into the XB-70.

Shock Waves and Control

Because shock waves so severely affect an airplane's stability, the greatest problem for a pilot at the sound barrier is the change in control characteristics. A wing has a slowly moving layer of air called the "boundary layer" that clings to its surface. Near Mach 1 shock waves can interact with the boundary layer to distort the airflow so that lift may be impaired and control surfaces made ineffectual. This disturbance also adds to the turbulent wake which is created by any wing, whatever its speed.

Wing shape is obviously important in controlling airflow, but other design solutions have been found. Some are ingeniously simple *(opposite, bottom)*; some involve radical changes. Tail surfaces, for example, may be moved up or down to get them out of the wings' troubled wake.

After a plane has negotiated the tricky transonic range, it still faces a paradoxical supersonic control problem: an excess of stability. At supersonic speeds the center of lift has moved back on the wing, improving the plane's aerodynamic stability. This stability is now so great that it takes several times as much control power to change the plane's attitude. Sometimes, too, unforeseen control problems arise from radical design changes *(below, right)*. The answer almost always lies in providing more sensitive and powerful control systems—so much so that in supersonic planes today mechanisms for flight control alone weigh two and one half times those of comparable subsonic craft—and cost four times as much.

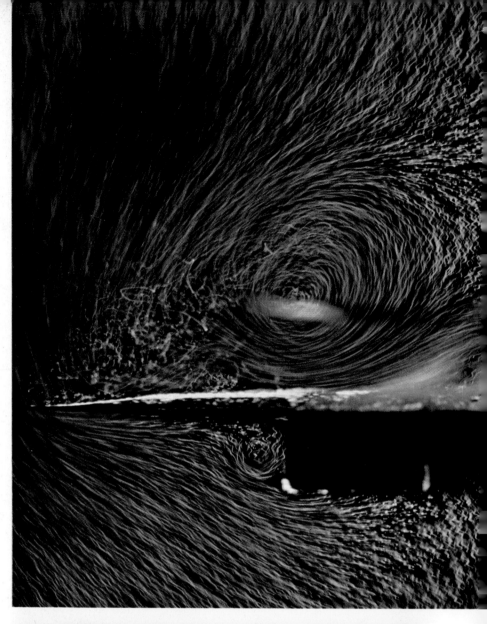

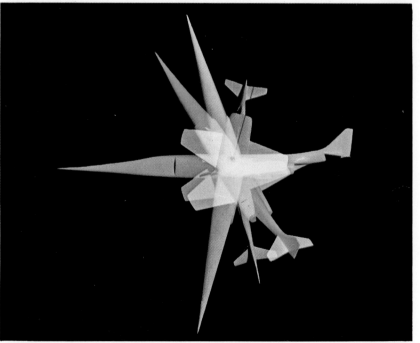

A PROBLEM OF STABILITY

The radically streamlined shape of the X-3 at right, designed to lessen drag at supersonic speeds, created unforeseen problems of stability. As this multiple-exposure demonstration illustrates, the plane developed serious yaw tendencies during a roll maneuver. Beginning a roll from level flight *(green)*, the model is seen first to yaw to one side *(blue, yellow)*, then to swing wildly in the other direction *(pink)*.

184

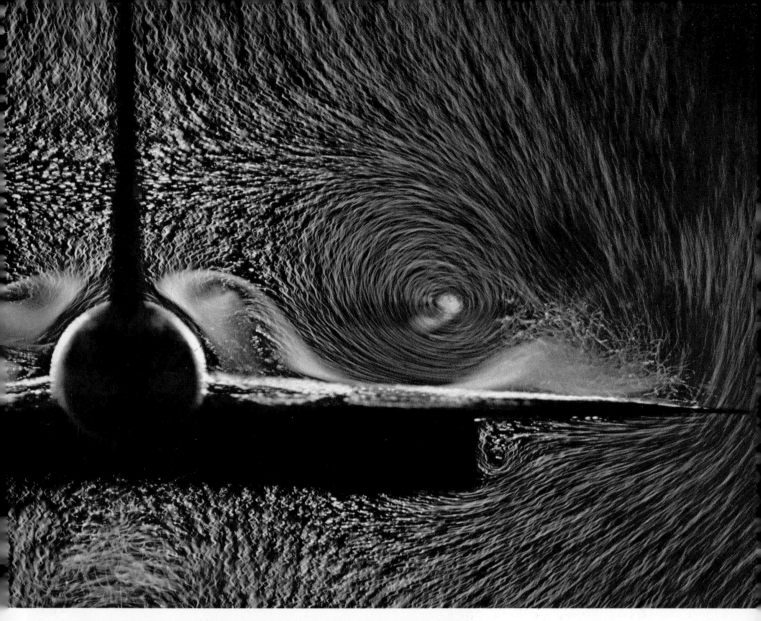

A STUDY IN AIRFLOW

This is how airflow over the wing looks in a model of the supersonic transport *Concorde* at the moment of landing. The wing is a radically modified delta type, with engine intake ducts at the bottom. The airflow, simulated by oil containing plastic particles, creates two big vortices over the leading edges which, at this speed, actually provide lift, improving handling qualities.

PRESERVING THE BOUNDARY LAYER

The boundary layer, the sluggish airflow right next to the skin of the wing, is vital to aerodynamic efficiency: it has to flow smoothly to maintain lift and control. In the top picture at left, a shock wave has caused it to separate from the wing: lift has been reduced and control impaired. A simple solution, seen in the bottom picture, a closeup of a Boeing 707 wing, is a row of vanes called vortex generators. These make small, controlled vortices that aid in keeping the boundary layer attached to the wing.

The Supersonic Look

On October 14, 1947, a slim, straight-winged hornet of a plane, the Bell X-1, dropped from the belly of its B-29 mother ship and streaked into a diving flight that carried man past the sound barrier for the first time. With a speed of 670 miles an hour, the X-1 set the pace for a parade of supersonic craft that have changed the look of aviation.

As the gallery of aircraft on these pages shows, that new look has many variations. Straight-winged, delta-winged or swept-back, needle-nosed or cigar-shaped, these craft all meet the demands of supersonic flight in different ways for different purposes. Like any plane, each is a compromise, but all have one thing in common: military or experimental, they provide experience and knowledge of the world beyond the speed of sound.

A

B

C

D

E

A   GENERAL DYNAMICS B-58 "HUSTLER"; U.S.A., 1956; DELTA WINGS, FOUR JET ENGINES, SPEED MACH 2; BOMBER.

B   DASSAULT "MIRAGE III"; FRANCE, 1956; DELTA WINGS, SINGLE JET, SPEED MACH 2.15; HIGH-ALTITUDE FIGHTER-INTERCEPTOR.

C   MCDONNELL F-101 "VOODOO"; U.S.A., 1954; SWEPT-BACK WINGS, TWIN JET, SPEED MACH 1.85; FIGHTER; HELD WORLD SPEED RECORD IN 1957.

D   DOUGLAS F-4D "SKYRAY"; U.S.A., 1951; DELTA WINGS, SINGLE JET, SPEED MACH 1.05; ADAPTED AS FIGHTER, INTERCEPTOR, BOMBER.

E   DOUGLAS X-3 "STILETTO"; U.S.A., 1952; STRAIGHT WINGS, TWIN JET, EXPERIMENTAL MACH 2 DESIGN.

F   ENGLISH ELECTRIC "LIGHTNING"; UNITED KINGDOM, 1954; SWEPT-BACK WINGS, TWIN JET, SPEED MACH 2; ALL-WEATHER INTERCEPTOR.

G   LOCKHEED YF-12A; U.S.A., 1962; DOUBLE DELTA WINGS, TWIN JET, SPEED MACH 3+; INTERCEPTOR; WORLD'S MOST ADVANCED SUPERSONIC AIRCRAFT.

F

G

Next Step for the Airlines

Today's jetliners fly at the top limit of subsonic speed, approaching Mach 1 as closely as their design will permit. Any advance will take commercial aviation into the supersonic realm—and a cloud of controversy. For while the supersonic transport, or SST, will carry passengers at two or three times the speed of sound, it will be a new breed of aircraft that could require a total revamping of commercial aviation. Design, materials, airports, air-traffic control—all will be subject to change.

The SST also carries with it the sonic-boom problem. Shock waves trailing along after a supersonic craft spread out and eventually hit the earth. Their effect is exactly that of pressure waves from a cannon shot—a loud boom. This thunder will constantly roll along a "boom carpet" beneath SST routes. A critic complains that "never . . . would so many have been disturbed so much by so few."

Yet, despite the opposition, SST projects are well under way. The Russians and a British-French combine have already flown prototypes. The chances are good that in the '70s tourists in New York will discover Paris to be only two and a half hours away.

THE CONCORDE GOES ALOFT
A joint venture of British and French builders, the Concorde roars off into its 28-minute maiden flight at Toulouse, France. Designed to carry 136 passengers at Mach 2.2, the 100-ton SST, less than 200 feet long, flies like a bird with wings that sweep back gracefully along its slender body.

A WINNING DESIGN
A competition between several U.S. companies produced this concept for an SST bigger and more efficient than the Concorde or TU-144. Boeing's plan calls for a 300-seat aircraft that can cruise over water at speeds up to 1,800 miles per hour and also fly at subsonic speeds over populated areas.

FIRST IN THE RACE
Looking more like a winged missile than a conventional aircraft, the Russian TU-144 (TU for the designer A.N. Tupolev) stands poised for its first flight in late 1968. The first commercial plane to break the sound barrier, it carries test instruments in the probe projecting from its nose.

The Last Frontier of Flight

It will be a few years before the casual traveler goes supersonic, but aviation pioneers have already pushed far beyond, into the ultimate domain of manned flight, the hypersonic range. This unimaginable realm begins at Mach 5, which is about 4,000 mph, or approximately three times the speed of a rifle bullet.

Though the sound barrier is a mere bump in the road for hypersonic craft, they face a technical problem fully as great: heat *(opposite)*. At Mach 6 air friction on a plane's skin produces temperatures of 1,200°, with some hot spots going as high as 2,000°. This is enough to melt any conventional aviation material now used, and to vaporize fuel or broil the pilot instantaneously in his cockpit, unless unusual design precautions are taken.

So far only one craft has been built that can cope with the problem of this "thermal thicket": the X-15 *(below)*. Special alloys, protective coatings and design features aimed at dissipating heat have been built into it, and though it is only a start, the X-15 flew at Mach 6.06, and to an altitude of 67 miles before it was retired in 1969. By the time the hypersonic range is more fully explored, man will have flown as far as he can fly in aerodynamic craft—to the very threshold of space.

THE X-15 TAKES OFF
Dropping from its carriage under a B-52 that has carried it to 35,000 feet, the X-15 blasts off on a flight that will reach Mach 5 or better. Though rocket-powered, the X-15 differs from a missile or space vehicle in that it is designed for aerodynamic flight: it still has wings. When its engine burns out, the craft will glide down to earth and a smooth landing at around 200 mph.

THE HYPERSONIC HAZARD
The experiment in heat resistance shown on the opposite page simulates friction problems during flight above Mach 5. A stainless-steel model is subjected to the 3,000°-blast of a rocket exhaust: at top the model is intact, but it soon begins to glow *(middle)*, and finally nose and wing surfaces are melting away. In flight, only parts of a plane would actually get this hot.

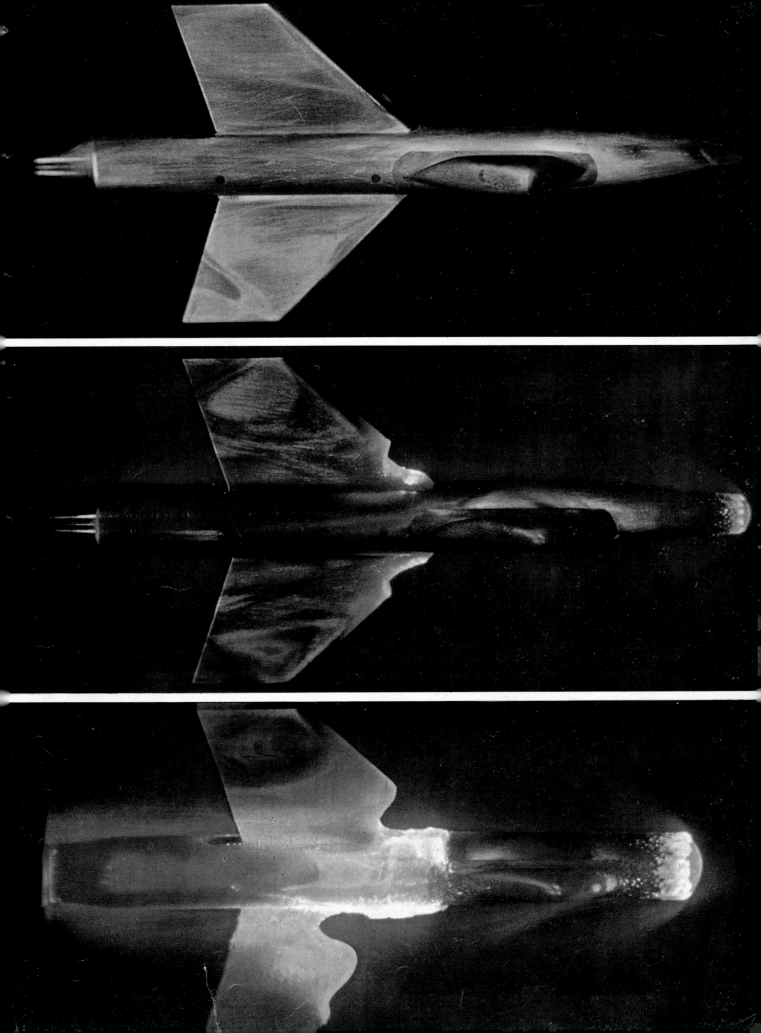

The Argot
of the Airman

Any group of specialists has its private language, and aviators are surely no exception. Ever since early "birdmen" began talking about "looping the loop" and "joystick," aviators have had a jargon of their own. Part of their vocabulary consists of technical words describing equipment, situations and maneuvers exclusive to the field of aviation. Other words reflect the tendency of any ingroup to invent a language that sets it apart from the uninitiated. Some of the more pervasive and colorful—if not the most pungent—words and phrases from this special vocabulary of flight are defined below.

BRIEF GUIDE TO THE LANGUAGE OF AVIATION

ABORT	Cancel a mission, takeoff, landing, etc., at the last minute
AUGUR IN	Have a major accident
BARREL ROLL	Acrobatic maneuver in which a plane does a complete roll on its longitudinal axis while flying level
BIRD DOG	Automatic direction finder (ADF) or radio compass
BLACK OUT	Temporary blindness from centrifugal pressure during steep turns
BLOWTORCH	Jet engine or jet aircraft
BOOM CARPET	Area on the ground where sonic boom from shock waves is heard
BUY THE RANCH (FARM)	Crash fatally
BUZZING	Diving close to the ground, especially near a house or people
CHOPPER	Helicopter
CREAMED (HIS BIRD)	Crashed (his plane)
DEAD STICK LANDING	Landing an aircraft without power
FEATHER THE PROP	Adjust the pitch of the blades of a propeller whose power has been cut off so they will offer the least air resistance
FIVE BY FIVE	Radio reception is loud and clear, loudness and clarity being measured on a scale from one to five
FLAME OUT	Loss of fire in the combustion chamber, resulting in power failure in a jet engine
FLAT OUT	Flying at full throttle
FLYING THE BEAM	Flying along a radio beam transmitted especially for aerial navigation
FLYING THE NEEDLES	Instrument flight
GEORGE	Automatic pilot
GREASE IT ON	Make a beautiful landing
LANDING HOT	Landing at too high a speed
MACHBUSTING	Flying faster than speed of sound
NO-GO GAUGE	Cockpit instrument indicating the malfunction of other instruments; also called the "idiot light"
NOSE OVER	Upending onto the nose
PANIC RACK	Ejection seat
PORPOISING	Pitching motion sometimes experienced by aircraft at transonic speeds
PRANG	Have an accident
PROP (OR JET) WASH	Blast of air behind engines; also, nonsensical talk
ROGER	Okay or yes; specifically, "Message received"
S.O.B.	Souls on Board; a term meaning the number of passengers and crew on board an aircraft
SCRUB	Cancel a flight
STACKED	Planes circling an airport in a holding pattern, waiting to land
THERMAL THICKET	Heat barrier at hypersonic speeds
THROTTLE JOCKEY	Pilot; sometimes irresponsible pilot
TOUCHDOWN	The moment of contact when landing
WEATHERED IN	Forced to stay on the ground by bad weather
WRINGING IT OUT	Performing aerial acrobatics
YOKE	One of many current terms for the control column of an airplane. Others are "wheel," "stick," or simply "controls." Once called "joystick"
ZERO-ZERO	No ceiling, no visibility

A Short but Crowded History

DURING THE 20TH CENTURY man has advanced faster and farther in the realm of flight than in any comparable enterprise in his history. Of course his preoccupation with the subject goes back through all the ages when he dreamed and schemed about ways to conquer the sky. He actually got himself into the air at the end of the 18th Century, when two Frenchmen sailed over Paris in a balloon. But not until 1903 and the Wright brothers did the real story of manned flight begin. After that, aviation milestones followed one another with such rapidity that six decades saw man fly from the sands of Kitty Hawk to the edges of space. Some of the highlights of this brilliant history are recorded here.

1783 Jean-François Pilâtre de Rozier and the Marquis d'Arlandes make the first aerial flight in history in a hot-air balloon made by the Montgolfier brothers.

1785 The first flight across the English Channel is made in a balloon by Jean-Pierre Blanchard and Dr. John Jeffries, from Dover to near Calais.

1809 Sir George Cayley publishes first part of *On Aerial Navigation*, a brilliant exposition of the principles of heavier-than-air flight that was later to have a profound effect on theories of aerodynamics.

1849 The first man-carrying plane, the Cayley-built triplane, flown as a glider with a 10-year-old boy as passenger.

1852 Henri Giffard pilots the first man-carrying engine-powered airship: a balloon fitted with a steam-driven propeller.

1900 Count Ferdinand von Zeppelin designs his first rigid airship, the LZ-1, forerunner of a long line of dirigibles.

1903 The first manned, powered airplane is built and flown by Wilbur and Orville Wright at Kitty Hawk, North Carolina.

1906 Alberto Santos-Dumont, a Brazilian expatriate living in Paris, makes Europe's first powered flights in a biplane named *14-bis*.

1909 The first airplane flight across the English Channel is made by Louis Blériot in his *Number XI*.

1910 First regularly scheduled passenger air service is begun in Germany, using zeppelin airships. The service carried a total of 37,250 passengers before it was canceled at the outbreak of World War I in 1914.

1910 A Curtiss biplane, piloted by Eugene Ely, takes off from a ship (the modified battleship U.S.S. *Birmingham*) for the first time.

1911 The first seaplane. Glenn Curtiss modifies a land plane by adding a single center float, and launches it at San Diego, California.

1911 Calbraith Perry Rodgers flies a Wright biplane from Sheepshead Bay, New York, to Long Beach, California, on first transcontinental flight. Flight takes 49 days, from September 17 to November 5.

1912 The first fighter plane. Englishman Geoffrey de Havilland designs the single-seat Farnborough B.S. 1, ancestor of all fighters and scout planes.

1913 Igor Sikorsky designs the first multiengined airplane, the four-engined biplane *Bolshe*.

1915 The first fighter with a fixed, forward-firing machine gun, Anthony Fokker's Eindecker Scout. The gun was synchronized to fire through the whirling propeller, and brought about a revolution in aerial combat.

1915 Hugo Junkers designs the first cantilever wing, low-wing and all-metal airplane, the J. 1 monoplane.

1918 An airmail flight is made from Long Island, New York, to Washington, D.C., on May 15, marking the beginning of U.S. airmail service.

1919 Lieutenant Commander Albert C. Read and a five-man crew fly a Curtiss NC-4 Navy flying boat in the first airplane-crossing of the Atlantic Ocean, traveling from New York to Lisbon, Portugal, via Newfoundland and the Azores.

1919 First nonstop crossing of the Atlantic is made by Captain J. Alcock and Lieutenant A. Whitten-Brown in a Vickers Vimy from Newfoundland to Ireland in 16 hours 12 minutes, averaging about 119 mph.

1923 Spaniard Juan de la Cierva builds the Autogiro, which takes off almost vertically on whirling blades and flies horizontally on wings using a conventional propeller—an ancestor of the helicopter.

1924 First aerial circumnavigation of the globe. Four U.S. Army Douglas biplanes leave Seattle April 6, two return September 28.

1925 Production of the Ford trimotor Stout, designed by William Stout, first American transport airplane to be built in any number.

1927 The Vega, a single-engined monoplane, goes into production by Lockheed, and becomes the first U.S. transport to compete successfully with European craft.

1927 Charles Lindbergh, flying *The Spirit of St. Louis*, a Ryan monoplane, makes the first nonstop solo transatlantic flight, from New York to Paris in 33 hours and 32 minutes. Distance: about 3,610 miles; average speed: about 122 mph.

1928 The first rocket-propelled airplane flight is made in a canard-type glider at Wasserkuppe, Germany.

1929 Lieutenant James Doolittle makes the first flight guided entirely by instruments in a Sperry-equipped Consolidated NY-2 biplane.

1929 Lieutenant Commander (later Admiral) Richard E. Byrd initiates the airborne exploration of Antarctica with the first flight to the South Pole in a Ford trimotor piloted by Bernt Balchen.

1933 Wiley Post flies the *Winnie Mae*, a Lockheed Vega, on the first solo flight around the world. Time: seven days, 18 hours.

1933 The first modern civil airliner, the Boeing 247, a twin-engined transport, is built.

1935 The most famous airliner in history, the DC-3 (Douglas Commercial) transport, is built. Still in service around the world 30 years later.

1937 The dirigible *Hindenburg*, filled with hydrogen gas, explodes and burns while approaching its mooring mast in Lakehurst, New Jersey, to mark the beginning of the end for rigid-airship transportation.

1938 The Supermarine Spitfire fighter, a low-wing, single-seat craft, goes into production in England. One of World War II's most famous fighters, it played a major role in winning the Battle of Britain.

1939 The Boeing B-17 Flying Fortress goes into quantity production. This four-engined heavy bomber, operating chiefly from air bases in the British Isles, helped put the World War II Allies on the aerial offensive.

1939 Pan American Airways initiates scheduled transatlantic airplane service with the four-engined Boeing 314. Capacity: 74 passengers; time: 29 hours.

1939 The first jet plane, the Heinkel He 178 with a single turbojet engine, is successfully tested in Germany, but little interest in its value for military purposes is shown by the Nazi high command.

1940 The first pressurized airliner, the Boeing 307-B, permits passengers to fly more comfortably at greater speeds for longer distances.

1942 Igor Sikorsky, living in the United States, successfully flies the first modern helicopter, the VS-300, capable of vertical and hovering flight.

1942 The first operational military jet, the Messerschmitt 262 fighter, is tested in Germany, but not put into operation until two years later.

1942 Battles of Coral Sea and Midway, turning point of the war in the Pacific, in which U.S. carrier-based planes shatter the Japanese fleet and establish the superiority of the aircraft carrier as a tactical naval weapon.

1944 The first operational rocket-propelled airplane is put into war service—the Messerschmitt 163 Komet.

1947 The first manned aircraft to exceed the speed of sound. Test pilot Charles Yeager flies the Bell X-1 to a speed of Mach 1.06, or 670 mph.

1948 The Vickers Viscount goes into service, the first airliner to use a turboprop, which is a combination jet and propeller-driving engine.

1952 The first jet airliner passenger service begins with the De Havilland Comet. Speed: 490 mph; range: 1,500 miles; capacity: 36 passengers.

1953 The North American F-100A Super Sabre becomes the first combat airplane capable of sustained supersonic performance.

1954 The Boeing 707, first U.S. jet transport, is tested. Speed: 550 mph; range: 3,500 miles; capacity: 150 passengers.

1954 The first airplane to take off and land vertically (VTOL), the Convair XFY-1, is tested.

1957 The Russians come up with the world's largest and heaviest airliner, the Tupolev Tu-114 Rossiya. Wing span: 177 feet; payload: 55,100 pounds; range: 6,000 miles.

1959 The North American X-15 is built for hypersonic flight. In the next four years it sets world records for speed: 4,104 mph, Mach 6.06; and altitude: 67 miles.

FURTHER READING

General

Desoutter, Dennis M., *Aircraft and Missiles*. John De Graff, 1959.

Gunston, W. T., ed., *Flight Handbook*. Aero Publishers, 1962.

Langewiesche, Wolfgang, *Stick and Rudder*. McGraw-Hill, 1944.

Mehrens, Harold E., *Aircraft in Flight*. Civil Air Patrol, Washington, D.C., 1956.

Murchie, Guy, *Song of the Sky*. The Riverside Press, 1954.

Rolfe, Douglas, and Alexis Dawydoff, *Airplanes of the World*. Simon & Schuster, 1962.

Van Sickle, Harold, Neil D., *Modern Airmanship*. Van Nostrand, 1961.

History of Flight

Canby, Courtlandt, ed., *A History of Flight*. The New Illustrated Library of Science and Invention, Vol. V. Hawthorn Books, 1963.

Davies, R.E.G., *A History of the World's Airlines*. Oxford University Press, 1964.

Dollfus, Charles, *The Orion Book of Balloons*. Orion Press, 1961.

Editors of *American Heritage*, *The American Heritage History of Flight*. American Heritage Publishing Co., 1962.

Gibbs-Smith, Charles H., *The Aeroplane*. Her Majesty's Stationery Office, 1960. *The Invention of the Aeroplane*. Faber and Faber, 1965.

Magoun, F. Alexander, and Eric Hodgins, *A History of Aircraft*. McGraw-Hill, 1931.

Miller, Francis Trevelyan, *The World in the Air* (2 vols.). G. P. Putnam's Sons, 1930.

Biography

Gibbs-Smith, Charles H., *Sir George Cayley's Aeronautics*. Her Majesty's Stationery Office, 1962.

McFarland, Marvin W., ed., *The Papers of Wilbur and Orville Wright* (2 vols.). McGraw-Hill, 1953.

Saint-Exupéry, Antoine de, *Wind, Sand and Stars*. Harcourt, Brace, 1940.

Aerodynamics and Propulsion

Chapel, Charles Edward, *Jet Aircraft Simplified*. Aero Publishers, 1950.

Dwinnell, James H., *Principles of Aerodynamics*. McGraw-Hill, 1949.

McMahon, P. J., *Jet Engines and Rocket Propulsion*. English Universities Press, 1964.

Animals That Fly

Augusta, Josef, *Prehistoric Reptiles and Birds*. P. Hamlyn, 1961.

Fisher, James, and Roger Tory Peterson, *The World of Birds*. Doubleday, 1963.

*Lanyon, Wesley E., *Biology of Birds*. Doubleday, 1964.

Pringle, J.W.S., *Insect Flight*. Cambridge University Press, 1957.

Design and Structure

Stack, John, "The Supersonic Transport." *International Science and Technology*. Oct. 1963.

Stevens, James Hay, *The Shape of the Aeroplane*. Hutchinson, 1953.

*Available in paperback edition.

ACKNOWLEDGMENTS

The editors of this book are especially indebted to Charles H. Gibbs-Smith, Honorary Companion of the Royal Aeronautical Society, London, England, and to Rudolf F. Lehnert of the Senior Technical Staff, and Acting Director, Subsonic Laboratory, Department of Aerospace and Mechanical Sciences, Princeton University, Princeton, New Jersey; and to the following persons and institutions: Aero Service Corporation; American Airlines, Public Relations Department; American Society of Photogrammetry, Falls Church, Virginia; Alexander Anderson, Public Relations, Lockheed Aircraft Corporation; Captain Ralph S. Barnaby, The Franklin Institute, Philadelphia; Peter Bowers, The Boeing Company; James S. Boynton, Assistant Public Relations Manager, Airplane Division, The Boeing Company; Elizabeth Brown, Librarian, American Institute of Aeronautics and Astronautics, New York City; Harold Carr, The Boeing Company; Louis S. Casey, Curator of Flightcraft Division, Smithsonian Institution, Washington, D.C.; Charles Dollfus, Honorary Curator of the Museum of the Air, Paris, France; Robert Dunn, General Dynamics Corporation; Jim Ean, Air Traffic Control Specialist, New York Air Route Traffic Control Center; Fairchild Aerial Surveys; James L.G. Fitz Patrick, Academic Dean, Staten Island Community College of the City University of New York; Duane Freer, Information Specialist, Federal Aviation Agency; Paul Garber, Head Curator and Historian, National Air Museum, Smithsonian Institution, Washington, D.C.; Geological Survey, U.S. Department of the Interior; Joseph P. Grandfield, Curtiss-Wright Corporation; Gordon Gray, Public Relations, North American Aviation; William Harris, Historian, National Park Service, Wright Brothers National Memorial, Kitty Hawk, North Carolina; Hunting Surveys Ltd.; Robert B. Jackson, Major, USAF; James E. Jones, Press Relations Manager, Greenfield Village, Dearborn, Michigan; Lyman Josephs, Director, Aircraft Development, Martin Company; John J. Knoll, Department of Transportation, Federal Aviation Administration; John Lee, former Director of Research, United Aircraft; Robert Lutz, General Dynamics Corporation; Marvin W. McFarland, Assistant Chief, Science and Technology Division, Library of Congress, Washington, D.C.; Walter E. Martin, Community Activities Division, Shell Oil Company; Vincent Modugno, Public Relations Representative at Kennedy Airport, American Airlines; Dr. Joseph Needham, F.R.S., Caius College, Cambridge University, Cambridge, England; Mark E. Nevils, Public Relations, The Boeing Company; James Ragsdale, Manager, Public Relations, Maintenance and Engineering Center, American Airlines; William J. Ratsch Jr., Chief, Information Section, Air Force Museum, Wright-Patterson Air Force Base, Dayton, Ohio; Joseph Stein, Public Information Office, National Aeronautics and Space Administration, Washington, D.C.; Vaughn Stephens, Information Specialist, ASEP, Wright-Patterson Air Force Base, Dayton, Ohio; C. Fayette Taylor, Professor Emeritus, Massachusetts Institute of Technology, Cambridge, Massachusetts; Robert Taylor, President, Antique Airplane Association, Ottumwa, Iowa; K. E. Van Every, General Dynamics Corporation; Irwin E. Vas, Gas Dynamics Laboratory, School of Engineering and Applied Science, Princeton University, Princeton, New Jersey; Daniel S. Wentz, Associate Public Affairs Officer, Langley Research Center, Hampton, Virginia.

For the picture essay on the Wright brothers, the editors are grateful for permission to use the original Wright home, bicycle shop, furniture and equipment now at Greenfield Village, Dearborn, Michigan. Other items photographed for this essay are from the collections of the Air Force Museum, Dayton, Ohio; The John Crerar Library, Chicago, Illinois; The Franklin Institute, Philadelphia; The Library of Congress and The Smithsonian Institution, Washington, D.C.; and the Wright Brothers National Memorial, Kitty Hawk, North Carolina.

INDEX

Numerals in italics indicate a photograph or painting of the subject mentioned.

PICTURE CREDITS

The sources for the illustrations which appear in this book are shown below. Credits for pictures from left to right are separated by commas, from top to bottom by dashes.

Cover—Ben Rose.

CHAPTER 1: 8—Courtesy Musée de l'Air from Terra Magica Picture Book *Schwingen*, Hans Reich, Munich. 10—From *Science and Civilization in China*, Vol. 4, by Joseph Needham with the collaboration of Wang Ling, Cambridge University Press—Photographie Bulloz courtesy Musée Carnavalet. 12—Derek Bayes courtesy Charles H. Gibbs-Smith except top courtesy The Science Museum, London. 13—Courtesy The Science Museum, London. 14—Derek Bayes courtesy Charles H. Gibbs-Smith. 15—Courtesy The Science Museum, London—courtesy Deutsches Museum, Munich. 17—Arnold Newman. 18, 19—Left courtesy The Henry Ford Museum and Greenfield Village, Dearborn, Michigan; right Arnold Newman courtesy The Henry Ford Museum and Greenfield Village, Dearborn, Michigan. 20—Arnold Newman. 21—Arnold Newman courtesy The Henry Ford Museum and Greenfield Village, Dearborn, Michigan—courtesy Library of Congress. 22, 23—Left and center Arnold Newman courtesy The Henry Ford Museum and Greenfield Village, Dearborn, Michigan; right Arnold Newman. 24, 25—Courtesy Library of Congress—Curtiss Wright Corporation, Arnold Newman. 26, 27—Arnold Newman. 28, 29—Courtesy Library of Congress, Arnold Newman.

CHAPTER 2: 30—Sandor Aldott. 32, 33—Robert E. Lackenbach from Black Star courtesy Zeppelin Museum, Friedrichshafen. 34—Courtesy New York Public Library, Slavonic Division. 36—Drawings by Otto van Eersel. 37—Drawings by Nicholas Fasciano. 39—Grant Haist. 40, 41—Left Leonard Lee Rue 3rd from Monkmeyer Press Photo—Peter Stackpole—Harold E. Edgerton from National Audubon Society, Robert B. Goodman from Black Star; right Karl W. Kenyon from National Audubon Society. 42—Torkel Weis-Fogh Zoophysiological Laboratory B, The University of Copenhagen. 43—Dr. Roman Vishniac except top drawing by Charles Mikolaycak adapted from an illustration in *Scientific American*. 44, 45—Gjon Mili except top David Goodnow. 46, 47—Left courtesy British Museum (Natural History); center Institut für Paläontologie und Museum, Berlin; right Gerhard Heilmann, *The Origin of Birds*, D. Appleton Co. 48—G. Ronald Austing from National Audubon Society—Andreas Feininger. 49—Stevan Celebonovic from Terra Magica Picture Book *Schwingen*, Hans Reich, Munich. 50, 51—Arthur Christiansen from Terra Magica Picture Book *Schwingen*, Hans Reich, Munich.

CHAPTER 3: 52—Rudolf Lehnert. 54—Drawings by Ronald de Vito. 56—Drawings by Nicholas Fasciano. 58—Drawings by Leslie Martin. 61—Drawings by Matt Greene. 63—Photograph designed by Matt Greene and photographed by Henry Groskinsky. 64, 65—Photograph designed by Matt Greene and photographed by Henry Groskinsky—drawings by James Alexander. 66, 67—Photograph designed by Matt Greene and photographed by Henry Groskinsky—drawing by George V. Kelvin. 68, 69—Photograph designed by Matt Greene and photographed by Henry Groskinsky, drawings by James Alexander. 70, 71—Photograph designed by Matt Greene and photographed by Henry Groskinsky—drawings by George V. Kelvin. 72, 73—Photograph designed by Matt Greene and photographed by Henry Groskinsky except top drawings by James Alexander. 74, 75—Drawings by George V. Kelvin, photograph designed by Matt Greene and photographed by Henry Groskinsky.

CHAPTER 4: 76—Norman Snyder. 78—Derek Bayes courtesy Royal Aeronautical Society. 79—Courtesy The Science Museum, London—courtesy The Smithsonian Institution National Air Museum. 80, 81—Drawings by Ronald de Vito. 82—Drawing by Leslie Martin—Eddy Van der Veen courtesy Charles Dollfus. 83—Eddy Van der Veen courtesy Charles Dollfus. 84—Drawings by Leslie Martin. 87—The Italian Ministry of Defense. 88, 89—Left drawings by Lowell Hess; center collection of Louis Vallin—Pratt and Whitney Aircraft, Division of United Aircraft Corporation and *The American Heritage History of Flight*; right collection of Louis Vallin—Bell Aerosystems Company. 90, 91—Drawings by Lowell Hess, courtesy The Smithsonian Institution (2)—John Bryson. 92, 93—Drawings by Lowell Hess, United Press International, courtesy The Smithsonian Institution—courtesy The Smithsonian Institution, Northrop Corporation. 94, 95—Drawings by Lowell Hess, J. R. Eyerman—courtesy The Smithsonian Institution, Lockheed Aircraft, Aero Spacelines, Inc. 96, 97—Drawings by Lowell Hess, United Press International—Flugarchiv H. u. B. v. Romer-Munich, Kyodo News. 98—Drawings by Lowell Hess—Fairchild Hiller Corporation. 99—J. R. Eyerman—Ling-Temco-Vought Inc.

CHAPTER 5: 100—Ralph Crane. 102—The Boeing Company, drawing by George V. Kelvin. 104—Courtesy Musée de l'Air. 105, 106, 107—Drawings by Leslie Martin. 109—Ivan Massar from Black Star. 110, 111—Ivan Massar from Black Star, drawing by James Alexander. 112—Drawing by James Alexander—Ivan Massar from Black Star. 113—Ivan Massar from Black Star—Henry Groskinsky. 114—Drawing by James Alexander—Ivan Massar from Black Star. 115—Left American Airlines; right Henry Groskinsky. 116, 117—Drawing by James Alexander, Ivan Massar from Black Star (2)—American Airlines. 118—Drawing by James Alexander, Henry Groskinsky. 119—Henry Groskinsky. 120, 121—Drawing by James Alexander—drawing by Patricia Byrne, Ivan Massar from Black Star.

CHAPTER 6: 122—Courtesy Aeronautical Chart and Information Center, USAF. 124—Courtesy Charles Dollfus. 125—Culver Pictures—courtesy Charles Dollfus. 126—Courtesy The Smithsonian Institution National Air Museum, drawing by James Alexander. 128—Drawings by Leslie Martin. 131—Ivan Massar from Black Star. 132, 133—Ivan Massar from Black Star, drawing by George V. Kelvin. 134, 135—Ivan Massar from Black Star (2)—drawing by George V. Kelvin. 136, 137—Ivan Massar from Black Star—drawing by George V. Kelvin. 138, 139, 140—Drawings by George V. Kelvin. 141—Lee Boltin—drawing by George V. Kelvin. 142, 143—Drawing by George V. Kelvin.

CHAPTER 7: 144—NASA. 147—Alan Clifton courtesy Royal Institution of Great Britain. 148—Courtesy Royal Aeronautical Society, London. 149—Musée Marey, Beaune. 151—Drawing by George V. Kelvin. 152, 153—Drawings by Matt Greene. 157—Fairchild Aerial Surveys. 158, 159—Aerofototeca M.P.I., Foto Vitale Valvassori. 160, 161—Left U.S. National Park Service, Yellowstone National Park, Wyoming; right Victor B. Scheffer and Karl W. Kenyon, U.S. Fish and Wildlife Service—California Department of Fish and Game. 162, 163—Lockwood, Kessler and Bartlett Inc. 164, 165—Canadian Department of National Defense except right National Air Photo Library, Ottawa. 166, 167—Bradford Washburn.

CHAPTER 8: 168—NASA. 170—Courtesy Sikorsky Aircraft Division of United Aircraft Corporation, drawing by James Alexander. 172, 173—Drawings by James Alexander. 174—Drawing by George V. Kelvin. 177—Office National d'Etudes et Recherches Aeronautiques. 178—NASA—drawings by Charles Mikolaycak. 179—Shell Oil Company *High Speed Flight* film series. 180—General Dynamics Corporation except top The Boeing Company. 181—J. R. Eyerman—General Dynamics Corporation. 182—General Dynamics Corporation—drawings by Patricia Byrne. 183—Ralph Crane. 184, 185—Office National d'Etudes et Recherches Aeronautiques—N.R. Farbman, Shell Oil Company *High Speed Flight* film series—Henry Groskinsky. 186, 187—Left General Dynamics Corporation—Photo Dassault—U.S. Air Force, Loomis Dean; right Loomis Dean—Ian Macdonald Photographers Ltd.—Lockheed Aircraft Corporation. 188, 189—The Boeing Company—Pierre Boulat. 190—NASA. 191—Yale Joel. 194, 195—Drawings by Charles Mikolaycak. Back cover—Patricia Byrne.

A
STONEHENGE
BOOK

PRODUCTION STAFF FOR TIME INCORPORATED

John L. Hallenbeck (Vice President and Director of Production), Robert E. Foy and Caroline Ferri
Text photocomposed under the direction of Albert J. Dunn

XXX